Creating Thinking Classrooms

Creating Thinking Classrooms

Leading Educational Change for This Century

Garfield Gini-Newman

Roland Case

With Contributions by Stefan Stipp and Warren Woytuck

CORWIN
A SAGE Publishing Company

FOR INFORMATION:

Corwin
A SAGE Company
2455 Teller Road
Thousand Oaks, California 91320
(800) 233-9936
www.corwin.com

SAGE Publications Ltd.
1 Oliver's Yard
55 City Road
London EC1Y 1SP
United Kingdom

SAGE Publications India Pvt. Ltd.
B 1/I 1 Mohan Cooperative Industrial Area
Mathura Road, New Delhi 110 044
India

SAGE Publications Asia-Pacific Pte. Ltd.
3 Church Street
#10-04 Samsung Hub
Singapore 049483

Publisher: Arnis Burvikovs
Development Editor: Desirée A. Bartlett
Editorial Assistant: Eliza B. Riegert
Production Editor: Melanie Birdsall
Copy Editor: Diane Wainwright
Typesetter: C&M Digitals (P) Ltd.
Proofreader: Barbara Coster
Indexer: Wendy Allex
Cover Designer: Dally Verghese
Marketing Manager: Nicole Franks

Printed in the United States of America

Library of Congress Cataloging-in-Publication Data

Names: Gini-Newman, Garfield, author. | Case, Roland, author.

Title: Creating thinking classrooms : leading educational change for this century / Garfield Gini-Newman - OISE, Canada, Roland Case - Simon Fraser University, Canada.

Description: Thousand Oaks, California : A SAGE Company, [2018] | Includes bibliographical references and index.

Identifiers: LCCN 2017049684 | ISBN 9781506398433 (pbk. : alk. paper)

Subjects: LCSH: Creative thinking—Study and teaching. | Thought and thinking—Study and teaching. | Educational change.

Classification: LCC LB1062 .G47 2018 | DDC 370.15/7—dc23
LC record available at https://lccn.loc.gov/2017049684

This book is printed on acid-free paper.

Certified Chain of Custody
SUSTAINABLE FORESTRY INITIATIVE
Promoting Sustainable Forestry
www.sfiprogram.org
SFI-01268

SFI label applies to text stock

18 19 20 21 22 10 9 8 7 6 5 4 3 2 1

Contents

Preface

This book is for classroom, district, and university educators who are working to make schools effective institutions for developing all students' capacity for rigorous and imaginative thinking so that they can become healthy individuals, contributing global citizens, thoughtful consumers of media, and adaptable learners who can thrive in a rapidly changing world.

Our goal is to help educators at all levels to understand and respond thoughtfully to the diverse and sometimes overwhelming calls for school reform that currently dominate public and professional attention. These calls are noisy, confusing, and not entirely coherent. We hope to separate the rhetoric from the reality surrounding many of the popular buzzwords and vague claims associated with learning in the contemporary world. In addition, we seek to unpack the widely recommended goals, initiatives, and pedagogical practices that advocates of reform are championing. Finally, we propose an approach supported with practical advice to educators in their efforts to navigate the substantial, often upsetting, challenges of educational change.

The most significant contribution of this book lies in its attempt to clarify and bring coherence to the current reform efforts. When distilled to its essentials, this movement represents a desire to shift the educational system in three important ways involving nine core ideas:

- **Shift 1:** Reorient the foundational beliefs about teaching and learning from the mindset characteristic of a discovery or didactic classroom to that of a thinking classroom.
- **Shift 2:** Refocus attention on more enriched versions of the three traditional educational goals, moving from fostering knowledge to deep understanding, from skills to real-life competencies, and from attitudes to genuine commitments.
- **Shift 3:** Align teaching practices with five key principles of powerful learning. These guiding principles are to engage students, sustain inquiry, nurture self-regulated learners, create assessment-rich learning, and enhance learning through digital technology.

The many other ideas associated with this reform movement are of secondary importance or negotiable means to achieve these ends. Understanding the importance and implications of these shifts and the nine ideas upon which these shifts are based form the main focus of this book.

Some insist that these needed changes require nothing less than a transformation of the educational system, while others have a more modest design. In our view, the extent of remodeling depends entirely on the state of individual schools and teacher practices. None of the ideas in the call for reform are brand new. Some have been around for a decade or more, others for centuries. This means that they are already present to greatly varying degrees in every school and classroom. For some, the educational renovations required to meet the called-for changes will be relatively modest; others may need to substantially refurbish aspects of their practice.

In the final chapter, we argue that educational leaders can best help teachers by looking upon the proposed shifts as invitations to teachers to affirm what they are doing well, refine those practices that can easily be adjusted, and, in the longer term, aspire to make more substantial changes in areas that require significant renovation. Our work with over 200,000 teachers encourages us to believe that this approach is feasible—perhaps the only realistic approach in the face of such a massive call for reform.

An earlier version of this book prepared for Canadian educators was published by The Critical Thinking Consortium (TC²) with the British Columbia Principals' and Vice-Principals' Association and the Ontario Principals' Council. All of our TC² colleagues have added in some way to the thinking that has created this work, and a few have actually penned the words that we have included. In this respect, we owe a special debt of gratitude to Stefan Stipp, Warren Woytuck, and Usha James. As well, we greatly appreciate the support and advice offered by Arnis Burvikovs and other members of the Corwin team, particularly Melanie Birdsall, Diane Wainwright, and Eliza Riegert.

About the Authors

Garfield Gini-Newman blends humor with a deep understanding of effective curriculum design centered around the infusion of critical thinking for all. As an associate professor at OISE/University of Toronto and a senior national consultant with The Critical Thinking Consortium (TC²), Garfield has worked with thousands of teachers across grades and subjects, helping them to frame learning around engaging and provocative activities and authentic assessments.

Requests for Garfield's services have taken him from Asia to the Middle East, Europe, the Caribbean, and across North America. His interest in effective teaching and learning has led him to actively explore the challenges and opportunities presented by teaching and learning in the digital age. Garfield has spoken across Canada and internationally on critical thinking, brain-compatible classrooms, curriculum design and effective assessment practice, and nurturing 21st century skills in a digital world. In addition to his work at the University of Toronto and delivering workshops, Garfield has also authored several articles, chapters in books, and seven textbooks, and has taught in the faculties of education at York University and the University of British Columbia.

Roland Case cofounded The Critical Thinking Consortium (TC²) in 1994 and has recently retired from a decade as its executive director. TC² is a not-for-profit association of over seventy school districts, schools, and educational organizations that has worked with over 200,000 educators to embed thinking into their teaching and professional practices. Prior to leading TC², he was a professor of curriculum in the Faculty of Education at Simon Fraser University in Vancouver, Canada. Roland has edited or authored more than 100 published works. Notable among these are the two-volume *The Anthology of Social Studies* and the multivolume series *Critical Challenges Across the Curriculum*—an award-winning set of TC² teaching resources. He has worked extensively with educators across Canada and in the United States, England, Israel, Russia, India, Finland, and Hong Kong. Roland is the 2006 recipient of the Confederation of University Faculty Associations' Distinguished Academics Career Achievement Award.

PART i
Understand
the Issues

1

Opportunities and Challenges

This chapter explores the range of initiatives championed by proponents of contemporary educational reforms and proposes the elements of a coherent response to the challenges and opportunities facing schools. More specifically, it discusses

- the main concerns fueling many current reform efforts;
- the urgency and uncertainties in addressing these concerns;
- the complexities and potential pitfalls of the many proposed initiatives;
- a three-part response to our enduring educational challenges.

When it was first becoming popular to talk about learning for the 21st century, I met a high school administrator who proudly announced that his school had pretty much resolved the problem of student engagement at the senior grades.[1] His solution was to allow for significant student choice. By dropping the requirement for students to complete mandatory senior courses, they had become free to pursue electives of their own choosing. I inquired about the kinds of courses students were opting for: Interesting topics? Courses that remediated gaps in their learning? He said "no." For the most part, students were taking easy courses, including online offerings, that they could waltz through without much effort, or they were redoing courses solely to improve their grades.

> If we are to understand a given educational reform movement, then it is more important to examine its basic values and principles than the type of pedagogical activities or structures it champions.
>
> —Jesse Goodman (1995)

It didn't seem that the school had done much to engage students educationally (except to reinforce a mark-driven mindset) or to better prepare them for a 21st century world. Their choices were not going to make them more successful engineers or mechanics, or better citizens and companions. These students weren't choosing courses that would help them develop personal or career interests; instead, they were navigating through the hoops in the system. Students who may have entered the system twelve years earlier filled with curiosity and wonder were now uninterested in learning. Rather than solving the challenges of learning for a complex world, this school's "solution" highlighted, or even compounded, the problems that must be overcome.

This incident reminded me of my own experience many years earlier as a beginning teacher in a high-risk elementary school. In an effort to interest my students, I promised that every Wednesday afternoon they would be allowed to choose what they would do, provided it was safe, feasible, and had some educational merit. Initially, students greeted the announcement with great joy, but soon after, some began to worry about what they would choose to do. After much prompting, almost every student brought something to do on the first afternoon. However, within minutes several students were bored, and by the end of the first period all but two students had abandoned their chosen activities. Because I had promised to allow this for the rest of the term, we had to continue the charade for a few more Wednesdays until the class agreed to abandon the plan. While school had taught students what they did not like, it had not engendered in them a curious spirit. My students couldn't even figure out what would challenge or interest them. Of course, this scenario would play out differently if I replicated this invitation in a contemporary classroom. The vast majority of students would likely show up with a mobile device eager to text or play video games for hours on end. If that is what contemporary students would choose to do with their school time, we have to ask what would be the point of their coming to school?

These two incidents illustrate a number of interesting points. Intuitively appealing solutions such as giving students choice or access to popular digital technologies are not silver bullets that will solve our problems in one easy step. Perhaps the deeper problems we currently face are not all that new: for many decades, schools have not been appealing places for many students, and what we are teaching them has not resonated outside of school. The contemporary crisis may simply be that the current generation is less willing than its predecessors to put up with irrelevance, especially since the digital age provides them with a host of more compelling ways to spend their time.

Defining the Challenges

Educators are confronted with a multitude of near constant and often conflicting or vague calls to improve schools. The scale of the challenge of bringing clarity to the volume of proposed reform initiatives is reflected in the Wordle image depicted in Figure 1.1. This graphic was created from a sampling of prominent recent policy documents (Ananiadou & Claro, 2009; Crockett, 2016; Fullan & Langworthy, 2014; National Education Association, n.d.; Partnership for 21st Century Learning, 2007; Rotherham & Willingham, 2009). Many of the terms are prone to conflicting interpretations, and collectively it is not at all clear if and how they are to be integrated into a workable system.

Perhaps the most important question we can ask is whether the calls for change are in response to new or to ongoing challenges. To what extent and in what ways are the root problems we face unique to this century, and to what extent are they manifestations of enduring problems and aspirations? Does this current call for 21st century reform derive its name from the timing of this particular movement, coming as it does at the dawn of a new millennium? Or does it signal the need for changes emerging from a new digital age that is unparalleled in the history of education?

Figure 1.1   The Range of Current Reform Initiatives

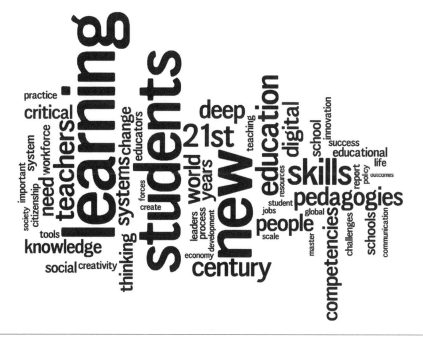

Source: Created by The Critical Thinking Consortium.

The answer to these questions is crucial and yet is still very much a matter of debate. There is little clarity as to what many of the proposed changes might actually mean and even less consensus on how they would play out in practical terms. This is because terms such as *21st century learning* are slogans. Slogans are ubiquitous in education, and like other educational slogans—authentic tasks, inclusive education, deep learning, visible thinking, personalized learning, integrated curriculum—they have two characteristic features. Slogans always sound positive—so everyone should be in favor of them. Who could possibly champion inauthentic tasks, superficial learning, invisible thinking, or disintegrated curriculum? In addition, slogans are notoriously vague, which means diverse groups can advocate for them without actually meaning the same thing. In fact, most educational initiatives began as slogans, and many never rise above being a slogan.

Contemporary calls to promote learning in a digital age don't gain traction unless they have considerable merit, but they are doomed to be largely ineffectual or, worse yet, aborted fads if we don't strip away the flash. The challenge is to identify the truly substantive elements behind the slogan and simultaneously expose the less helpful and perhaps dangerous elements that have attached themselves to these inherently vague ideas. While it is important to understand how various advocates use these terms, there is no definitive version to be found—slogans can and will come to mean what people decide they want them to mean. The goal of this book is to help thoughtful educational leaders at the system, district, and school levels give substance to the breadth of widely used contemporary slogans by exploring what they could and perhaps should be interpreted to mean. Without this kind of clarity, efforts to implement 21st century learning will look a lot like attempting to nail jelly to a wall.

Before discussing what educators and others identify as the reasons why we need to improve schooling in the United States, it is important to remind ourselves of our successes. There is much that goes on in schools that deserve celebrating. It is not widely appreciated that American elementary school students typically score among the upper ranks on international tests, and middle school students' scores are generally above average (as cited in Steinberg, 2015). Results from the 2012 National Assessment of Educational Progress (NAEP) assessments show that test scores in reading and mathematics have improved for fourth- and eighth-grade students since the 1970s (National Center for Education Statistics, 2013). Many of the world's best and brightest thinkers, entrepreneurs, and artists have been educated in American schools. In addition, all of us can recount inspiring stories of teachers who made profound differences in the lives of their students. In short, there are many wonderful things going on in schools, and there are many students for whom schooling is already a positive and rewarding experience.

The point in drawing attention to our educational successes is that we stand to lose ground if we disrupt the system. We must ensure that our reform efforts do not undermine the practices that contribute to our current level of success. For example, opponents of inquiry learning have claimed that this reform initiative is undermining acquisition of basic content knowledge (Hirsch, 2009–2010). Equally troubling if we get the reform wrong is the impact on teacher morale. Many of us who work extensively with teachers have noticed increasing levels of teacher burnout. It is an abuse of the goodwill and commitment of teachers if we urge upon them a range of difficult reform initiatives that are eventually found to be ill-conceived or fruitless. Finally, reform efforts are expensive. The nation can ill afford to squander scarce financial resources.

The Urgency to Improve

Despite its successes, there are many areas in need of improvement within the educational system. Our analysis of the dissatisfaction among educators that is fueling many reform efforts suggests that the concerns concentrate around three significant problems.

Poor Achievement

Despite the evidence suggested earlier, there is a pervasive feeling that U.S. schools are failing to generate acceptable student performance. These perceptions are fueled by significant weaknesses in achievement results on various standardized tests. For example, according to the World Economic Forum, the United States ranks 48th in the world on mathematics and science achievement tests (Klein, 2011). The 2010 NAEP—called the Nation's Report Card—found that barely one-third of eighth-grade students were proficient in math, science, or reading. On the same test, only 13 percent of high school seniors earned solid results in knowledge of American history (CBS News, 2011).

While there is undeniable room to improve the quality of learning in schools, our goal can't simply be to secure higher scores on achievement tests. Simply because students' scores on pen and paper standardized tests improve does not mean that we are getting better at teaching our students what they really need to learn to succeed in life. As one observer noted,

> Many of the students in high-poverty classrooms—both in charter schools and traditional public schools—have been relegated to classrooms where cramming for standardized tests was the norm and students were taught to pass a specific test rather than gain any real understanding of the material. (Rotberg, 2014)

Standardized tests have been sharply criticized for their inability to measure many of our most important educational goals (A. Kohn, 2001). The gap between what is measured and what really matters may be worsening as teachers are pressured to spend more time teaching to the test. We may be improving our test results at the expense of genuine student learning. This point was brought home recently when I asked a talented student who was just graduating from high school with top marks what she had learned from her schooling. Much to my dismay, she said, "I think what I most learned in school was how to write multiple-choice exams."

The challenges in overcoming poor achievement are twofold. First, we need to identify the outcomes and benchmarks that truly are worth pursuing. Second, we must understand what each involves and how best to achieve them. These questions are the focus of our discussions in Chapters 5, 6, and 7.

Disaffected Students

Many students do little within school or leave school entirely because it is boring and irrelevant. According to a study sponsored by the Bill and Melinda Gates Foundation, one-third of all high school students and nearly 50 percent of blacks, Hispanics, and Native Americans fail to graduate with their class (Bridgeland, Dilulio, & Morison, 2006). In explaining these results, the study found that for 47 percent of these students, a major reason for dropping out was lack of interest in school—they were bored and disengaged. Almost 70 percent stated that they were not motivated to work hard. A 2012 Gallup survey of 5,000 American students in fifth to twelfth grades found that 75 percent of elementary students are engaged by school, but by high school that figure is down to 44 percent (Busteed, 2013). Other reports paint an equally depressing picture: "Between 40–60 percent of high school students in the US are chronically disengaged; they are inattentive, exert little effort, do not complete tasks, and claim to be bored" (National Research Council and Institute of Medicine, 2004, p. 18).

Dissatisfaction may be widespread but is not a new phenomenon.

> Nearly half a century ago, educational philosopher John Dewey and others claimed that if schools were to succeed in preparing the great majority of young people, not just a select few, to be responsible and productive citizens, they would have to do a better job of motivating and engaging the broad spectrum of students in learning. (as cited in National Research Council and Institute of Medicine, 2004, p. 16)

Before we can decide on a prudent course of action, we need to understand why we are in this situation. There are two explanations we will consider.[2] One hypothesis is that the root problem resides in what we are teaching students. Some critics call for a more relevant set of outcomes or suggest that we abandon a common prescribed curriculum and let students decide what and when they need and want to learn. A second hypothesis is that the problems reside not so much in what we teach but in how we instruct and engage students in the things that schools currently are trying to teach. Later in this chapter, we offer our analysis of the extent to which we need to change our pedagogy and methods, and the extent to which the content of the curriculum is the source of this problem.

Ill-Prepared Graduates

A third concern driving 21st century reform is the perception that successful graduates don't have the knowledge and skill set that parents, professors, employers, and governments consider essential given the new realities of global economics and a digital world. For example, the national organization that administers college admissions tests concluded that 76 percent of high school graduates "were not adequately prepared academically for first-year college courses" (Klein, 2011). Here, too, there are alternative explanations of the problem. Are "successful" students not learning what the current system has to offer, or is the system not currently offering the kinds of things that are actually needed by students and society?

The hypothesis that students aren't learning what schools currently are trying to achieve is supported by evidence that many "good" students seem driven by a desire for high marks rather than by a desire to learn. One study found that a mark-driven mentality undermines significant learning.

> Students who attend class and complete assignments to avoid punishment or bad grades are less likely to become engaged beyond a superficial (just get it done) level, whereas students who complete assignments because the material captures their interest or because they experience a sense of pride in accomplishment are more likely to go beyond the minimal requirements and become actively and deeply engaged. (National Research Council and Institute of Medicine, 2004, p. 32)

If we accept this evidence, then the problem is rooted to some extent, at least, in a failure to create teaching, learning, and assessment conditions that engage students and foster in-depth understanding and high-level skill development.

Alternatively, many critics claim that the bigger problem is that schools are teaching the wrong things. It is often suggested that the digital age has significantly shifted what students need to learn. The more critical voices in this camp suggest that an entirely new set of skills are needed, and some even suggest that "mastery of bodies of knowledge or content has become less important, even pointless" because of the explosion of new knowledge and changing information (Sener, 2011). These radical views seem exaggerated when we remind ourselves that many of the most commonly advocated 21st century competencies, such as literacy, numeracy, critical thinking, creativity and innovation, and problem solving, have been educational goals for decades, even centuries. Furthermore, the kind of information that is changing at an exponential rate has not been the primary focus of the intended curriculum. The tendency with educational standards is to emphasize more enduring concepts, such as sustainability, interdependence, democracy, and theories of thermodynamics, evolution, and anatomical functioning, which will continue to have currency for generations to come, even if modified from time to time.

Our analysis of the situation aligns with the view expressed by two prominent educators:

> The skills students need in the 21st century are not new. . . . What's actually new is the extent to which changes in our economy and the world mean that our collective and individual success depends on having such skills. . . . This distinction between "skills that are novel" and "skills that must be taught more intentionally and effectively" ought to lead policymakers to different education reforms than they are now considering. If these skills were indeed new, then perhaps we would need a radical overhaul of how we think about content and curriculum. But if the issue is, instead, that schools must be more deliberate about teaching critical thinking, collaboration, and problem solving to all students, then the remedies are more obvious, although still intensely challenging. (Rotherham & Willingham, 2010, pp. 17–18)

A similar point may be made about the contents of the curriculum. Reliance on multiple-choice tests and fact-focused textbooks has often pushed recall of a litany of facts ahead of the broad conceptual understanding recommended in the curriculum. Rather than throw out the curriculum, the more sensible option is to do a better job of aligning our examinations, resources, and teaching practices to the intended outcomes.

The need to recognize the urgency to improve the system and to ensure that we diagnose the causes accurately has never been greater. For the first time in history, there are viable alternatives to public education. Private schools and homeschooling were never realistic options for most families, but a digitally delivered alternative education is now feasible. As well, the large-scale outsourcing of educational services to commercial interests has placed even greater pressure on schools to perform or be replaced. A failure to address the identified problems may have significant consequences for the educational system as we know it.

The Many Directions for Change

There are a surprisingly large number of diffuse initiatives proposed by reform advocates. In times such as these, when the calls are for wholesale reform, it is not surprising that change initiatives span all aspects of the system. A first step in making sense of the breadth and interrelationships among these initiatives is to recognize that they function at different levels of generality and purpose.

Four Operational Components of an Educational System

Popularly recommended initiatives are directed at changing the operations of the school system in four domains:

School and Classroom Practices. These refer to the individual strategies and procedures, and the comprehensive programs that teachers and administrators implement, to achieve the desired outcomes. Practices define almost every aspect of what educators do in schools, including assessment (use of rubrics), instruction (use of advance organizers, use of textbooks), group work (use of think-pair-share or placemat strategies), school structures (flexible timetable), and grading policies (no penalty for late assignments, no letter grades before Grade 4). Many contemporary reform initiatives are aimed at school and classroom practices. These include inquiring learning, flipped classrooms, blended classrooms, problem-based learning, one-to-one mobile devices, and open questions. Their direct focus is on the particular actions and policies that teachers and principals implement in classrooms and schools.

Guiding Principles. These refer to the instrumental values that inform the practices that teachers, principals, and other educators adopt. They are instrumental in that they are not the goals of education that we hope students will achieve but instead identify the desired conditions that need to be created to enable students to achieve the desired goals. Student voice and choice, student engagement, authentic assessment, and differentiated instruction are some of the principles associated with 21st century reform. As principles, they do not typically specify particular classroom strategies or school programs. In fact, educators may act on the same principle by adopting very different practices, even contradictory practices. For example, some teachers may promote student engagement by making assignments easier for students to complete; other teachers may make assignments more challenging to complete. Both practices are motivated by the principle of promoting student engagement. As we will see, the different direction that each of these practices takes is grounded in basic beliefs about students and about the nature of learning.

Educational Goals. These refer to the ultimate outcomes that we hope students will acquire from their education. The most discussed goals in the current reform discourse are so-called 21st century competencies, including digital literacy, social responsibility, critical thinking, creativity and innovation, and collaboration. Deep understanding and developing essential habits of mind or dispositions, such as curiosity, open-mindedness, and flexibility, have also been mentioned. As was suggested earlier, some reformers advocate for an entirely new set of educational goals, whereas others recommend that current goals in education be revised or reemphasized.

Foundational Beliefs. A less obvious dimension of the educational landscape is the embedded assumptions or basic tenets held about teaching and learning. These form the core of one's philosophy or educational worldview. They are often broad generalizations or belief statements about the most basic elements of schooling. The foundational statements found in contemporary reform focus on various themes:

- **The Nature of Learners and Learning:** Foundational beliefs of this type include "Students are inherently curious," "Students need to be motivated to learn," and "Learning requires active participation."
- **The Role of the Teacher:** Foundational beliefs of this type include visions of the teacher as a mentor, guide, expert, or facilitator of learning.
- **The Nature of Knowledge:** Foundational beliefs of this type include "Information is obsolete" and "Knowledge is changing at exponential rates."
- **The Purpose of Schooling:** Foundational beliefs of this type suggest "Schools should nurture the interests and needs of each child" and "Schools should give priority to the needs of society and business."

These core assumptions inform almost every educational decision about what goals to pursue and what practices and principles to implement.

Focusing on the Most Appropriate Aspects

One reason for distinguishing the various components is to ensure that change efforts target the most appropriate aspects of the system. For example, differing assumptions about the reasons for the perceived state of ill-prepared graduates will determine whether we revise our educational goals (e.g., adding new digital literacy outcomes), adopt new principles of learning (e.g., making tasks more realistic and authentic), or institute specific teaching practices (e.g., adopting a problem-based approach to learning). Many initiatives that focus on particular classroom practices or principles of learning don't have the desired effect because the root problem stems from questionable or incompatible foundational beliefs. For example, enhancing student engagement may look very different depending on educators' beliefs about the nature of learners. Educators who believe that students are inherently curious will try to fuel children's curiosity by creating a stimulating learning space but will otherwise try to stay out of students' way. Conversely, educators who presume that students are not inherently motivated to learn will pursue a more activist role. Awarding grades for extra work or using social media to arouse student interest may be among the practices that these educators might use. Identifying the most suitable locus within the system at which to direct our reform efforts is key to successful reform.

Ensuring That All Aspects Are Aligned

A second reason for distinguishing various components stems from the fact that schooling is an interactive system. Each of the parts must align with one another if the system is to be effective. For example, much of the pressure on educators to change assessment practices or to reduce the amount of content in the curriculum is to ensure that these practices and goals do not undermine efforts to support inquiry learning and student engagement.

The interrelated balance needed among these four components is analogous to the core structures in a building. As Figure 1.2 illustrates, foundational beliefs are the platform upon which all other aspects of the building rest. The roof is the pinnacle of the building. Educationally speaking, it represents the goals we aspire to achieve. The guiding principles are the equivalent of the pillars or framing that are anchored to the foundation and reach up to the roof. They provide the supports that keep the building

Figure 1.2   Structural Components of a Building With Parallels to Education

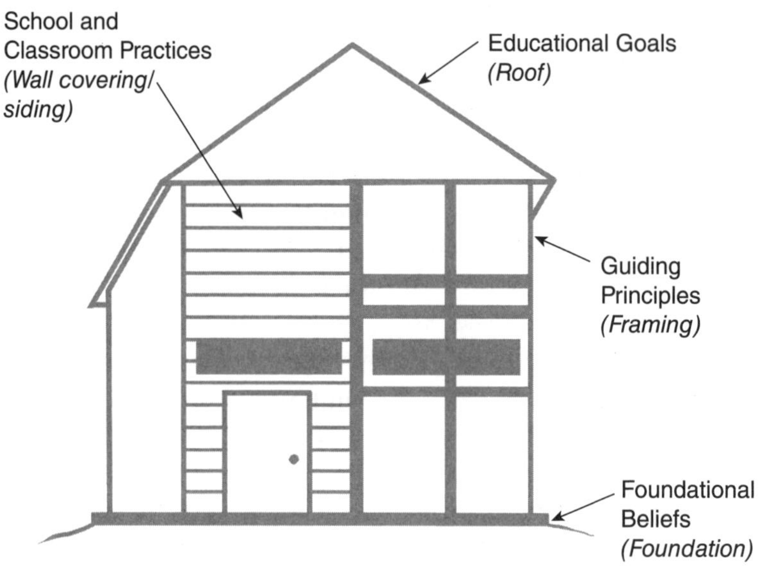

School and Classroom Practices *(Wall covering/siding)*

Educational Goals *(Roof)*

Guiding Principles *(Framing)*

Foundational Beliefs *(Foundation)*

Source: Illustrated by Kirsten Nestor, Corwin.

intact. Finally, school and classroom practices are the equivalent of wall coverings and sidings. They are the most visible aspects of a building, and they determine its "look and feel." However, as with the façade of a building, they must be attached to the infrastructure; otherwise they will fall away or crumble.

Three Potential Pitfalls

The conundrum when confronted with so many different kinds of change initiatives is in figuring out which ones are most needed and in what combinations they should be implemented. What would a blueprint for change look like that included all the essential design features? Before outlining the three-pronged response that we propose in this book, let's consider three pitfalls that educational leaders will want to avoid.

Looking for a Simple Fix

One reaction to the call for reform has been to champion one or a few core changes that are purported to transform the system. In some respects, limiting focus to a handful of initiatives is highly commendable, since it increases the likelihood of a sustained effort that will be well understood by those who must implement these initiatives. The danger is that the particular initiative is seen as "the" answer to the problems facing schools—as though all the important shortcomings can be addressed by these few changes. In addition, this approach underappreciates the interactive nature of the educational system. Or, to use the building metaphor, changes may introduce new elements without ensuring that they align with the other structural components of the system.

We can see the limitations of a singular response by considering the popular recommendation to establish a handful of new goals often referred to as 21st century skills. These typically include critical and creative thinking, collaboration, and communication, including digital literacy. While we believe that efforts to promote these competencies are worthwhile and important, implementing this solitary initiative in isolation from an array of other components will not alleviate crucial challenges facing the educational system. The emphasis on new competencies seems to address the concern that graduates are ill-prepared for the world beyond school. But are we sure that this solution addresses this completely? Perhaps preparing graduates for a rapidly changing world has as much to do with instilling lifelong habits of mind such as flexibility, curiosity, and perseverance as it does with promoting a new set of abilities. As well, it leaves open the extent to which this initiative addresses the other major concern that we identified, namely lack of student engagement. Can we expect that students will actually benefit from the new emphasis on these competencies if many students remain disengaged by schooling and seem largely motivated by doing things only for marks? At another level, the focus on competencies leaves open the implications for alignment with other aspects of the system. Researchers have noted the overwhelming prevalence of a didactic orientation to teaching in many secondary school classrooms.[3] This deeply rooted foundational belief about teacher-directed learning may conflict with the goal of developing 21st century competencies. If so, then changing the goals will have marginal impact unless teachers' philosophy of teaching and learning is more closely aligned with the conditions for competency development.

School choice is another popular "fix" proposed to improve our educational system. While individual parents and students will no doubt be presented with particular choices that may have obvious benefit to them, the idea that school choice offers a systemwide solution is less certain. The assumption is that the competition created by allowing for school choice will lead to an improved system. However, the evidence does not support this premise. The Organisation for Economic Co-operation and Development has reported that once students' prior achievement and socioeconomic background are taken into consideration, there is little difference between private and public schools in many educational systems (Hattie, 2015, p. 10). As it turns out, there is far greater variation between teachers with a single school than there is variation between schools. The presumed problem underlying the call for competition is that educators lack the motivation to improve schools. Yet encouraging competition motivates schools to improve their students' results on standardized tests. This can be counterproductive for two reasons discussed earlier: the gains in scores have often been purchased at the expense of student understanding of the material, and relatively high scores on pen and paper tests may mask the fact that these students are not actually being prepared for the world they will face. School choice leaves unanswered the more important questions about what directions we want schools to head and how best to support educators in achieving these goals.

In short, the simple fix approach won't address all of the most important issues fueling the challenges facing schools, and the interrelated nature of the educational system necessitates supporting any single initiative with complementary initiatives at various levels within the system.

Implementing a Grab Bag of Improvements

Another potential pitfall—one that is in some respects the opposite of the search for a simple fix—is the danger of proposing a grab bag of changes. Rather than focus on a few initiatives, the tendency is to recommend a multitude of divergent initiatives. To its credit, this approach acknowledges the multidimensional nature of the challenges by enumerating a host of changes ranging from foundational beliefs to pedagogical principles and goals, and individual practices. The danger, however, is their failure to articulate the connections among the changes proposed or appreciate the extent of missing or incongruent elements within their lists. Consider, for example, the challenges that emerge when trying to reconcile two commonly cited initiatives: personalized learning and 21st century competencies. If personalized learning allows for significant student choice of topics delivered through nontraditional learning situations, how can educators ensure that students master all the competencies they need and not simply the few competencies that the students favor? As suggested by the stories that open this chapter, what other changes in the system are required in order to prepare students to make responsible, productive choices? Can we expect students to successfully navigate self-directed independent learning if they have not already developed an ability and inclination to effectively self-assess their learning on assigned tasks and to responsibly initiate remedial efforts without waiting for the teacher to prompt them?

In short, a grab bag approach may lack coherence. Individual initiatives must be supported with often unacknowledged, complementary initiatives at various levels of the system, and collectively, the initiatives must be brought into alignment.

Rushing to the Practical

The final pitfall to consider is what we call *rushing to the practical*. The most visible elements of schooling are the practices—the activities, routines, and procedures—that occur within the school and classroom. These are the equivalent of the paneling in a room or the exterior siding of a building. As soon as you approach the space, this is what you will notice. Teaching practices are understandably the most pressing focus of teachers' attention—their survival depends on what they do and what they have their students do each day. It is therefore predictable that, when faced with calls for educational change, attention turns to what this means in terms of their practical implications. It is not that attention to practices is wrong-headed. Our concern is that the practices get "hollowed out"—they start off well intended but often become cardboard versions of their original selves. In short, they get lost in translation.

A particularly alarming failure of an early widespread attempt to personalize learning was an attempt by a group of 3,000 schools to introduce individual guided learning. Despite their efforts, researchers found that only twenty schools experienced a substantive change in teaching practices. Implementation in 99 percent of the schools was at a superficial level that left untouched the core assumptions and habits that entrenched the old practices. Although the vast majority of the teachers espoused the language of individual guided education, their routines and arrangements were unchanged (as cited in Goodman, 1995, p. 3). Similar concerns have been expressed about the lack of impact of billions of dollars of spending on digital technologies. It has been reported that little has changed inside most classrooms. Instead of innovating, most teachers use technology "to sustain their existing practices and pedagogies" (Ferriter, 2010).

More recently, we have seen the hollowing out of various efforts to implement inquiry learning. Without a deep understanding of the principles and purposes of inquiry, this complex orientation to teaching and learning can be reduced to a five-step method for conducting independent research. Inquiry understood in this way is likely to have minimal impact: the difference may simply be that instead of using the textbook to find facts, students search for them on the Internet. Properly understood, to inquire is to ask questions where the answers are not already known—requiring students to draw their own critical conclusions. This interpretation of inquiry need not involve formal steps to follow nor does it require directing students to the Internet. Inquiry can be conducted with and about the textbook. Only if teachers understand the principles behind inquiry will adopting this initiative make any real difference to student learning.

The worry with rushing to the practical is that educators may be caught up in the procedures without thoroughly understanding the principles that should guide their use.

Three Promising Directions

Answering the calls for school reform will require a sustained and coherent response that remains mindful of the big picture and takes the long view on educational change. Our focus in this book is less on recommending particular initiatives and more with articulating the constellation of broader kinds of goals, principles, and foundational beliefs—and the practices that support them—that must anchor, orient, and enrich whatever initiatives are chosen. Regardless of the particulars, we advocate for a three-pronged response: build on enriching the goals that we strive for, invigorate existing practices with powerful pedagogical principles, and instill thinking as the fundamental orientation to teaching and learning.

Pursue Richer Not New or Higher Results

In our view, preparing students for a complex world is not a matter of getting more students to score in the upper percentiles on standardized tests. What most of these tests measure is not what will empower students in the ways needed for success in a changing world. This is the reason that many educators and parents are calling for less reliance on these kinds of measures. Nor will instituting an entirely new set of topics or skills provide the preparation that our students require. There is no magic and revolutionary skill set that will transform students. Students still need to be able to read, write, and do mathematics. If not new or higher results, what is the solution?

The notion of richer results directs us to reinterpret the existing curricular goals—whether they are knowledge, skills, or attitudes outcomes—in more authentic and robust ways. We believe that the emerging preference for the term *competencies* in place of *skills* is intended to signal a shift in emphasis from pen and paper to real-life abilities. Teaching students to solve word problems where all the variables are provided to them has not enabled students to solve open-ended real-life mathematical problems even when the same mathematical processes are involved.

The same can be said of the shift in emphasis from talking about promoting knowledge to engendering deep understanding. Research suggests, for example, that a large proportion of university students who have passed examinations in physics are unable to provide credible explanations for simple real-world problems, such as which of two dropped balls, one heavier than the other, would hit the floor first. In explaining this anomaly between advanced study in a subject and lack of basic understanding, Nobel Prize-winning physicist Richard Feynman (1997) concludes:

> After a lot of investigation, I finally figured out that the students had memorized everything, but that they didn't know what anything meant. When they heard "light that is reflected from a medium with an index," they didn't know that it meant a material such as water. They didn't know that the "direction of the light" is the direction in which you see something when you're looking at it, and so on. Everything was entirely memorized, yet nothing had been translated into meaningful words. (pp. 212–213)

In short, the issue is not that there is a new body of knowledge to master as much as we want students to understand the core areas of knowledge more thoroughly so that they can actually use them to inform their lives.

A similar point can be made about the teaching of attitudes. Flexibility, open-mindedness, perseverance, and other such dispositions have been long-standing attitudinal goals prized by educators. Teachers exhort students to adopt these virtues and invite students to discuss their importance. However, it is one thing for students to espouse the virtues of open-mindedness, but what really counts is that they live this out in their day-to-day lives. The problem is not with the attitudes that we seek to promote in schools, but that our efforts to nurture attitudes don't consistently translate into commitments that translate into student actions.

Our analysis suggests that the failure to prepare students for the world may largely be because we have been interpreting and teaching the existing goals in ways that don't lead to deep understanding, real-life competence, and genuine commitment. The solution is not to change the curriculum radically—most of the essential goals already exist in curriculum documents. Our more pressing challenge is to reframe how we understand and promote the existing goals so that we produce richer results.

Invigorate Rather Than Invent Practices

The tendency in education when something isn't working well is to replace it. Fortunately, this is not the pattern in medical practice. Health practitioners are more likely to modify the dose or alter the regimen before implementing a brand-new treatment. The thinking in medicine is that the original treatment was adopted for a reason, and a new regimen may have more unintended negative consequences than the existing practices. Rather than quickly abandoning practices, medical professionals will first do what they can to make them work before deciding that they must be dropped. The cumulative effect of this approach is growth in the collective wisdom of the profession by building on progressively refined practices.

Things are different in education. To use a cliché, the tendency here is to "throw the baby out with the bathwater." We start anew when existing practices don't achieve everything we want them to. Because there are only so many practices to draw upon, we revive old methods that have been revised and renamed, only to reabandon them a few years later. The effect is not a progressively refined practice as much as it is a perpetually supplanted practice. Many educators recognize this as the proverbial educational bandwagon.

The power of principles to invigorate our practices can be illustrated by a simple example of etiquette. The practice of saying hello to people we greet is motivated by our respect for the principle "Be gracious and polite to others." When a practice becomes a hollow ritual, it means the principle behind the practice has been lost. All of us can distinguish a perfunctory, often grumpy, greeting and a sincere, cheerfully delivered one. The solution is not to discourage the former person from saying hello but to help the person rediscover the missing or neglected principles behind his or her practice.

Similarly in education, principles identify the features or values that guide the intended action. Practices that deviate from sound guiding principles are unlikely to produce a desirable result. Reconsider the example of letting students choose their electives or their learning activities. Students who choose easy courses or courses involving already covered material to secure higher marks miss the intentions—which were to support students in pursuing areas of passion and in bettering meeting their educational needs. This failure is not an indictment of the practice of student choice per se, but of our lack of success at empowering students to make responsible and effective choices about their educational needs and at awakening students to potentially fruitful interests. In other words, the focus should be on instilling these principles so they guide teachers and students in implementing student choice.

We believe that many existing practices and the proposals for new practices will succeed only if they embody powerful principles of effective teaching and learning. Our reading of the literature on 21st century reform highlights five such principles that are widely mentioned and that address the key complaints that critics offer about the system:

- engage students;
- sustain inquiry;
- nurture self-regulated learners;
- create assessment-rich learning; and
- enhance learning through digital technology.

It is instructive that these five principles are also the core principles of digital game design. Designed around such principles, games such as *Minecraft* and *Angry Birds* have become the most popular games among young people. It has been claimed, for example, that at its zenith, each day *Angry Birds* was played for 140,000 hours—the equivalent of 16 years each day. Coincidentally, this is the length of time a youth spends in public school.

These five principles, powerfully embedded in the structure of *Angry Birds*, are not specific methods but guiding principles or essential features for virtually all effective learning. Later, we look in depth at each of these principles, explaining what they mean, why they are important, and how they can be embedded in teaching practices.

Embedded in the structure of *Angry Birds* are five powerful features (guiding principles) that empower users to develop increasing proficiency at hitting their targets as they launch projectiles of various bird species.

- The game engages users by challenging them to increase their ability to achieve a complex task that they are freely willing to devote their time toward. It is not played because it is compulsory but because it offers a challenge. The game presents a differentiated challenge to everyone who wishes to play by mastering greater levels of difficulty.
- The game requires sustained inquiry by users in order to succeed. There is continuous trial, diagnosis, and proffered solutions as users track the launched birds' trajectories and experiment with various strategies. Each new configuration and advanced level presents users with new challenges to figure out.
- The game offers assessment-rich learning by providing timely and helpful feedback on how to improve. Every launch of a bird is accompanied by an immediate indication of what works and what doesn't work. The tiered level of the game offers evidence of the greater skill users are able to demonstrate.
- The game requires and supports self-regulated learning. With timely feedback, students learn that they can't simply repeat what they've done before.

(Continued)

> (Continued)
>
>> Without adults standing over them explaining how the game is to be played and what to do to improve, students learn to take charge of their learning: they learn to use what they know and the data they receive to make thoughtful decisions about what's working and what's not, and why, and how to improve.
>
> • The game illustrates the potency of digitally enhanced learning. The technology enhances user abilities to launch the projectiles, receive instantaneous feedback, and test revised strategies in ways they could not do as quickly and effectively in a nondigital learning environment.

Instill Thinking as the Foundation to Teaching and Learning

Fundamental beliefs and assumptions are often the least visible but the most pervasive aspect of a classroom. No structure will stand without a solid foundation. It is our view that a "thinking classroom" ought to orient every activity in school if we are to create a more effective school system. It might seem rather simpleminded to suggest that thinking is foundational to schooling. After all, thinking is fundamental to being human, so of course it is central to virtually everything we do, especially in intellectual endeavors such as schooling. Despite the obvious connection, it is not clear, however, that rigorous thinking permeates the practices in many classrooms.

One reason for the current state of affairs is the widespread influence of Bloom's taxonomy as a basic tenet of teaching and learning. Popular interpretations of the taxonomy, which is the most widely known theory in education (Shulman, 2002), has encouraged teachers to teach subject matter through direct transfer of information before asking students to think about the content. At least initially, students are simply asked to recall or summarize what they have been presented with. In addition, this theory fuels the belief that rigorous thinking is best reserved for more able students because of a presumption that mainstream or at-risk students who struggle with knowledge and comprehension tasks shouldn't be taxed with "higher-order" tasks. In one case, a curriculum document for an applied history course replaced the higher-order verbs found in the mainstream curriculum with lower-order verbs. Thus, instead of being asked to assess, synthesize, and apply, students in the applied course were asked merely to list, summarize, and recall (Antonelli, 2004, p. 38).

The implications of a regurgitation mindset were brought home when working with a seventh-grade class. I had challenged them to decide whether the 9/11 World Trade Center bombers were crazed martyrs or masterful strategists. Students were asked to use a briefing sheet on the topic to help them identify reasons for and against each conclusion and to record their ideas on a pro and con chart. Partway through, one student pointed to a passage in the briefing sheet and asked me, "Where do I put this?" At first I didn't understand what he meant. After some probing, I realized that his idea of reading for information was to identify key words that directly matched the question on the worksheet and to transfer the phrases to the suitable blank space on the student page. He did not understand that he was being asked to think for himself: to judge the relevance and implications of the information on the briefing sheet in order to arrive at his own conclusions about the issue. Apparently, thinking was not a regular expectation.

> One gains knowledge only through thinking.
>
> —Richard Paul (1993, p. 277)

Similarly, it is not at all clear that skill development is a "thinking" exercise in many classrooms. To make this point, consider two approaches to teaching how to kick a penalty shot in soccer:

- **Rote Practice:** Coaches show their players exactly where they should stand and how they are to move forward, strike the ball, and follow through. They practice identical actions exactly as instructed hundreds, if not thousands, of times until they master "the" way to execute a penalty shot. The coach's role throughout is to remind and correct the players' technique whenever it deviates from the "correct" approach.
- **Thoughtful Repetition:** Coaches introduce players to the principles of how to kick a soccer ball and suggest various techniques. Players are expected to practice penalty kicks repeatedly. But instead of mimicking one prescribed way, they are asked to experiment and test out variations: to consider what happens if they stand farther back or kick with different parts of their foot; to experiment with what they need to do to keep the ball on the ground or to lift it a few inches or several feet; to see what difference it makes to approach the shot from a standing position or while moving; and so on. The coach's role throughout is to suggest options and to exhort players to refine or change techniques when the current one isn't working.

With rote practice, there is no real thinking—merely countless drills of the same gestures—whereas thoughtful repetition involves mindful repeated testing of options. Repetition and instruction are evident in both approaches. But how these are used differ significantly. With rote practice, players repeat an action time after time exactly as before without necessarily understanding why each gesture must be done as directed. The coach's instructions are offered as prescriptions to follow verbatim. Within a thinking approach, instruction is intended to provide a platform from which players can explore options and variations. The repetition is thoughtful in that the players are imagining possibilities, observing the effects of each trial, and making further critical adjustments as needed.

Many of us will recognize that the rote practice approach was how we learned many basic skills in school, from shooting a basketball to solving math problems. The presumption of thinking has not been present in many skills-based lessons. As one teacher recently recounted, she was taught to divide fractions by memorizing the phrase "'Tis not for me to question why, just invert and multiply."

The point that we want to make here and extend in the next section is that beliefs about what students can be expected to do and how learning should best occur are powerful determinants of teaching practices. Despite the countless formal endorsements, thinking is not embedded as thoroughly into our teaching and learning practices as it should be.

Concluding Thoughts

The daunting challenge facing educators is to make sense of the multitude of reform initiatives they are confronted with. While we may agree in general terms about the failings of our system, there is less consensus on the underlying causes and the most appropriate directions to take. To avoid the pitfalls that may hamper or derail reform efforts, we offer a three-pronged coherent response:

- **Establish a Thinking Orientation:** Because teachers' educational worldviews determine virtually every decision they make, it is imperative that their foundational beliefs are compatible with and supportive of the desired direction for reform. An orientation that places thinking at the center of all teaching and learning is foundational to all other changes. This is the focus of our discussion in Part II, "Reorient the Foundations."

- **Enrich Our Goals:** Current interest in educational reform is more profitably viewed as a call to rehabilitate classic goals and not an attempt to superimpose entirely new goals for schooling—many of the so-called 21st century goals have been long-standing educational objectives. A global, digitally connected world has changed the environment in which these classic goals must be nurtured and made them even more valuable. In Part III, "Refocus the Goals," we discuss what is involved in a more robust understanding of the three traditional goals that schools strive to achieve.

- **Invigorate Our Practices:** Rather than focus on a new array of practices, educators should ensure that existing practices support powerful principles of sound teaching and learning. We offer five principles that are especially relevant to addressing the challenges facing schools. In Part IV, "Align With Guiding Principles," we explain these principles and show their potential to guide and invigorate teaching practices.

The book's closing chapter in Part V, "Support Teacher Growth," suggests how educational leaders might conceptualize and plan to support teachers in this journey using a three-tiered approach: invite educators (1) to affirm those aspects of their teaching that support and advance the goals, principles, practices, and foundational beliefs; (2) to refine those aspects of their teaching that can easily be modified to bring greater coherence; and (3) to aspire over time to tackling those more substantial changes that may take years to nurture.

At the end of each chapter, we suggest a few practices that educational leaders might implement to support teachers in coming to understand and adopt the ideas discussed in the chapter. The following three strategies help teachers approach any of the reform initiatives they may be asked to implement.

Opportunities for Leadership

Refine Rather Than Replace

Before deciding to redirect efforts to introduce a new initiative, determine what aspects are working well and which could be improved with a few refinements. Then consider what more significant changes educators might aspire to bring about. Only then is it appropriate to consider which new initiatives might best serve these goals.

Anchor Initiatives to Guiding Principles

When adopting a new initiative, formulate the principles that should guide how it is translated into classroom practice. For example, when implementing problem-based learning, educators might set the following principles to direct their efforts: make sure students are on board at every step of the way; let the project drive all of the learning, not just the final days of the unit; and check that the project actually supports the desired outcomes in a powerful, noncontrived manner.

(Continued)

(Continued)

Anticipate Ambiguity

Recognize that educational initiatives are often wrapped in ambiguous language and vague directions. Rather than looking elsewhere for a definitive definition, seek to interpret the proposal in ways that align with the best of the beliefs and principles that lie at the core of one's teaching practices. This requires walking a fine line between simply making a pretense of changing one's practices and imposing an initiative that is inconsistent with the best of one's practices.

Notes

1. For linguistic convenience, we use the first person to indicate that one of the authors had the experience.
2. There are two other causes worth considering. One pertains to the physical, social, and emotional conditions that students are raised in. Poverty, malnutrition, and parental and community neglect clearly influence student performance and engagement. A second cause may be the working conditions in schools. Relatively large classes with many high-needs students and inadequate training and support for teachers also undermine success at school. These issues are not addressed in this book since our focus is on the curricular and pedagogical dimensions of educational reform—but this in no way diminishes their importance as obstacles faced by schools.
3. Larry Cuban (2010) estimates only 10 to 15 percent of history teachers have incorporated "student-centered techniques" into their largely teacher-centered repertoire. The widely cited and extensive study of 1,000 American classrooms by John Goodlad (2004) concludes that from the early grades, school-based activities and environments condition students to reproduce what they are taught (p. 241) and not to use and evaluate information (p. 236).

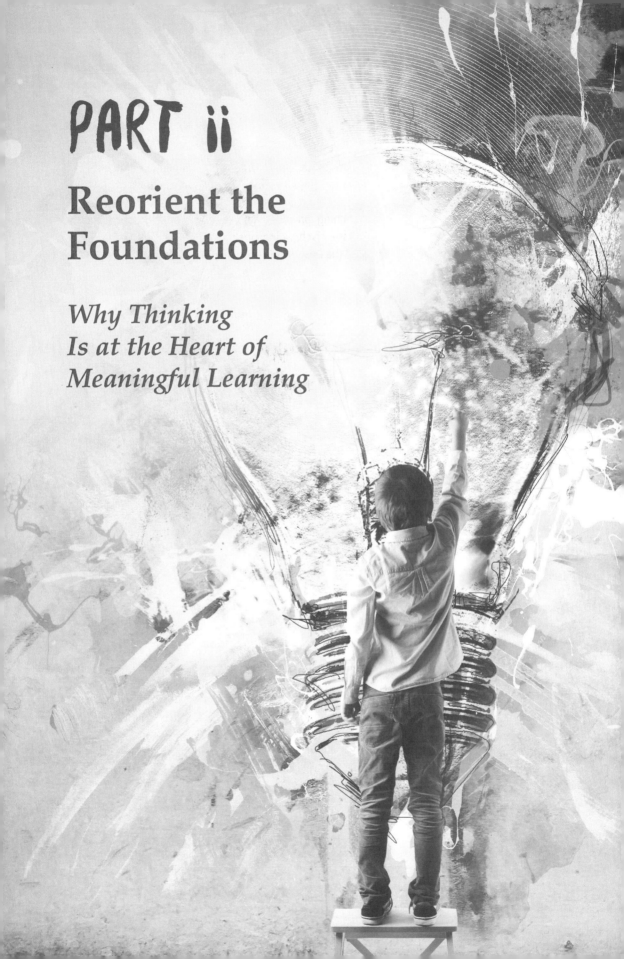

PART ii

Reorient the Foundations

*Why Thinking
Is at the Heart of
Meaningful Learning*

2

Thinking Is the Key

This chapter explains why thinking is foundational to teaching and learning—not as a dominant goal but as an overriding orientation to schooling. More specifically, it discusses

- key assumptions behind two long-standing orientations—what we call "discovery classrooms" and "didactic classrooms"—and behind our recommended orientation—what we call "thinking classrooms";
- implications of each orientation for curriculum content, the nature of student learning, and the role of the teacher;
- evidence of the benefits for student achievement and engagement in adopting a "thinking classroom" as the dominant orientation to teaching and learning.

My most successful experience in supporting students in thinking for themselves began on the first day of a university methods course. Early on I explained the two kinds of requests that students can make of any teacher: "Tell me what I should think and do" and "Support me in advancing my own thinking and actions." I shared a few examples of "Tell me" questions related to our first assignment: "How long does the analysis have to be?" and "How do you want us to record our answers?" I announced that students were allowed to ask these kinds of questions for the first three weeks of class, but after that time I would

As I reflect on critical thinking and what I am learning, I am realizing more and more that critical thinking is a form of teaching, embedded in every aspect of life in the classroom. It doesn't happen in isolation, or in specific subjects, but it permeates the curriculum.

—Journal entry of an elementary teacher working with The Critical Thinking Consortium respond only to "Support me" requests. Initially, they struggled to grasp how to ask a question that didn't simply seek the answer but was designed to assist them in thinking through the matter for themselves. We practiced reframing "Tell me" questions as "Support me" questions.

The unexpected result over the next weeks was that students were asking fewer questions as they grew better at thinking through issues for themselves without my help. On the occasions when they did ask a question, it was to seek guidance on a particular issue that they and their colleagues had discussed but couldn't agree upon. They might ask questions such as "If our students don't know enough about a topic to come up with criteria on their own, is it better simply to tell them, let them struggle initially, or spend time codeveloping criteria?" Even in these cases, my stock response was "Well, what do you think?" followed by "Why do you think that?" Depending on the answer, I might prompt further thinking by proposing a hypothetical scenario or complication. I was delighted to see how thoughtful and independent students were becoming. My refusal to provide answers outright helped students realize that they could work out most issues on their own and they didn't need me to do their thinking for them. Ironically, turning their questions back on them led to a much deeper understanding of and fluency with the course material than I had witnessed from previous classes. Despite my doing less explicit teaching, students had learned more.

The point of this story is not simply to describe a particular practice for encouraging thinking, but to draw attention to a mind shift or orientation that began to pervade everything I did in class. My students and I stopped seeing me as the expert to consult when they did not know something. Not only did they learn to be better thinkers, but the very act of thinking through the issues enriched their understanding of the subject matter. The distinction between promoting thinking as an educational outcome and promoting thinking as an orientation to all teaching and learning is an important one. Thinking is one of the competencies we discuss in Chapter 6, "From Skill to Real-Life Competency." However, thinking is not simply one goal among others; it needs to be at the heart of everything we do in schools—as a fundamental approach that underpins how we conceptualize the very nature of schooling. The inclusion of thinking in the title of this book signals that the most basic and important change that educators can make is to embed thinking as the engine of teaching and learning.

> The most basic and important change that educators can make is to embed thinking as the engine of teaching and learning.

The focus of this chapter is on what it would mean to position thinking at the center of the ongoing business of the classroom and the benefits of doing so in terms of enhanced student achievement and engagement. Chapter 3, "Critical, Creative, and Collaborative Dimensions of Thinking," explores in greater detail what is involved in thinking. Chapter 4, "A Framework for Nurturing Thinking Classrooms," introduces a four-pronged approach to systematic implementation of thinking as the dominant orientation.

Basic Orientations to Teaching and Learning

Over the centuries, various educational philosophies have been put forward as the defining approach to teaching and learning. The two most prevalent and deeply debated orientations are often referred to as *child-centered* (or learner- or student-centered) and *subject-centered* philosophies. Since there are many versions of these philosophies, we will focus on a few central pedagogical assumptions and implications of each camp. We suggest that learning by discovery is the characteristic pedagogy of a child-centered approach, and learning through didactic instruction typifies the pedagogy of a subject-centered approach. We contrast these with the pedagogical orientation that forms the core of this book—learning by thinking. We refer to these as *discovery, didactic*, and *thinking classrooms*.[1]

We consider three assumptions represented by these contrasting foundational beliefs:

- the source of curriculum content;
- the nature of student learning; and
- the role of the teacher.

To sharpen the contrast between the options, simplified accounts of these diverse constellations of fundamental beliefs are offered. Within any given classroom, elements of all three orientations will be present, and no one orientation will best serve all conditions and every situation. Figure 2.1 outlines key implications of these approaches on the decisions educators make about curriculum content, student learning, and the teacher's role in the classroom.

Alternative Sources of Curriculum Content

The traditional basis of a student-centered (or learning by discovery) curriculum is student interests and needs. It is thought that each student's uniqueness requires that learning be individually tailored. For example, the introverted, academically inclined budding mathematician has different

Figure 2.1   Contrasting Foundational Beliefs About Teaching and Learning

Learning by Discovery	Learning Through Didactic Instruction	Learning by Thinking
Source of Curriculum Content		
Curriculum is built from students' interests and needs.	Curriculum is based on requirements of the disciplines and society.	Curriculum is co-constructed from disciplinary and societal requirements and students' interests and needs.
Nature of Student Learning		
Students experience, explore, and realize for themselves.	Students receive, replicate, and retain for later use.	Students consider, assess, and conclude.
Role of the Teacher		
The teacher is an animator who stimulates and nurtures.	The teacher is an instructor who motivates and transmits.	The teacher is a choreographer who frames and guides.

interests and needs from the gregarious, practically inclined budding artist. The curriculum, to the extent possible, should respect this diversity. When it comes to curriculum decision making, individual students are in the best position to know what will interest and satisfy them.

On the other hand, the basis for a subject-centered (or learning through didactic instruction) curriculum are societal needs for responsible and productive citizens, and the intellectual requirements of the various disciplines (e.g., an understanding of the principles and processes of mathematics, the laws and methods of science, and the major developments in history). Since subject-centered advocates believe that these common needs should guide curriculum development, educators—whether curriculum designers or teachers—are best positioned to determine what is needed.

Clearly, there are merits to both views: there are common abilities and understandings that all students can benefit from (including knowing how to read, write, and calculate), and there are important differences that distinguish each student's educational needs. What we refer to as the learning by thinking orientation offers a middle-ground position between a child- and subject-centered approach. According to this view, curriculum should be a jointly negotiated program based on what would be most valuable and realistic, balancing common societal and disciplinary requirements and individual students' interests and needs. In terms of curriculum decision making, both educators and students have expertise that must be respected.

Implications for Student Control of Curriculum Content

The notions of student-centered learning and student choice are regularly used in tandem. Significantly, the responsibility is placed on school authorities to interpret what this will mean in practical terms. At the very least, we are left with uncertainty about who makes the decisions about how best to meet learner needs. Does the language of student-centered learning signal that learners will be given greater say? Or are these decisions largely to be made by educators on behalf of students? This ambiguity is reflected in another popular term—*student voice*. This term has two branches: one is to listen much more intently and more regularly to what students are saying so that educators can better tailor programs to meet student interests and needs; the second is to give students greater say in their learning. This last interpretation is variously referred to as "sharing ownership for learning," involving students as "partners in decisions about their learning," putting "learners in the drivers' seat," and promoting "learner autonomy."[2] Does this mean that students will negotiate with educators about these decisions or be free to exercise considerable discretion on their own? Which interpretation of student choice will prevail will in many cases depend on educators' fundamental beliefs and assumptions about the source of curriculum decision making.

To illustrate how these orientations shape differing educational practices, consider varying implications for student control of curriculum content as seen through the lens of each set of beliefs.

Student Choice Within a Discovery Classroom. Students would be encouraged to direct their own learning path since they are seen to be in the best position to know what they want to learn.[3] The decision to pursue band over basket weaving or physics over psychology would depend on what individual students wished to explore—provided it was feasible and safe. Up to a certain age, expectations may be set by authorities, but after, there would be progressively fewer prescribed courses of study: students would eventually be free to pursue packaged courses prepared by educators or assemble their own courses of study. Within a given subject, students would choose the novels or other literary works to read and select which historical events or science topics to explore more deeply. Students would be encouraged to decide for themselves how they would complete their learning tasks, whether it was developing their own method of throwing a basketball or solving a math problem.

Student Choice Within a Didactic Classroom. Within this orientation, students could select from a fixed and relatively narrow array of authorized choices. Since educators are seen as the curriculum experts, they should determine what is most valuable for students to learn and how best to learn it. Students' limited choices might involve selecting, for example, a biology or a physics elective as the way to meet their science requirement. Alternatively, students might be permitted to take face-to-face or online self-paced versions of approved courses. More extensive options might be available after students had satisfied prerequisites across core subjects. For example, after junior high school, students might be allowed to develop expertise in an area of strength by pursuing a strand or concentration (in math and science, fine arts, technical arts, or athletics). But each of these options would be built around a packaged array of courses that experts had created. Within a given subject, students could be allowed to choose a novel from an authorized list that the teacher had assembled. Independent research projects would allow students to delve more deeply into a teacher-approved set of historical events or science topics. Students would generally be shown the correct or best way of completing learning tasks, such as throwing a basketball or solving a math problem. However, if there were several recognized methods, students would be instructed in each of these options and allowed to decide which one they would prefer to use. The scenario depicted here is the kind of personalization already available in many school districts. With a greater push for use of technology, the list of approved online options that students may choose will likely expand.

Student Choice Within a Thinking Classroom. Within this approach, students, in consultation with teachers, would be free to select, modify, and create options provided they satisfied agreed-upon expectations. Since educators and students are both seen to have expertise in the design of curriculum, they would negotiate what is most valuable and realistic for students to learn and how best to learn it. Students may have a wide but not completely open-ended set of options from which to select. Students would likely be required to master the basic foundations within each subject area, and all choices would need to satisfy specified expectations. For example, it might be stipulated that the course of study had to promote critical thinking, the ability to communicate effectively using various media, or perseverance and understanding of everyday scientific phenomena. It would be up to students in consultation with their teachers to justify how to meet these expectations in a realistic manner given the student's strengths, needs, and interests. Within a given subject and where feasible, students could be allowed to choose their novel or independent inquiry topic provided it supported the core expectations for the course. Although not as freewheeling as those available in a discovery classroom, the options would be far less restricted than those available in a didactic classroom. Students would be encouraged to decide how best to complete learning tasks; however, they would need to demonstrate that their chosen method was effective and efficient for the purpose and context.

As this comparison suggests, fundamental beliefs about who should make decisions about curriculum content range from open-ended student choices, to student selection among narrowly prescribed options, to varied options negotiated by teacher and student in light of established expectations.

Deciding on the Extent of Student Control Over the Curriculum

A thinking classroom approach offers a middle ground that recognizes the value of significant opportunity for student choice without foregoing the value of common expectations about what students should know and be able to do. The core weakness in the discovery approach is the assumption that students are always in the best position to realize what they need. While many students may know what they want, they may not all be in the best position to decide on what would be most important to learn. John Hattie's analysis of student control over learning shows a very low correlation with student achievement because students fail to master the basics before embarking on more ambitious learning (Case et al., 2015). Furthermore, it is not clear that all students know what will interest them in the long run, and many things that interest students may not be pursuits that will justify going to school.

Although the didactic orientation recognizes the importance of setting common learning goals, it leaves little room for the legitimate choices that students often want and should be able to make. Research suggests that narrowly restricting choices has significant consequences for engagement. Student effort and learning are negatively affected when forced to choose among fixed options. This is because students feel they are being controlled and not able to exercise self-determination (National Research Council and Institute of Medicine, 2004, p. 38).

A didactic orientation expects student to do things because it's good for them more than because it appeals to their developed interests. The use of external rewards and punishments, such as marks and entrance to a university, are seen to be necessary to keep students on track. Yet researchers caution that "'carrot and stick' approaches can be particularly problematic for secondary students, who, for many reasons, do not value the rewards typically available in schools, and may want to appear independent rather than compliant" (National Research Council and Institute of Medicine, 2004, p. 41). Not only are external motivators not particularly effective, but they are often counterproductive. There is considerable research demonstrating that reliance on extrinsic motivation decreases the likelihood of developing intrinsic interest in an activity (National Research Council and Institute of Medicine, 2004, p. 48). In other words, if we did not repeatedly pressure students to complete assignments for marks, they would be more likely to find enjoyment and fulfillment in these tasks (A. Kohn, 2011).

A thinking classroom orientation allows for significant, but not unbridled, student choice by requiring that jointly negotiated decisions be made in light of students' and society's legitimate needs and interests. This approach is to be preferred over ones where either students decide for themselves or educators decide for students.

Differing Views of Student Learning

Learning involves making sense of the world. Let us examine what this means and how it occurs when viewed through the three orientations.

Learning in a Discovery Classroom. This orientation strives to help students create their own individual sense of the world. It is believed that learners are so unique that each of them must make their own meaning from the world as they encounter it—the key is to experience the world for themselves. The notion of discovery suggests that no one can know all the things that another learner knows, so no one can make sense for another or truly explain things to others. It is less important that learners arrive at a "correct" impression than it is for learners to reconcile newly formed ideas with their broader worldview. Advocates of a discovery orientation believe that learners are inherently inquisitive and generally eager to ask questions and explore things around them. They believe that learning best occurs by experiencing things for oneself. The more stimulating and varied the experiences, the richer the learning opportunity.

Learning in a Didactic Classroom. This orientation strives to imprint a shared sense of the world. It is believed that although learners may differ in many ways, the reality of the world around them is based on established facts and real objects. There is so much that learners are unaware of and misinformed about. Making sense of the world means sharing in the insights and accumulated wisdom of experts. The notion of didactic teaching implies that educators who have accumulated vastly greater knowledge of the world will impart or pass on their knowledge. Often, this requires correcting myths and misconceptions that learners have developed. Advocates of a didactic orientation believe that learners are generally receptive to new ideas that are interesting and relevant, but it may take time for the ideas to sink in. The learners' primary role is to attend to and absorb the content that is presented to them, and to retain and replicate the ideas and skills for subsequent use.

Learning in a Thinking Classroom. This orientation seeks to guide students in internalizing a reasoned and grounded sense of the world. While the world is based on established facts and real objects, what these mean and how to respond to and understand these realities is not a predetermined matter. If learners' interpretations are to be useful and justifiable, they cannot simply invent their own; sense-making must be grounded in rigorous investigation, not playful exploration. Making reasoned sense requires building upon what is known about the world, but learners who simply accept the views of others won't have internalized and digested these ideas.

> In the book of life the answers aren't in the back.
>
> —Charlie Brown

Learners' primary responsibility is to reach their own conclusions based on careful and informed assessment of the possibilities. Learners may be mistaken in their conclusions not because they have the "wrong" answer but because their reasoning may be flawed or incomplete. Advocates of a thinking orientation believe that learners are willing to be challenged to think for themselves. Learners' primary responsibilities are to seriously entertain (but not necessarily accept) what they are presented with, to assess options and implications, and then to reach a conclusion for themselves.

Deciding Upon an Orientation to Student Learning

According to the three orientations, learning is either experienced, imprinted, or internalized. While there are occasions when one or another orientation may offer more useful direction and insights, we believe that challenging students to rigorously think through their own conclusions offers a more powerful approach to learning than the other two approaches. This is supported by research that suggests that students are more engaged when they are "pushed to understand," which includes "being required to explain their reasoning, defend their conclusions, or explore alternative strategies and solutions" (National Research Council and Institute of Medicine, 2004, p. 49). Or, as a student in another study reported, "What made math more engaging were activities where 'you had to work out for yourself what was going on, and you had to use your own ideas'" (Boaler, 2002, p. 68; as reported in National Research Council and Institute of Medicine, 2004, p. 50).

Increased cognitive engagement has been shown to translate into higher achievement. A large study involving 5,000 students in 117 Chicago-area schools found that providing challenging intellectual work resulted in greater than average scores on standardized measures of basic numeracy and literacy skills. These researchers found that third-, sixth-, and eighth-grade students in disadvantaged as well as mainstream classrooms benefited from these challenging tasks. In fact, students with low prior achievement levels in mathematics experienced greater gains from this approach than did students with high prior achievement levels (Newmann, Bryk, & Nagaoka, 2001).

Qualitative data and anecdotal evidence emerging from our own work with thousands of teachers each year offer a similar picture (Hattie, 2015, p. 10). A number of schools have reported improved results on standardized tests in areas such as literacy, mathematics, and student engagement. These schools have attributed these results in large measure to the power of a thinking approach to deepen student understanding and increase engagement. The improvements are often dramatic. One school reported a 54 percent increase in combined third-grade reading and writing scores on provincial standardized tests. The same school saw a 75 percent increase in sixth-grade students' procedural and conceptual understanding in mathematics. Four elementary schools in one district reported an increase of 15 percent in the number of third-grade students and an increase of 36 percent in the number of sixth-grade students achieving level 3 (B or B+) or level 4 (A- to A+) in mathematics. These positive results are found with students from across the spectrum of ability. For example, a school with students considered to be at high social risk reported slightly less than a twofold increase in the number of students reporting that they liked math most of the time. Not surprisingly, the number of those students achieving at or above the provincial standard tests increased from 15 percent to 50 percent during the same period. In another school with a challenging school population, among the four classes of sixth-grade students, 85 percent were performing at or above the standard in mathematics after working with our team. In the previous year, only 49 percent of sixth-grade students had reached this level.

Collectively, these results offer a compelling glimpse of the potential of a thinking classroom to increase achievement and engagement across the spectrum of the student population.

Contrasting Roles for Teachers

Each orientation has clear implications for the role of teachers. We offer three overarching metaphors to characterize these differences: animator, instructor, and choreographer.[4] All have a place in learning, but which role should dominate?

Animating a Discovery Classroom. Teachers are expected to bring learning to life and evoke student interest. Animators create stimulating learning spaces and tasks that ignite and feed into students' curiosity. They encourage and prompt students but do not introduce ideas without being invited. Animators step aside to enable students to go in directions they choose and are ready to answer student questions if asked. Play, manipulation, firsthand experiences, and unstructured experimentation are powerful activities that animators design to help learners figure things out and develop knowledge.

Instructing in a Didactic Classroom. Teachers are expected to inform—give form to students' minds—and instruct—imparting to students what is intended to be learned. Instructors endeavor to communicate the learning in the most effective and interesting manner to ensure that students master the desired content. They encourage and prompt students, and correct their errors when they arise. Instructors design and lead students through a planned course of study with a clear sense of the conclusions that students should reach. Explanation, examples, demonstration, repetition, and practice are effective ways in which instructors impart knowledge.

Choreographing a Thinking Classroom. Teachers are expected to orchestrate a rich sequence of thinking activities for students to undertake while developing the conditions that enable learners to succeed at these tasks. Choreographers frame challenging activities where students are doing much of the talking and the thinking. Choreographers encourage and question students, and probe faulty reasoning when it arises, but they do not stipulate the conclusions that students will reach. They actively manage the sequences of activities that enable students to think their way through the curriculum. Choreographers support learners in developing their own reasoned conclusions through challenging tasks, probing questions, aids to support thinking, and opportunities for deliberation and dialogue.

> Lecturing [is the] ... best way to get information from teacher's notebook to student's notebook without touching the student's mind.
>
> —George Leonard (as cited in A. Kohn, 2004)

While there is room for instruction and animation when teachers play the role of choreographer, these functions do not epitomize the powerful teaching that is needed. Neither giving students an established answer nor coaching students to invent their own is as effective as supporting students in thinking things through to a reasoned conclusion. As argued previously, research on student engagement and achievement points to the effectiveness of a thinking classroom orientation to curriculum and learning.

Implications for an Inquiry Unit

Educational leaders often ask us, "If I went into a thinking classroom, how would it look different from other kinds of classrooms?" Figure 2.2 offers a realistic but fictionalized comparison across the three orientations of a partial inquiry unit on community similarities and differences. While the account is simplified, it does highlight what to look for. It is clear that the content and resources are nearly identical across the three versions. What distinguishes each are the expectations of what students will learn, how they will be supported, and what will be assessed. In the discovery unit, there is no predefined outcome but a general topic around which students pose and answer questions of their own making. The goal is to develop their own impressions of community similarities and differences. In the didactic unit, students extract evidence from sources to support a specific conclusion that the teacher has offered as the outcome for the unit. In the thinking classroom, students research and justify their own conclusions to a question that has no "right" answer. The goal is to deepen students' understanding of community similarities and differences by inviting them to judge the significance of the information they uncover.

Concluding Thoughts

Foundational beliefs are the bedrock of any educational system. In this chapter, we have discussed three alternative sets of fundamental beliefs associated with discovery, didactic, and thinking classrooms. We have looked at the assumptions related to curriculum, learners, and teachers that underlie these orientations. We have seen that the practices associated with personalized learning and inquiry take significantly different directions depending on these assumptions. While each of the orientations may have a place in education, research suggests that the thinking classroom offers significant promise for increased student achievement and engagement. In the next chapter, we look more closely into the kinds of thinking that are to be nurtured in a thinking classroom.

Figure 2.2   Inquiry in Three Different Classrooms

Unit Components	Discovery Classroom	Didactic Classroom	Thinking Classroom
Big Idea The teacher expresses the big idea in terms of . . .	an open-ended theme for students to explore: "Similarities and differences in our community."	a broad generalization that all students should understand: "All of us are similar in some respects and different in other respects."	a critical question that each student must decide upon: "In areas that really matter, are we more similar or different?"
Resources The teacher assembles a range of materials, including pictures, stories, artifacts, field trip opportunities, and class guests. Her goal is to provide students with . . .	stimulating resources that will evoke a full range of sensorial experiences.	various resources where it is easy to identify similarities and differences, and other resources where it is more difficult to identify similarities and differences.	a range of resources that students must scrutinize where similarities and differences are rather trivial, and other resources where the similarities and differences are significant.
Unit Task Each day in different ways, students explore and discuss various resources that have been assembled or arranged. Students record their ideas on . . .	a KWL chart (what I Know, Want to know, and have Learned) to record their ideas and questions about community similarities and differences.	an activity sheet with places where students identify two similarities and differences they notice from each resource.	an activity sheet organized around a scale (ranging from "very different" to "very similar") to record similarities and differences they notice, assign a rating to each, and indicate reasons for their ratings.
Introductory Activity The teacher introduces the unit by . . .	inviting students individually to select one of the assembled resources about the community and to think of what they already know and what more they might want to know about it.	discussing two deceptive images: one where the people seem to be nearly identical but on closer examination are seen to have differences, and another where people look to be completely different but actually have similarities.	inviting students to look at one of the community images and decide on the most significant similarity between the people in the image and themselves, and then decide on the most significant difference between the people in the image and themselves.

(Continued)

Figure 2.2 (Continued)

Unit Components	Discovery Classroom	Didactic Classroom	Thinking Classroom
Initial Instruction The teacher scaffolds the learning by . . .	inviting students to share what similarity and difference mean to them, and to give an example.	providing definitions of similarity and difference, and modeling how to locate similarities and differences from the provided resources.	providing examples that students use to draw out criteria for deciding when a similarity or difference would be important or significant to the community.
Teacher Guidance During the unit, the teacher will circulate around the class to . . .	encourage students and prompt them to reflect on their thoughts, feelings, and questions about the similarities and differences in the community.	help individual students notice some of the similarities and differences that they may have overlooked.	ask students to explain their ratings of the importance of similarities and differences, and posing questions to gently invite students to wonder about some of their ratings.
Concluding Activity The unit concludes with . . .	a carousel where students circulate around the classroom looking at the display each student has created on the theme "What I've learned about similarities and differences in our community."	a think-pair-share activity where students share the evidence they have found initially with a partner, and then the pair shares their ideas with two other students.	a four corners debate where students assemble initially with students who share their conclusions (very different, mostly different, mostly similar, or very similar) and then with students from other groups to discuss their respective positions.
Assessment The teacher assesses whether students are able to offer . . .	three imaginative insights or feelings about similarities and differences in their community.	three accurate pieces of evidence to support the generalization "All of us are similar in some respects and different in other respects."	three relevant and convincing reasons to support their personal conclusion and one plausible counterargument as a response to someone who might disagree with their conclusion.

The following are selected strategies for educational leaders to use with teachers to encourage to explore and harmonize the assumptions underlying their practices.

Opportunities for Leadership

Clarify Basic Assumptions

It is helpful for educators, individually and as a staff, to be aware of the range of assumptions that form their core beliefs about teaching and learning, and to appreciate the implications that these assumptions have for the choices they make.

Drill Down to the Root Issue

Educational disputes about specific practices are often not about the practice per se but reside in differing assumptions. Recognizing that the disagreement lies more deeply is helpful in its own right. As well, it provides an opportunity to explore which set of assumptions is more warranted or fruitful. Research can be brought in to shed light on fundamental beliefs such as the motivational value of marks or the capacity of young students to think critically.

Draw Upon Basic Beliefs to Interpret Ambiguous Recommendations

Many educational initiatives are open to significant interpretation. As we saw with conflicting interpretations of personalized learning and inquiry, one's fundamental beliefs can give direction to inherently ambiguous ideas.

Build Coherence Among Practices

Because teachers acquire diverse practices over the course of their careers, these may not all be consistent with one another. Selecting a few of the basic beliefs about teaching and learning can be useful in combing through those practices to highlight possible incompatibility.

Notes

1. The term *thinking classroom* has been used by educators at Harvard University and elsewhere for a while, but not necessarily in the way in which we use the term. See, for example, Tishman, Perkins, and Jay (1995).
2. These phrases are from Student Achievement Division (2013).
3. It might be suggested that a discovery approach could allow for the teacher, and not individual students, to determine what best meets each student's

needs. Yet this, in effect, acknowledges the teacher as the expert on student needs. This is not very different from what curriculum planners do when they determine that literacy and numeracy are necessary skills. They make judgments about what students need in order to be functioning and fulfilled members of society.

4. We avoid the more commonly used term *facilitator* because it is ambiguous. Some interpret it in ways that are similar to the animator role described here; others have a highly proactive interpretation that approximates what we call "choreographer." See, for example, Case, Harper, Tilley, and Wiens (1994).

3

Critical, Creative, and Collaborative Dimensions of Thinking

This chapter explains the interrelated nature of three dimensions of thinking—critical, creative, and collaborative. More specifically, it discusses

- the value and merits of an integrated approach to thinking;
- common misconceptions associated with each of these dimensions;
- ways in which the three dimensions powerfully reinforce each other.

The power of an integrated approach to thinking became evident while working with mathematics teachers in India. By Grade 6, students in the school we were assisting had in two previous years memorized the formula for calculating profit and loss, and applied the formula to countless problems. Despite repeated drills, many students were unsuccessful with the problems, and most didn't really understand the formula. With support from our team, teachers created several scenarios featuring simple commercial ventures where the profit or loss was to be calculated. Working in groups, students were asked to figure out the answers as best they could, and then to produce a formulation using as few words as possible

> The ability to learn new things is more important than ever in a world where you have to process information at lightning speed. Students need to be able to think creatively, critically, and collaboratively.
>
> —Don Tapscott (2008, p. 127)

(or only symbols if they were able) that represented all of the variables and the relationships among them. Students came up with varied and, in some cases, imaginative ways to represent their formulas. Working again in their groups, students tested their draft formulas using different problems to see if they worked in each case. They shopped their version around to other groups to see if they could arrive at more complete, reliable, and concise formulations. In reflecting on this experience in a learning log, one student remarked that while this was the third time he had been exposed to the topic, for the first time he understood what he was doing. He wasn't worried that he would forget the formula at exam time, because now that he understood it, the formula was more memorable to him. He went on to explain that even if he did happen to forget the formula, he was confident he could reconstruct it because of this learning experience.

Most of us can readily appreciate that this experience would not have been nearly as effective if students had worked entirely on their own. This testifies to the value of thinking collaboratively. As well, we can imagine the inferior results if students were not expected to test and revise their ideas but simply arrive at conclusions based on hunches. This is a testament to the value of thinking critically. And finally, without the expectation that students try to offer original formulations, the activity would have been diminished. This is a testament to the value of thinking creatively. Considered together, they illustrate the synergy and value of seeing effective or quality thinking as a composite achievement.

Our discussions thus far have intentionally referred to thinking rather generally, without trying to define it precisely. In recent years, educational literature has emphasized the three forms highlighted in the previous scenario: critical, creative, and collaborative thinking. As is the case with many complex concepts, their meanings and interrelationships are variously interpreted. When we say we want our students to think, what do we mean? Which form or forms of thinking do we have in mind? Creative thinking has often been framed in opposition to critical thinking. The former is typically characterized as spontaneous, productive, and nonrational, whereas the latter is often described as deliberative, reactive, and logical. Is this a fair and helpful classification? Many discussions of collaborative thinking immediately move to references to cooperative learning. Are these two terms synonymous? Answering these and other questions about the meaning and interrelationships among critical, creative, and collaborative thinking (C3 thinking) is an important step in conceptualizing and implementing a thinking classroom.

The Power of an Integrated Approach to Thinking

There is little consensus about the relationship between critical, creative, and collaborative thinking. Three alternative interpretations of the concepts are

- as distinct and opposing forms of thinking;
- as distinct but complementary forms of thinking; and
- as intertwined and mutually reinforcing dimensions of one form of thinking.

Figure 3.1 illustrates each of these interpretations. As these examples show, there is nothing incompatible about wanting to be rigorous in one's thinking, seeking to come up with

> Quality thinking is rigorous thinking that is both productive and reactive, done alone and in concert with others.

new or innovative ideas, and building on the ideas of others to further our own thinking. This is why we define quality or C3 thinking as rigorous thinking that is both productive and responsive, done alone and in concert with others. Each dimension of thinking reinforces and is relied on by the

Figure 3.1   The Interrelationships Among Critical, Creative, and Collaborative Thinking

Distinct and Opposing Modes If they are distinct and opposing forms of thinking, no one would use all three at once, and different people might typically rely on one form over the others. For example, philosophers might rely most on critical thinking, artists on creative thinking, and negotiators on collaborative thinking.	
Distinct but Complementary Forms If they are distinct but complementary forms, all three are helpful, but each serves a discrete function. One form would be used at one time and another in another context. Students would need to be introduced to each form of thinking and helped to figure out when to use each one.	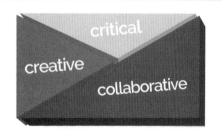
Intertwined and Mutually Reinforcing Dimensions of One Form If they are intertwined and mutually reinforcing dimensions of one form of thinking, it would be hard to function effectively in any situation without relying on all of them. Students would need to be introduced to each dimension and helped to effectively deploy all three dimensions in almost every situation.	

Source: Images created by The Critical Thinking Consortium.

others. When asking students to think, we want them to understand that they are expected to be rigorous, imaginative, and collaborative (even if only to consult a resource for greater background knowledge).

There are at least two practical reasons for looking upon C3 thinking as intertwined and mutually reinforcing dimensions of one form of thinking:

- **More Economical:** A composite form of thinking is simpler and more efficient than multiple forms. If they are discrete forms, thinking about a task would require applying a critical lens, then a creative lens, and finally a collaborative lens. Alternatively, if they are intertwined, we can approach a task concurrently with one composite lens.

- **Greater Effectiveness:** An integrated conception is likely to be more effective. If there are, in fact, discrete forms of thinking, then each can be done effectively on its own, without need of the others. Alternatively, if they are mutually reinforcing, we could not do one well without mobilizing the others. Consider what happens when each of the forms is absent. Thinking that is missing a critical dimension would be unsupported and thoughtless. Without creativity, thinking is limited to what is already known and predictable. Without collaborative input, thinking is solitary and isolated. To what extent would we be satisfied with individuals who thought critically about interpretations of a text or about solutions to a problem if their conclusions were always predictable? While we want individuals to think for themselves, how effective are critical thinkers who are always thinking by themselves and never drawing on the insights of others? Similar points can be made about creativity. Do we want creative solutions that are unsupported and thoughtless? It is said that great innovations are built on the shoulders of giants. If this is true, what are the prospects for creative output if people are consistently isolated from the ideas of others? And finally, who would want collaborative thinking that was entirely predictable and unsupported?

Let us now look in greater detail at each of these dimensions of thinking and how misconceptions have caused people to view them as discrete, even opposing, forms.

The Critical Dimension

In our view, individuals are thinking critically if, and only if, they are attempting to judge or assess what would be reasonable or sensible to believe or do. And any assessment must always be done in the face of criteria. The close relationship between the terms *critical* and *criteria* is instructive. The word *critical* should be seen as a synonym for *criterial*. In other words, critical thinking is criterial thinking—thinking in light of or using criteria (Lipman, 1988). The grounding in criteria is what gives our judgments rigor. When thinking critically about a solution to a problem, we are not asserting a personal preference ("It's good simply because

---

Critical thinking involves judging or assessing in light of relevant criteria what would be reasonable or sensible to believe or do.

I like it") or reaching a conclusion based on a dubious set of considerations ("It's a good solution because it is easy, even if it does work"). Rather, we are offering a reasoned assessment of the merits of the solution—we are making a judgment based on an ample set of relevant criteria.

Critical Is Not the Same as Criticize

A common misconception equates critical thinking with criticizing: teaching students to think critically means encouraging them to criticize everything. This concern typically takes two forms: critical thinking teaches students (1) to be disparaging or judgmental and (2) to question and reject all authority. Both are misleading characterizations of the purpose and necessary effect of promoting critical thinking.

It is understandable, given the connotation of the term *critical*, that some may equate critical thinking with being negative, harsh, and mean-spirited. However, this connection is not inevitable and in fact distorts the intention behind critical thinking. Although making judgments is essential to critical thinking, making a thoughtful judgment is not identical with being judgmental. In fact, being judgmental implies rash, one-sided conclusions based on inadequate evidence. These qualities are the antithesis of the attributes of a good critical thinker. Thinking critically is essentially to engage in critique. Good critical thinkers are like respected critics. They are not simply disparaging of things but look fairly at both the merits and shortcomings. In fact, the inclination to belittle and to tear down everything marks the absence of key attributes of a good critical thinker.

Another misleading tendency is to equate critical thinking with being cynical—with doubting or discounting everything one reads and hears. This perception may stem from a tendency among some to stress questioning the opinions of others over self-questioning. The cynical student who discounts the opinions of all authority is no less uncritical than the student who accepts whatever any authority says. Or, as one philosopher observed, "[T]here are two ways to slide easily through life: to believe everything or to doubt everything—both ways save us from thinking" (as cited in Ruggiero, 1996, p. 84). A trait of a good thinker is an ongoing attitude of self-reflection. Teaching students to think critically includes getting them to question why they disagree with the opinions of others, and it does not mean teaching them to discount the opinions of others. The irony of promoting critical thinking, especially among adolescents, is that it may lead them to be less dismissive of generally accepted views because they may be helped to appreciate that facile rejection of an opinion is no less thoughtless than is facile acceptance.

Thinking Critically Applies to Everything, Not Just Argumentation

Another misperception is that critical thinking is largely focused on logic and argumentation. Properly understood, thinking critically is usefully applied to any task we may want to undertake. Even seemingly rote tasks such as taking notes can be opportunities to think critically (and creatively and collaboratively). Consider first thoughtless note taking. This happens when students write down virtually everything the teacher says or when they record ideas unsystematically without consideration of importance, relevance, or accuracy. On the other hand, students can be assisted in treating note taking as a thoughtful task by introducing them to the criteria for judging good notes and by suggesting various strategies—circling key words, webbing of ideas, paraphrasing. Students are thinking critically about their note taking as they judge whether or not their suggested entries are accurate, relevant, comprehensive, and concise. Recognizing that critical thinking is a way of engaging in virtually any task is a reason why all teachers—from art to zoology, and from arithmetic to woodworking—should care about helping students think critically.

Creative People Need to Think Critically

It is common among writers who espouse different forms of thinking to sharply contrast critical and creative thinking. This division is often painted in terms of the relentless deliberation and technical rationality of the critical thinker versus the intuitive sensitivity, spontaneous impulse, and imagination of the creative thinker. Artists, writers, inventors, and other creative people often deliberate about their work, considering whether or not their creations meet the aesthetic and technical criteria they seek to effect (e.g., is their work imaginative? balanced? evocative? functional?). Even when following their intuitions, creative thinkers are likely at some point to step back and assess whether or not their hunches or impulses are worth pursuing. Someone once suggested that an intuition is simply a hypothesis that has yet to be tested. The frequency with which writers and other creators discard drafts of their work and start over is a testament to the role of critical introspection in creative endeavors. Conversely, the image of the critical thinker as unimaginative, unfeeling, and overly analytic is a stereotype. Critical thinkers need to be creative—they must anticipate potential implications, generate original approaches, and view things from novel perspectives.

The Creative Dimension

The concept of creativity has been even more contested than critical thinking. Until rather recently, it was largely relegated to the arts (and to some extent to science). However, growing concerns about rapidly changing global conditions and competitiveness in a knowledge-based economy have increased the perceived importance of design thinking, innovation, and creativity. In this section, we define creative thinking and explore some of the misconceptions that surround it.

> Creative Intelligence is about tools, not lightbulbs. It's something we do, not something that happens to us. It's about what happens during those moments of insight, but also after; it's the hard work and the collaborations that can help bring your idea out of your mind and into the world.
>
> —Bruce Nussbaum (as cited in 800ceoread blog, 2013)

Creativity Is Purposeful, Unique, and Significant

We believe that creativity involves purposeful creation of ideas or products that are novel or unique and have value or significance. Let's consider what each of these terms means and why they are relevant to understanding creativity.

Creativity Requires Purposeful Creation. Creativity is something that people do intentionally. The root of "creative" is to create, meaning that the purpose is to produce something—whether it is an idea, a novel argument against a position, a work of art, a new dance move, or an original solution to a problem. If creativity is intentional, how can we account for famous inventive accidents such as Archimedes' discovery about the displacement of water by submerged objects while sitting in his bathtub? Saying that Archimedes' principle—which he had been exploring for years—was a great creative advance is not incompatible with saying that the insight that triggered his discovery was a fluke. This is because creativity is attached to the ideas, actions, and things we create, and not to how we got there. Countless others have sat in their baths observing objects—there is nothing inherently creative here. The Archimedes incident became creative only because of the nature of the product that emerged, not because of any special type of activity—one may be creating while sitting at one's desk, feeling the sensations on walks in the woods, or when meditating. Often, people will perform certain tasks such as listening to music, brainstorming with others, or thinking through "what if" scenarios with the explicit hope of producing original ideas. But it is not the inherent nature of the thinking that makes any of these activities creative. A designation as creative depends on the qualities of the product that emerges.

> Creativity involves purposeful creation that is novel or unique and has value or significance.

Creations Must Be Original or Unique. Only things that are novel or unique in some way can be considered to be creative. We do not use the term *creative* when the creation is indistinguishable from what already exists or is widely known. There must be some novelty to justify use of the term.

Creations Must Have Value or Significance. Not every unique idea, thing, or action is creative. It is generally thought insufficient to warrant designating something as creative even if it had never happened before. The novelty must have value or contribute something that is in some way or in some circles deemed useful or significant. For example, we don't characterize the configuration of scattered pieces created by dropping a glass on the floor as creative. It may be a unique design—broken glass may never previously have been distributed in exactly this array—but it has no particular value or merit. The significance may be very tangible, such as curing a devastating illness or designing a cutting-edge mobile device, but it can also be ethereal, for example, producing something of great beauty or containing important insights. Debates in the art world over controversial paintings or performance art are very much a question of the aesthetic merits of a work. Typically, subjects of such debates are unusual pieces, but that is not in itself a sufficient reason to warrant placing them in a gallery. Although conclusions about the value of an original work may be subjective, the fact that the debate occurs is proof that providing value is an aspect of creativity. The concern that creative efforts have some value or significance—even if only in a modest way—is particularly important for educators. There is little point in devoting educational resources to encourage students to think differently if nothing of value is expected to emerge from it.

Creativity Doesn't Require Genius

There is a perception that something must be truly original and of profound value before it qualifies as creative. Contemporary talk about the importance of creativity and innovation is often accompanied with stories of the Steve Jobses and Bill Gateses of the world who have transformed the lives of billions of people. Teachers also often discuss creativity in the context of scientific and artistic geniuses who radically changed the world. If our goal is to nurture the critical, creative, and collaborative dimensions of thinkers, focusing on the creative giants is akin to setting an expectation that students in physical education classes will become world-class athletes and students in English classes will become Nobel Prize-winning writers. Clearly, this is an unrealistic expectation for the vast majority of students. Is creativity to be understood as an elitist goal that applies only to the best and the brightest? What place, if any, does creativity have in the lives of the vast majority of students?

We can better understand the sense in which creativity is an achievable goal for all students by distinguishing two categories of creativity:

"Big C" Creativity. This term indicates that the product must represent a significant departure from what existed before anywhere in the world, or have huge value or merit on a very broad scale. "Big C" creative innovations are the ones that get described in books on the history of business, science, and art, and that enrich the lives of millions of people. We typically refer to "Big C" creators as geniuses. Certainly schools should do everything they can to nurture individuals with this potential, but this is not a realistic goal for most of us. Nor is it what we have in mind when we describe the creative dimension of a thinking classroom.

"Little c" Creativity. This term indicates that the product must represent a departure from what the individual or local circle has been doing and have value or merit for the person or group. It refers to the ways in which people solve everyday problems by going beyond what they have typically done to bring about useful or insightful solutions. These "Little c" creative moments arise when parents find imaginative ways to prepare tasty meals using leftovers, or children invent new playground games with whatever is at their disposal, or the stranded driver rigs a twig to temporarily fix the engine of her car until she can get to a service station. While these achievements may seem modest on a grand scale, they are essential to our functioning in the world around us. Think of the countless situations our students encounter each day that could be solved with a little bit of creativity. This includes deciding what to do when they have lost their pencil and no one is around to provide one, or when their zipper is stuck and pulling hard doesn't work, or when their best friend won't talk to them and they have asked three times why not. In school, "Little c" opportunities arise within almost every learning situation—when students are asked to think of possible explanations beyond the obvious reasons, to generate an interesting title for their paragraph, or to figure out how to solve a math problem when the conventional approach isn't working. While their solutions won't transform the world, they will enrich almost every idea or product students create in school and beyond.

Nurturing Creativity Is About Tools, Not Lightbulbs

For centuries, it was suggested that creativity arises from the possession of a unique mind or a mysterious spark of inspiration, often divinely sent. While there is no doubt that some individuals are imbued with a natural ability to generate creative ideas, it is equally true that schools can cultivate "Little c" creative capacity within every student. We readily acknowledge that some students are inherently more intelligent thinkers than others and will likely be much better students than most. This does not mean that we do not try our best to raise everyone's ability. The same can be said about creativity: while some individuals will be naturally more gifted, creatively speaking, all can improve with support.

At the heart of creativity is the ability to see the unusual in the ordinary, to reconfigure accepted ideas into new and fresh combinations. This requires two things: a steady supply of new ideas that may stimulate our thinking and mechanisms for juggling the possibilities in unique ways. Naturally creative people are instinctively disposed to see the world differently. To put it another way, they are hardwired to generate new ways of seeing the familiar. It is suggested that the downside of naturally creative individuals is a difficulty in seeing the world in conventional ways—they may struggle to see the world as the majority of us do. The rest of us—the more conventional thinkers—can leverage our limited naturally creative instincts by employing idea-generating strategies. Talking to others, especially people who are dissimilar to us, brainstorming alone or with others, reading widely, and even travel are ways in which each of us can access new ideas to think about. We can also employ strategies to help us reconfigure the ideas we have. These strategies include looking at an idea or object from different physical and intellectual points of view, physically reconfiguring elements or components in different ways, exaggerating features, or sometimes simply putting things aside and coming back later with a fresh pair of eyes. The point is that creativity is not simply a matter of being inspired; it can be nurtured. What is worth noting is that many of these so-called creative strategies are also useful in thinking collaboratively and critically.

The Collaborative Dimension

It has never been more important than it is in the present for students to learn to think for themselves—but not by themselves. This means being open to deeply engaging with and building on the ideas of others but also being able to filter and assess these ideas in light of one's own values and beliefs. The fruitful interchange of ideas is the essence of collaborative thinking.

> Collective intelligence will always trump individual intelligence.
>
> —Einstein

Collaborative Thinking Is Different From Cooperative Learning

There are important points of connection between cooperation, cooperative learning, and collaborative thinking. All are concerned with increasing people's ability to function effectively together. Cooperation is the most general of the three terms and is concerned with enriching how people work and live together. Cooperative learning is the next broadest with its concern for enriching how students learn together. Collaborative thinking is the narrowest of the three in its concern for enriching how people think together. Thinking together is and should be a part of the other two, but it is not always the case. In discussion, students may simply offer their opinions without building on anyone else's ideas, and while they may be listening, no one may actually be thinking seriously about what the others are saying. In other words, students may be highly cooperative without thinking collaboratively. A focus on collaborative thinking calls attention to a potential gap between cooperating and thinking together. Consider the following examples:

Class Debates. One of the hallmarks of a cooperative group is the ability of members to respectfully disagree with each other. Nowhere is this more in evidence than in the conventional

> Collaborative thinking involves deeply engaging with and building on the ideas of others for mutual benefit.

class debate. While debates are useful activities, they may not support students in learning to think effectively with others. The implied messages in debates are threefold:

- issues are black and white (you are either for or against the issue, and the other side is the enemy);
- the objective is to win the argument; and
- students are discouraged from changing their minds (they can't switch sides halfway through the debate).

Unfortunately, these lessons are antithetical to collaborative thinking. To think collaboratively, students need to appreciate that

- most issues involve many shades of gray spanning a spectrum of legitimate perspectives;
- the goal is to arrive at the most sensible position for the person on the issue; and
- being open to others means changing one's mind in the face of new ideas and evidence.

In short, while class debates encourage cooperation, they do not necessarily promote collaborative thinking. A more productive alternative that teaches about collaborative thinking, called the U-shaped discussion (see Figure 3.2), is described in the following box.

U-Shaped Discussion

Figure 3.2   U-Shaped Discussion Strategy

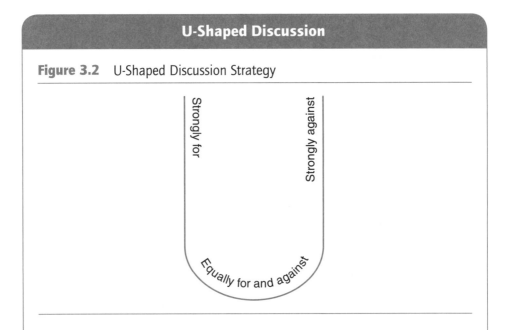

The U-shaped discussion strategy can be used with students and adults to help them appreciate the spectrum of views on an issue and to encourage a genuine exchange of ideas.

- Arrange the chairs in a U-shape.
- Ask the participants to situate themselves along the "U" based on their initial position on an issue. Participants with polar views (that is, who strongly agree or strongly disagree with a position) would seat themselves at either tip of the "U." Individuals with mixed opinions would sit at appropriate spots along the rounded part of the "U."

- Begin by inviting individuals at each tip of the "U" to state their opinion and offer a few reasons only (if there is an imbalance in strong support for one side or the other, locate yourself temporarily in a polar position to get the discussion going).
- Alternate from side to side as participants from all parts of the "U" offer their views.
- Encourage participants to physically move along the spectrum if they have heard reasons that cause them to want to shift their thinking on the issue.

Afterward, debrief the discussion. Ask students: What comments made you think the most? Did the discussion cause you to change your position? Do you now think differently in any way about the issue?

Assigned Group Roles. A popular cooperative learning strategy involves assigning students to play a specific role in a group assignment—say, as a checker, note taker, encourager, and so on. While each student's role complements the work of the others, they are not supported in putting their minds together. In fact, it is more likely that they will be distracted from the thoughtful exchange of ideas because of a preoccupation with fulfilling their primary role. In short, each group member may do their job effectively and still the give-and-take of ideas among them could be rather low and of poor quality. Collaborative thinking would be enhanced if overlaid on their assigned roles was a structure to encourage students to engage with each other's ideas. The placemat structure, described in the following box and illustrated in Figure 3.3, is an example of an activity that reinforces collaborative thinking.

Placemat Discussion Structure

The placemat structure can be used with students and adults to help them formulate their own ideas before discussing them with others and then to encourage a genuine exchange of ideas when they share them with others.

Instructions

- Divide students into groups of three to five with a large piece of chart paper at each table. Groups draw a placemat on the chart paper with one section for each group member and a common section for a collaborative response.
- Students write quietly on their own for several minutes in a section of the placemat immediately in front of where they are seated.

(Continued)

(Continued)

- Students listen as they share one by one what they have recorded in their respective sections of the placemat.
- The group tries to agree on shared concerns, concepts, and ideas, and records these in the common section of the placemat.

Afterward, debrief the discussion. Ask students: What comments made you think the most? Did the activity alter your thinking in any way about the topic?

Figure 3.3   Sample Placemat Formats

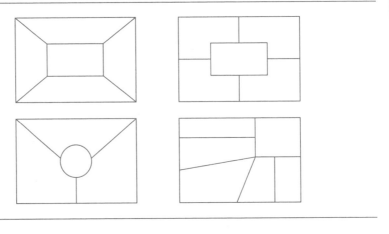

There are several ways to draw a placemat depending on the number of group members and their seating arrangement.

Thinking Collaboratively Is Not Simply Conferring With Others

One of the most powerful means for thinking collaboratively is the exchange of ideas with others in direct conversation. But one can think collaboratively without talking to anyone. In fact, thinking collaboratively can occur, metaphorically speaking, with someone who has been dead for centuries. These conversations with the past are typical of what scholars do when they probe the views of great thinkers: What would Einstein have said about a particular issue if he were alive today? How does Plato's view differ from mine? While we cannot expect the same level of analysis from students, the reality of the so-called information age is that students are accessing the ideas of countless historical and contemporary people they will never meet. The popular impression of the Internet is that the answers to all of our questions are simply out there waiting to be retrieved. Rather than treating information from digital sources as static entities, students can engage with the ideas they access digitally: Do I really understand what it says? Are these ideas consistent with my own experiences and beliefs? What implications might this new information have for my other beliefs? What questions might I have about the ideas expressed? It is worth noting that none of these questions invite an overt critical assessment of the views; they simply seek to explore their meaning and implications. In short, they seek to establish a conversation in one's own mind with the author. This is not a fanciful expectation, but rather it is what, for example, teachers of literacy do when they encourage their students to read between and beyond the lines.

Collaborative Thinking Is an Important Method of Learning

Collaborative thinking is one of the many competencies discussed in Chapter 6, but along with critical and creative thinking, it is also a fundamental engine of learning. Students need to learn how to think collaboratively so they can learn effectively with and from others. This is why collaboration needs to be at the center of a thinking classroom.

Understanding Requires Hearing From Multiple Perspectives. The importance of sharing perspectives in building understanding is famously captured in the story of the six blind men who each encounter a different part of an elephant. The person touching the tail thinks the object is a vine, the man touching the leg thinks it is a tree trunk, and so on. Although there is an independent real world, our ability to make sense of and interpret that world, illustrated by the partial view held by each man in this story, is limited by our perspective. To a logger, a tree is an economic resource, to a squirrel a tree is a home, and to a believer in animism, it is a living entity whose life is as sacred as any person's. No one has to accept everyone else's view of the world, but it is impossible to understand the world—to understand why some people will risk their lives to cut down a tree and others will risk their lives to save a tree—without some understanding of each other's perspectives. Learning to understand the world includes learning how others see the world and informing our own perspective with those of others.

Innovation Occurs by Building on the Ideas of Others. As was seen in the previous discussion, one of the myths of creativity is that great creators simply invent their discoveries out of the blue. Virtually every significant achievement has been arrived at because a number of individuals have been able to build on the ideas and experiences of their predecessors and peers. Collaborative thinking is the engine of creativity. But we must be careful to recognize that, in a didactic classroom, the ideas of others, especially those in authority, may undermine creativity if they are accepted without question or modification. In a thinking classroom, the intention is to learn from others but not be limited by the views of others. Developing the capacity for collaborative thinking is key to learning to think for oneself but not by oneself. Creativity can develop only in such an environment.

Concluding Thoughts

We have suggested that critical, creative, and collaborative thinking are profoundly interrelated: considerable creativity is required for good thinking, and considerable critical reflection is involved in being creative, and both are aided by building collaboratively on the ideas of others. Our interest in these dimensions of good thinking is not exclusively because they are important 21st century competencies. There is, as well, an orientation through which students can approach all learning. When asking students to think as they work through the curriculum, we want them to understand that they are expected to be rigorous, imaginative, and collaborative in this pursuit. The next challenge in nurturing a thinking classroom is to help educators effectively implement all three mutually reinforcing dimensions into their day-to-day practices. This is the focus of the next chapter. The following are selected strategies for educational leaders to use with teachers to support them in coming to understand and implement C3 thinking.

Opportunities for Leadership

Model Thinking Strategies in Staff Deliberations

One way to enhance the quality of staff deliberations and to encourage teachers to use effective strategies in their own classes is to employ selected thinking strategies for use in teacher and parent meetings.[1]

Create Regular Expectations for C3 Thinking

Encourage teachers as a matter of course to embed in their assignments explicit invitations for students to demonstrate how they were rigorous, imaginative, and collaborative. Encourage teachers to do the same when they propose ideas for consideration in staff meetings.

Build Toward Shared Understanding

Because of the diverse conceptions surrounding critical, creative, and collaborative thinking, it is likely that there will be divergent views among the teaching staff. If thinking is foundational, it would be useful to try to develop a shared understanding of the meaning of these terms and their interrelationships.

Note

1. Thinking strategies for use with parents and staff are described in Planche and Case (2015).

4

A Framework for Nurturing Thinking Classrooms

This chapter introduces a framework for systematically implementing a thinking classroom. More specifically, it discusses

- four questions to guide implementation of any initiative;
- the role of school and classroom climate, and a range of practices that shape the culture of a thinking classroom;
- how to create opportunities to support a thinking classroom;
- ways to build student capacity within a thinking classroom;
- ways to provide guidance to support a thinking classroom.

Tami McDiarmid's primary class was to learn about the importance of commemorating the contributions and sacrifices of veterans of various wars. She planned to invite her stu-

> To do good work, one must first have good tools.
>
> —Chinese proverb

dents to create questions to ask of a classroom guest who was a World War II veteran. Left to their own devices, many students could have asked rather trivial or irrelevant questions. Tami systematically supported her students in thinking about the questions they might ask in four ways: fostering a supportive climate, creating rich opportunities, building student capacity, and providing timely and helpful guidance.

Preparation for this event began long before the planned visit by the classroom guest. From the beginning of the year, Tami had been nurturing a climate of trust and building student confidence about sharing their ideas. She had also established an expectation that students would regularly think for themselves—but not by themselves. In planning for the guest speaker, she decided that creating their own powerful questions would provide students with an authentic opportunity to think about the outcomes she hoped to promote. Explicit development of students' capacity to formulate powerful questions began three weeks prior to the guest's visit with the reading of children's stories set during the war. Without the background knowledge acquired from these stories, many students would have been incapable of asking a thoughtful question. A few days prior to the visit, Tami invited the class to consider the attributes of a powerful question. Students were able to generate thoughtful and relevant criteria: "gives you lots of information," "is open-ended—can't be answered by yes or no," "may be unexpected," and "is usually not easy to answer."

Tami supported students in collaborative brainstorming to generate possible questions. Working in pairs, students assessed which of the brainstormed questions best met the agreed-upon criteria. Some weaker questions were rejected; others were modified to make them more powerful. Tami quietly guided students' thinking by inviting them to consider criteria they may have overlooked. On the day of the guest's visit, each student had a question to pose. Their questions were far ranging and probing: *Why did you fight in the war? What memories do you have of your friends from the war? What roles did women play in the Second World War? What were their jobs? What was your safe place?* Students listened intently as the veteran answered the questions they had so thoughtfully constructed. He admitted that they caused him to think more deeply about the war than he had in 60 years.

This teacher succeeded in helping her students develop a deeper understanding of the events and conditions surrounding World War II, competence in framing powerful questions, and an intimate appreciation for the significance of veterans' contributions. These outcomes were so successfully achieved because of the systematic way in which she approached the task. The myriad of specific decisions about how to frame the learning opportunity, what tools to teach students to build their capacity, when and what guidance to offer, and how to nurture a supportive climate were all informed by her commitment to a thinking classroom—a commitment to make critical, creative, and collaborative thinking the way in which her students would learn.

If thinking is to become a mindset or worldview that permeates all aspects of teaching and learning, it needs to be implemented systematically and thoroughly. This chapter explores a recommended framework for undertaking this journey.

A Comprehensive Approach to Implementation

The four-faceted approach outlined in Figure 4.1 can be applied when implementing any innovation, not simply a thinking classroom. In fact, this framework is used throughout this book to organize the recommended practices associated with each of the structural elements discussed. These facets are not procedures to follow but broad areas for consideration when implementing anything in schools:

- **Shape Climate:** What can we do to foster a culture within the classroom or school that supports . . . (e.g., student choice)?
- **Create Opportunity:** How can we frame invitations and organize opportunities to implement . . . ?
- **Build Capacity:** How can we grow the ability of all concerned to succeed at . . . ?
- **Provide Guidance:** What, how, and when might we seek or offer feedback on . . . ?

We have highlighted the importance of a coherent response to any educational change effort: fundamental beliefs should align with guiding principles, goals, and practices. So too must each principle or practice be internally coherent. In other words, for any particular initiative, all the facets (climate, opportunity, capacity, and guidance) must align with each other. Inattention to these facets can undermine efforts. For example, educators may create many opportunities for thinking but neglect to build student capacity to do so. As a consequence, students will likely become frustrated. Similarly, classroom debates and discussions may falter because the norms

Figure 4.1   A Framework for Systematic Implementation

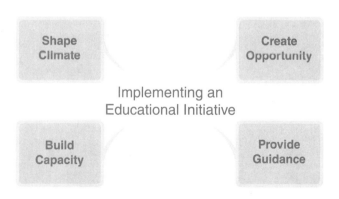

Source: Created by The Critical Thinking Consortium.

of a thinking classroom have not been established. Students may still be looking to the teacher for the "right" answer or not appreciate the need to be open to and respectful of other viewpoints. Thinking, or any other initiative, is unlikely to succeed unless all four facets are in place and aligned.

This conceptual framework is especially useful in helping educators build on what they are already doing and avoid throwing the baby out with the bathwater. As described in Chapter 13, we encourage educators to look upon efforts to improve their practices as an ongoing renovation rather than a short-lived abrupt change. As part of a sustained inquiry into their practices, educators may consider three questions in the context of each of these four facets of implementation:

- **Affirm:** What am I currently doing to . . . (e.g., to nurture climate) that effectively supports the initiative I wish to implement (e.g., student choice)?
- **Refine:** What can I easily modify what I currently do . . . that will more effectively support the initiative I wish to implement?
- **Aspire:** What more substantial changes might I undertake over the longer term . . . that would effectively support the initiative I wish to implement?

Figure 4.2 identifies how the four general facets of implementation apply in the case of promoting thinking. Let us consider in detail how

Figure 4.2   A Framework for Implementing a Thinking Classroom

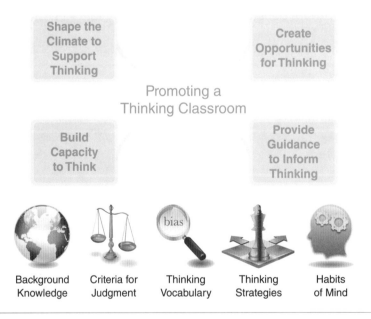

Source: Created by The Critical Thinking Consortium.

each of these facets informs the practices that characterize a thinking classroom.

Shape Climate to Support Thinking

Implementing a thinking classroom depends significantly on the culture or atmosphere in the classroom. Whether face-to-face or virtual, teachers need to actively manage the conditions for thoughtful learning to flourish. This entails considering the physical space in which the learning takes place, setting clear expectations that support thinking, establishing routines to nourish thinking, managing positive interactions with and among students, and modeling the traits of a good thinker. Let's explore what is involved in implementing each of these practices.

> Unless the learning environments of our classrooms nurture and support student thinking, especially higher-order thinking, our students are unlikely to be very receptive to continued efforts on our part to help them improve their thinking.
>
> —Barry Beyer (2001, p. 418)

Create a Physical Environment Conducive to Thinking

Physical space is an important factor in establishing a thinking classroom. The class arrangement sends a message to students about the way they are expected to learn. A study conducted by the Public Education Foundation found, among other factors, that highly effective teachers did not stand still and lecture but moved about the room monitoring student learning; their rooms were covered in student work, and the classrooms were virtually never arranged with desks in rows but were arranged in ways that promoted regular interactions among students (Darling-Hammond & Bransford, 2005, p. 6). Classrooms organized in rows with the teacher's desk at the front of the room send an implicit message to students that learning flows from the teacher to the students, and interactions among students are limited.

Configuring aspects of the physical space to support a thinking classroom may include the following:

- Arrange student seating flexibly so that students can discuss and work comfortably with their peers in various groupings.
- Use U-shaped and circular seating to enable whole-class discussions.
- Adorn classroom walls with examples of student thinking and other displays that support thinking.
- Reduce the likelihood of disruptive physical conditions such as uncomfortable temperatures, distracting noise, and unwanted movement.

Set Clear Expectations for Thinking

The expectations that educators set for their students influence the tone of their classrooms. Properly established, they set the norms for student behavior. For this reason, each September, teachers are careful to establish a range of behavioral expectations such as being punctual, keeping the classroom clean, and treating each other respectfully. Equal attention needs to be paid to the intellectual expectations that teachers set for students. The following kinds of expectations support a thinking classroom:

- Students are to make up their own minds and not simply take someone's word for things.
- Students are to initiate plausible answers or solutions to questions or problems and not expect to be told the answer.
- Students and teachers will provide reasons or examples in support of their observations, conclusions, and actions.
- Students and teachers will seriously consider other perspectives on an issue and alternative approaches to a problem before reaching a firm conclusion.
- Students are expected to try to think of possibilities beyond those that have been expressed in class or are widely known.

Establish Routines That Support Thinking

In addition to framing clear expectations about thinking, teachers can further support a thinking classroom by building into the daily operations various routines and activities that habituate students to particular frames of mind and expectations. Ongoing practices to support thinking may include the following:

- Use the vocabulary of thinking as a matter of course in classroom discussion (e.g., ask "What can you infer from this picture about the individual's state of mind?" or "What assumptions are you making?").
- Provide students with adequate time to reflect on their learning, alone and with others, and to think about their answers before being asked to respond, or to revise their work before submitting it to the teacher.
- Provide time for students to "muck about" with their thinking: to explore ideas, try out solutions, and make revisions or even start anew when their initial ideas don't work out.
- Scrutinize textbooks, news articles and reports, and other reputable sources of information to identify bias, stereotyping, overgeneralizations, inaccuracies, and so on.

Foster Personal Interactions That Nurture Thinking

There are three levels of personal interactions at play in a classroom: teacher interactions with the entire class, teacher interactions with individual students, and student-to-student interactions. All three kinds of interactions can be fostered in ways that support thinking. For example, teachers can help students learn to interact with each other in a manner that is productive, respectful, and collaborative. When responding to students individually, teachers can answer students' questions directly and end the opportunity for further thinking, or support students in answering their own questions—to think for themselves. Practices that support thoughtful interactions in the classroom include the following:

- Facilitate whole-class discussions that are not dominated by teacher talk but involve widely distributed, respectful interaction among students.
- Use exchanges with individual students to probe and support their ability to reach their own conclusions and understand the reasons for their beliefs.
- Foster respectful and fruitful student-to-student conversations by teaching students how to offer constructive and focused feedback.

Model the Traits of a Good Thinker

Teachers are integral members of a classroom community, and their actions provide important models for students. Albert Schweitzer is reported to have noted: "Example is not the main thing in influencing others, it's the only thing." This principle applies to thinking. If we want students to be good thinkers, teachers must model the attributes themselves. Here are some ways to model exemplary thinking:

- Sincerely attempt to base all comments and decisions on careful and fair-minded consideration of all sides.
- Be willing, if asked, to provide good reasons for decisions and actions.
- Avoid making gross generalizations and stereotypical comments, or using books, pictures, films, and other learning resources that reinforce stereotypes.
- Regularly acknowledge different positions on an issue (for example, by looking at events from different cultural, gender, or class perspectives).

Create Opportunities for Thinking

At the core of a thinking classroom are regular invitations for students to thoughtfully respond to challenges in reactive and generative ways both alone and in collaboration with others. Framing challenges that drive the learning is a key factor in making thinking a routine but powerful part of students' classroom experience.

Problematize Learning Through Curriculum-Embedded Critical Challenges

A critical challenge is a question or a task that invites a reasoned response. This is to be contrasted with questions that invite guessing, sharing of uninformed opinions, retrieval of information, or rote applications of a formula. A reasoned response is invited only if there is a problem to be resolved. As John Dewey wrote in *How We Think*, only when a routine is disrupted by the intrusion of a difficult obstacle or challenge are we forced to think about what to do. If a situation is not problematic (i.e., there is only one plausible option, or a correct answer is obvious), then it does not call for critical thinking. Thinking will never be adequately addressed if it is an add-on to the curriculum; thinking must be the *way the curriculum is taught*.

> Only when a routine is disrupted by the intrusion of a difficult obstacle or challenge are we forced to think about what to do.

A curriculum-embedded approach to learning invites teachers to present questions or tasks that challenge students to reflect thoughtfully about and with the curriculum content and skills. Simple refinements to questions and tasks can make a powerful difference in problematizing what is to be learned. Instead of asking students to locate information to answer the factual question (e.g., "What did Native Americans traditionally use to make tools?"), the teacher might ask students to judge the more significant source of tools (e.g., "Which animal—the bear or the deer—contributed more to traditional Native life?"). Similarly, instead of writing a report on a famous scientist, students might assess whether da Vinci, Newton, or Einstein had the greatest scientific mind. Instead of simply picking a title that students would like for their paragraph, students might decide which of several options was the most informative and engaging. In all these cases, students go beyond locating facts or espousing a personal preference. They are not merely reporting what they know or like but judging or assessing possibilities in light of criteria, with the aim of reaching a reasoned response.

Learning to Problematize the Curriculum

Too often, teachers focus on the verb as the means to create richer questions or tasks for students, believing that asking students to analyze rather than list will require deeper thinking. In fact, an analysis question may not lead students to make a reasoned judgment, while a list question can be framed to require it. The key is not in the verb but in the addition of an "evaluative" adverb or adjective. For example, consider the effect of adding "significance" to the question "List four battles from World War II." Rather than citing the first four battles that come to mind or are found by skimming the textbook or conducting an Internet search on the topic, students need to assess various battles in light of the criteria for significance to support their list of four significant battles. It is instructive to see how teachers can elevate the depth of thinking expected of students for any of the questions in Bloom's taxonomy simply by adding appropriate evaluative terms.

Embedding Thinking Throughout Bloom's Taxonomy

	Sample Questions Using Bloom's Taxonomy	Critically Thoughtful Versions of the Tasks
Remember	Describe where Goldilocks lived.	Describe where Goldilocks lived *in a way that makes me see and feel what the place was like*.
Understand	Summarize what the Goldilocks story was about.	*Select the five most important details that tell* what the Goldilocks story was about.
Apply	Construct a theory as to why Goldilocks went into the house.	Construct a *believable* theory *based on clues in the story* as to why Goldilocks went into the house.
Analyze	Differentiate between how Goldilocks reacted and how you would react in each story event.	Differentiate between how Goldilocks reacted and a *sensible (street-safe) response to* each story event.
Evaluate	Assess whether or not you think this really happened to Goldilocks.	Assess *which of the story events* could really happen and *which are fantasy*.
Create	Compose a song, skit, poem, or rap to convey the Goldilocks story in a new form.	Compose *and perform a well-crafted* song, skit, poem, or rap that *conveys the core message to students your age* of the Goldilocks story.

Build Capacity for Thinking

We offer the notion of intellectual resources or tools to explain the development of good thinking. The scope of tools to be developed over time are discussed below. However, as the primary teacher did in the opening story, tools need to be introduced individually and methodically in the context of preparing students to successfully complete one thinking task at a time.[1]

Teach the Range of Intellectual Tools Needed for Each Task

> Neither the hand nor the mind alone would amount to much without aids and tools to perfect them.
>
> —Francis Bacon,
> *Novum Organum* (1620)

Much of the frustration teachers experience when attempting to engage students in thinking critically stems from the fact that students often lack the required concepts, attitudes, knowledge, criteria, or strategies—in short, students lack the tools needed to do a competent job. It is often assumed that students have the tools required for success, or that repetition will improve students' reflective competence. No doubt some will improve by repeatedly trying to figure things out for themselves, but most will be more successful if they are taught the requisite tools for the task. Although the specific tools depend on the nature of the challenge facing the thinker, promoting thinking is largely a matter of helping students master an ever-broadening repertoire of five types of intellectual resources.

Background Knowledge. This tool refers to the relevant information about a topic that is required for thoughtful reflection. Students require sufficient understanding of the context within which the challenge is situated. For this reason, students need information relevant to the range of topics that we want them to be able to think about. Presumably, this range of topics is (or should be) found in the subject matter of the curriculum. This point speaks strongly for embedding the teaching of critical thinking within the teaching of curricular content. The need for background knowledge is as important for creativity as it is for thinking critically, and more knowledgeable people have more to contribute to the thinking of others.

Criteria for Judgment. This tool refers to the appropriate criteria or grounds for judging the reasonableness or merits of available options or possibilities. To think critically is essentially to engage in deliberations with the intention of making a reasoned judgment. And judgments inevitably are made on the basis of criteria.

For example, in deciding whether or not ice cream ought to be part of our diet, we would want to go beyond whether we personally like the food and consider whether it is nutritious, affordable, readily available, and easy to keep. This larger set of factors forms the criteria involved in making a reasoned judgment on the merits of including ice cream in one's diet. For this reason, an important category of tool is the range of context-sensitive criteria spanning the diverse intellectual tasks found in the curriculum, from what makes for a good argumentative essay, a sound solution to a business problem, or a thoughtful question, to the qualities of a reliable scientific experiment, an accomplished artistic performance, or effective lecture notes.

Thinking Vocabulary. This refers to the concepts and distinctions that help us understand and think about thinking. Although other tools also refer to concepts, *thinking vocabulary* refers to concepts that expressly address distinctions foundational to thinking. These include distinguishing concepts such as

- conclusion and premise,
- cause and effect,
- innovative and different, and
- consensus and unanimity.

Teachers have long recognized the importance of concepts—especially teachers of students who are not native speakers of the language of instruction. For example, we teach students key vocabulary prior to reading a story in language arts and explain concepts in science or social studies prior to analyzing physical or social phenomena. What has not been as widely appreciated is the need to teach the vocabulary of thinking. Students cannot enter very deeply into conversations about their thinking if they do not have the words to identify or recognize key distinctions. For example, if students cannot distinguish a premise from a conclusion or do not know what a reason is, they are less likely to provide sound justifications for their opinions. Knowing the difference between cause and correlation is crucial when analyzing phenomena and events.

Understanding the subtle but important distinction between the concepts of like and worthwhile is key in students' ability to think critically and creatively. For example, when asked to determine the better dietary choice—hamburger or salad—many students, especially younger students, will select what they would like to eat. In doing so, they do not think about the relative merits of each option; they merely report their preference. Thoughtful reflection is likely only when students have the conceptual lens to distinguish between considering what is worthwhile—what would be a sound dietary choice (i.e., nutritious, environmentally sound, easy to prepare, tasty, widely available, inexpensive)—and what is likable—what is merely a pleasing personal choice. Conceptual distinctions such as like and worthwhile, premise and conclusion, or cause and effect allow us to see important features of good thinking without which we are left in a conceptual haze.

 Thinking Strategies. These refer to procedures, learning tips, organizing tools, algorithms, and models that may be used to guide or support thinking. This category of tool is most closely aligned with what others call *skills*, although we believe they are more appropriately viewed as *strategies*. Good thinkers draw upon a great variety of strategies to think critically, creatively, and collaboratively through the challenges facing them. Thinking strategies may be elaborate, such as following a comprehensive decision-making model (e.g., when tackling a complex problem, begin by identifying the issue, then consider the consequences, research each option, and so on). Alternatively, they may be very focused strategies addressing a specific task (e.g., to gain clarity about a problem, restate it in your own words, ask others for clarification, or graphically represent the problem).

Habits of Mind. These are the range of commitments to the values and principles that characterize a careful and conscientious thinker. Although more commonly described as *dispositions*, we prefer the term *habits of mind* to refer to the intellectual ideals or virtues that orient and motivate thinkers in ways that are conducive to good thinking, such as being inquisitive, consultative, open-minded, fair-minded, tolerant of ambiguity, self-reflective, and attentive to detail. An individual's attitudes—or habits of mind—are key constituents of good thinking. People who are, for example, closed to new ideas or inflexible in their thinking are seriously impaired in their ability to arrive at justifiable resolutions of issues.

Acknowledging the role of attitudes in thinking challenges a popular perception that thinking is a skill or set of skills. This perception is unfortunate since no amount of skill will overcome the limitations of closed-minded, prejudicial thinking. The case of people who deny the Holocaust illustrates this point. These individuals may be very clever, have extensive knowledge of the events, and be able to marshal persuasive arguments. Despite considerable thinking ability, these individuals are fundamentally mistaken in their belief that the Holocaust did not happen because, in many cases, their racial prejudice prevents them from impartially considering the evidence. Open-mindedness is but one of an array of habits of mind needed by thinkers. The tendency of some individuals to rashly leap to conclusions underlies yet another crucial mental habit of a good thinker:

the inclination to deliberate—to think before acting. Successful thinking is significantly (but by no means exclusively) a matter of attitude.

Provide Guidance That Informs Thinking

In a thinking classroom, educators will want to ensure that everyone is aware of how well they are thinking and what they might do to further enhance the quality of thinking. The use of the term *provide guidance* is to signal that feedback need not come from the teacher primarily but can be generated by the individual, other students, and the teacher. Also, in a thinking classroom, guidance can be provided in multiple forms including "feedforward" or advice on how to proceed, feedback on work completed, shared observations, collaborative conversations, supporting new learning, and critiquing each other's products or performances.

Assess Thinking and Performance

From a young age, children come to understand that what is valued in schools gets assessed. This seemingly simple equation—what matters gets assessed—often creates a disconnect between stated curriculum goals and where students put their energy. When assessments focus on recall of information or the rote application of formulas, students come to believe that memorization is the best route to success. If we are to take thinking seriously, it needs to be a focus for our assessment practices. Teachers will want to assess whether students competently completed the assigned task and demonstrated the desired understanding—what we have called the *performance of the task*. For students to recognize the importance of thinking, they need to receive timely critiques of the quality of the thinking that gave rise to the completed product or performance. A concern when assessing thinking is deciding on what to look for in a student's answer. If there is no single correct response, we may well ask, "On what basis, then, can we reliably assess students?" In the case of thinking, the key is to see how well students exhibit the qualities of a competent thinker. Thus, the intellectual tools for thinking become the criteria for assessing students' thinking. Figure 4.3 suggests specific assessment criteria related to the five types of critical thinking tools that may be used to evaluate a persuasive essay and a creative work.

Involve Everyone in Providing Effective Feedback

Equally important to student success is the variety of ways in which students receive guidance to improve the quality of their thinking. Guidance should neither come exclusively from the teacher nor be provided exclusively

Figure 4.3   Criteria for Assessing Thinking

	Evidence of Thinking in a Persuasive Essay	Evidence of Thinking in a Creative Work
Background Knowledge	• makes use of accurate information • understands the key facts	• understands the mechanics of the creative medium
Criteria for Judgment	• provides ample evidence • arranges arguments in a logical sequence	• work is imaginative • work is clear and compelling
Thinking Vocabulary	• distinguishes arguments from counterarguments • understands what is implied by a sense of place	• represents point of view
Thinking Strategies	• uses appropriate strategies for developing persuasive arguments (such as an essay outline, a graphic organizer)	• uses appropriate strategies for preparing work (for example, a rough sketch, a rehearsal)
Habits of Mind	• demonstrates an openness to alternative perspectives	• refrains from forming firm opinions where the evidence is inconclusive

through formal assessments. When students themselves become effective assessors, they contribute to making timely and helpful guidance a routine part of learning. The following suggestions may help to guide students during such feedback sessions:

- Emphasize peer feedback as an invitation to see the positives, not just the negatives.
- Ensure that all feedback is specifically focused on the criteria of the task or assignment.
- Begin by critiquing the work of those not in the class, and before asking students to put their work forward, involve the class in critiquing something you have done (for example, an essay you wrote as a student, a class presentation you made) or an Internet-sourced work.
- When it is time for peer critique, start with group assignments so the responsibility is shared among several students.
- In the early days of peer critique, do not allow negative comments—only allow remarks on positive features. A good indication of the time to make the transition to concerns or areas to consider is when

students voluntarily ask each other for what is wrong with their work.

- Model and set a few simple guidelines for peer critique: perhaps insist that each student start with two (or more) positive comments before offering a (single) concern and that negative comments be phrased in the form of a query (e.g., "I'm unclear why you did it this way. Could you explain what you had in mind?").
- Ensure that the early instances of peer feedback are low risk, relatively easy to perform, and have an obvious benefit.

Concluding Thoughts

Educators need to systematically build the conditions that nurture a thinking classroom where critical, creative, and collaborative thinking powerfully drives student learning. This includes creating thinking opportunities in an environment conducive to thinking, and focusing instruction and assessment in a way that enhances student capacity for good thinking.

Practices That Nurture a Thinking Classroom

Shape Climate	• Create a physical environment conducive to thinking. • Set clear expectations for thinking. • Establish routines that support thinking. • Foster teacher–student interactions that nurture thinking. • Model the traits of a good thinker.
Create Opportunities	• Problematize learning through curriculum-embedded critical challenges.
Build Capacity	• Teach the range of intellectual tools needed for each task.
Provide Guidance	• Assess thinking and performance. • Involve everyone in providing effective feedback.

The following box contains selected strategies for educational leaders to use with teachers to nurture a thinking classroom.

Opportunities for Leadership

Use the Framework as a Guide to Implementation

When developing plans to implement or support a new school or district initiative, think of what might be done to help shape the climate, create opportunities, build capacity, and provide guidance in relation to the initiative.

Pool the Collective Wisdom

Every teacher has something to offer that supports the practices discussed in this chapter. Arrange for them to share these ideas and resources as part of affirming what they are currently doing that supports a thinking classroom and to collectively build on what they are doing to refine their practices.

Don't Try to Do It All at Once

Teachers may be overwhelmed if efforts are made to tackle all four facets of a thinking classroom at once. It may be advisable to focus initially on refining or aspiring to one or two of the practices within one of the facets (e.g., establishing expectations and routines to support thinking, or problematizing learning tasks).

Note

1. The Critical Thinking Consortium has developed an online resource, *Tools for Thought*, which contains tutorials on teaching a wide range of individual tools, http://tc2.ca/t4t.php.

PART iii

Refocus the Goals

What Schools Must Achieve to Better Prepare Students

5

From Knowledge to Deep Understanding

This chapter explains what is involved in deep understanding and why educators should care to promote it. More specifically, it discusses

- the difference between having knowledge about and understanding the subject matter of the curriculum;
- two factors that have undermined our success in developing widespread understanding;
- the importance of understanding if we want to prepare students for learning in school and for the world beyond school;
- practices to implement that nurture student understanding of what they are studying.

A few years ago, my niece came home with the results of an end-of-unit quiz on thirty of the most difficult concepts in social studies. The concepts included capitalism, communism, totalitarianism, liberalism, and dozens of other complex political ideas. She received 96 percent on the quiz. Seeking to celebrate her success and engage her in political conversation,

> Understanding always entails personal invention; it can never be simply transmitted from a generator to a recipient but must be constructed from the learner's own experience and intellectual work.
>
> —Martha Stone Wiske
> (1998, p. 83)

I asked her what capitalism meant. She recited a dictionary-perfect definition in a rather hypnotic tone. I responded, "Yes, but what does it actually mean?" and my niece said she wasn't exactly sure. So I agreed that it was a difficult concept to explain and asked if she knew whether or not our nation was a capitalist country. My niece responded, "How should I know?"

I asked if she understood what capitalism meant. She replied, "Not really." How did she feel about this? It had been an end-of-unit test. She wasn't sure if the definitions would be asked on the final exam, and she was worried that she might forget one of them. She "knew" the definitions but not the meaning. She had acquired knowledge of the terms but not understanding. She had the top mark in the class.

The opening chapter of this book suggests that the challenges in preparing students for a 21st century world were not essentially about changing the topics taught in schools or getting higher results on the current measures of student achievement. Rather, we have presented the need for richer results involving the current goals of the curriculum. This chapter deals with the first of these enriched goals—the move from promoting knowledge to engendering deep understanding.

The terms *knowledge* and *understanding* are sometimes used as synonyms. For example, we might mean similar things by asking "Do you know the meaning of the word?" and "Do you understand the definition of the word?" However, as the opening example illustrates, there is an important difference between remembering and understanding a definition. Teachers will explain facts, concepts, rules, formulas, and principles to students and assume that they "get" what we are saying. We may assess whether they remember the key points that we explained for a subsequent test or quiz, but we should not presume that they have understood in any deep way what these ideas mean.

In this chapter, we explore why we are in a situation where many students don't understand what they are learning. We discuss what it would mean to deeply understand, why it is important that students understand most of what they learn in school, and what kinds of practices foster deep understanding.

What Does It Mean to Understand Deeply?

What exactly would it mean to understand rather than merely possess (or recall) information about something? Three conditions must be present in order for someone to truly understand a body of information.

Understanding Implies Basic Comprehension of Information. Understanding a fact is not merely patter off the lips of a definition memorized by rote. At the least, understanding implies that students can thoughtfully rephrase an answer in their own words. This problem is illustrated in an amusing history of the world drawn from students who so poorly understood what was taught that they got their facts completely wrong. Here is one student's account of ancient Rome:

> Eventually the Romans conquered the Greeks. History calls people Romans because they never stayed in one place very long. At Roman banquets, the guest wore garlics in their hair. Julius Caesar extinguished himself on the battle fields of Gaul. The Ides of March murdered him because they thought he was going to be made king. Nero was a cruel tyranny who would torture his poor subjects by playing the fiddle to them. (Lederer, 1987)

Understanding Implies Appreciation of Significance and Interconnections. The etymology of a word is instructive. The word *understanding* descends from the Old English word *understandan*, which meant "to stand in the midst of." While students can recall definitions, events, labels, and formulas, they won't understand them until they connect this information with a constellation of related concepts and facts. Remembering that the United States is a capitalist country is not the same as understanding this fact. Understanding something about U.S. ties to capitalism requires appreciating the significance of this economic system and how it fits into the larger picture. Students must have some appreciation of the ideas that interconnect with a specific event or phenomenon. For this reason, amassing discrete facts adds little to understanding. The student's inability to recognize the United States as a capitalist country described previously was a symptom of her lack of understanding of the connection of this concept with related concepts such as controlled and mixed economies, and with basic facts about U.S. economic operations.

Understanding Implies Some Grasp of the Warrants for Belief. A final aspect of understanding is the need to appreciate, to some extent at least, what kind of evidence is required before one decides whether one should accept or reject a proposed statement of fact. If students have no idea whatsoever what might count as supporting or refuting evidence for claims, then we might wonder how well they understood what these claims signify. For example, even if the student mentioned previously happened to remember that the United States was a capitalist country but could not cite one piece of evidence to justify this label, we would doubt her understanding of the concept.

The challenge for educators who are concerned to promote understanding is to help students comprehend, connect, and be able to justify or explain the information they receive.

Why Do We Have This Problem?

Although many students are supported by their teachers in understanding what they are being taught, many other students memorize but don't understand large parts of what they are studying. This is not to say that teachers don't try to engender understanding despite facing constraints beyond their control. The point of our discussion is to consider what might be done to increase our collective success in teaching for understanding. Two obstacles undermine teacher efforts: transmitting information or covering material (characteristic of the didactic approach) remains an accepted practice in many circles; and mandated curricula and examinations are so packed that covering the material is perceived to be the only way to get through the content.

> Coverage is the enemy of understanding.
>
> —Howard Gardner (as cited in Antonelli, 2004, p. 4)

Transmit First, Think Later

There is a long-standing belief, often attributed to Bloom's taxonomy, that suggests learning requires moving up a hierarchy of thinking: teachers are to begin by front-end loading information acquired through lower-order tasks before engaging students in more complex tasks.[1] For example, when developing comprehension, teachers are directed to invite students to describe, express, locate, explain, or summarize the information. Or to put it another way, students are expected to understand material without being asked to interpret, distinguish, relate, or question the subject matter. But what does it mean to explain if there has been no opportunity to analyze parts, synthesize diverse sources, or apply ideas in novel situations?

The effect of equating understanding with low-level comprehension has been to encourage a transmissive approach to content knowledge—that is, to encourage teachers to teach subject matter through direct transfer of information to students. Answering comprehension questions after reading a text or taking notes while listening to the teacher merely involves receiving of transmitted information.

This transmit-first approach is at odds with a thinking classroom approach, which requires that students digest or work with ideas in order to understand them. Resistance to the didactic approach has been a long-standing theme in education. In the early 20th century, John Dewey (1938) concluded that students must, in some fashion, digest the ideas they encounter—they must put knowledge into use and assimilate or own the ideas if they are to understand them. Rather than seeing learning as the warehousing of facts, it is better seen as the progressive construction of understandings. Teaching is not the telling of fact but can be thought of as a construction project in which the teacher acts as a contractor—not actually building the house but contracting to students the sorts of labor that will culminate in their building a house (Parker, 1989). To highlight the point that understanding requires rigorous thinking, some recommend flipping Bloom's taxonomy on its head. Instead of positioning understanding as the product of lower-order thinking at the bottom of the taxonomy, it is best seen as the outcome of significant thinking and therefore deserving of placement at the apex of a hierarchy of learning (see Wineburg & Schneider, 2010).

Covering a Crowded Curriculum

The pressure to cover course content remains one of the enduring impediments to successful teaching, especially in the senior grades. A high school student offered the following telling remark on the volume of material covered in his courses: "Sometimes these classes can be like trying to take a drink from an open fire hydrant" (James Leming, as cited in Soley, 1996).

There is a commonly shared perception that even if teachers want to teach differently, they are unable to do so because of curricular and testing constraints. It is certainly the case that in many jurisdictions the curriculum is full. For example, the Common Core prescribes seventy-one standards and substandards for Grade 4 English/Language Arts (National Governors Association Center for Best Practices and the Council of Chief State School Officers, 2010). Compounding the curricular overload is the pressure of high-stakes testing, which drives teachers to "cover subject matter even when they know spending more time on certain topics is needed in order for students to understand them" (Osborne, 2004, p. 36). Even in jurisdictions where the content expectations in the curriculum and on tests are less onerous, many teachers nevertheless feel compelled to cover much more information than they are formally required to do. Some perceive the need to work through an entire textbook or address all the main features of every topic mentioned in the curriculum.

Whether the conditions are actual or largely imagined, there is a widely shared impression that a transmissive, less probing approach to teaching enables teachers to cover the curricular terrain they feel bound to address. As a consequence, many students experience large gaps in their understanding of what they study.

Why Is Teaching for Deep Understanding Important?

Given the constraints that schools face, it may be tempting to feel that understanding is a wonderful outcome if one can achieve it, but, more

> At the first it is no great matter how much, but how well you learn it.
>
> —Erasmus (as cited in Ryerson, 1847, pp. 56–57)

realistically, educators may have to settle for less. Let's consider two reasons to challenge the view that understanding is an educational luxury, not an imperative.

It's Harder to Learn If You Don't Understand

The need to understand what we are studying lies at the heart of all learning. It is much harder for students to learn something when they don't understand what they are being exposed to. This is true even if the goal is to get students to remember something. Consider the following sentences:

- My best friend is Peter Pan.
- Gy hepl gfiern iv Qelef Qaw.

Most will agree that the first sentence would be easy to remember, whereas the second sentence would be very difficult. This is true even though all the vowels are identical and there are the same number of words and letters in both sentences. The more we help students comprehend what we want them to remember, the less students need to learn by memorization (Sternberg, 2008). Before expecting students to memorize number facts such as 5 + 5 = 10, we should ask them to visualize this fact, manipulate objects to demonstrate it, and predict the result and justify their answer to help them understand its meaning. Not only does understanding increase the likelihood of recall, but it saves time in the long run. Many students struggle in mathematics and science because they lack understanding of the principles upon which subsequent ideas are developed. Without an understanding of the basics, every new concept becomes more and more like the gibberish sentence considered earlier.

You Can't Use What You Don't Understand

If we are content that students remember information long enough to successfully complete school requirements, then it might be acceptable to produce students with considerable recall of information but little understanding. However, since schools must prepare students for a world beyond school, significant gaps in their understanding of the curriculum are problematic. Some level of understanding is a prerequisite; otherwise, as David Perkins explains, the ideas remain inert—that is, "knowledge that learners retrieve to answer the quiz question, but that does not contribute to their endeavors and insights in real complex situations" (Perkins, 1993).

In other words, ideas that aren't understood can't be used to make sense of the world.

It is sometimes suggested that in an Information Age, we can prepare students for the world beyond school without them amassing bodies of knowledge since students can simply find what they need to know on the Internet. Certainly students can locate any definition, fact, and explanation in an instant. But it would be unwarranted and perhaps dangerous to assume that students will understand what any of what they find really means. Let's consider the role that prior understanding has on students' ability to benefit from information available from the Internet. The following summary of *Romeo and Juliet* is from the popular website SparkNotes (n.d.), which provides short factual summaries of commonly studied school topics:

> In the streets of Verona another brawl breaks out between the servants of the feuding noble families of Capulet and Montague. Benvolio, a Montague, tries to stop the fighting, but is himself embroiled when the rash Capulet, Tybalt, arrives on the scene. After citizens outraged by the constant violence beat back the warring factions, Prince Escalus, the ruler of Verona, attempts to prevent any further conflicts between the families by decreeing death for any individual who disturbs the peace in the future. Romeo, the son of Montague, runs into his cousin Benvolio, who had earlier seen Romeo moping in a grove of sycamores. After some prodding by Benvolio, Romeo confides that he is in love with Rosaline, a woman who does not return his affections. Benvolio counsels him to forget this woman and find another, more beautiful one, but Romeo remains despondent. ("Plot Overview")

While the information in this summary may be accurate, it will likely be confusing and possibly useless unless students understand the class structure that prevailed during the Italian Renaissance and the context in which the scene is set, both historically and as part of a play from the Elizabethan era. In other words, students can always look up the information, but if they don't understand the context and key related concepts, the information is largely meaningless. Significantly, *Merriam-Webster* defines *understanding* as "the power to make experience intelligible by applying concepts and categories" ("Understanding," n.d.). If schools are to prepare students for a digital world, they must foster understanding of a wide range of topics that will enable students to make sense of what they encounter on the Internet and not simply retrieve and parrot facts that mean little to them.

What Practices Nurture Deep Understanding?

The practices recommended in the previous chapter that support a thinking classroom are clearly relevant and important in promoting understanding. What follows are additional practices that are especially tailored to nurturing understanding.

Shape a Climate That Supports Understanding

Recently, while observing various high school classes, I was struck by how consistently classroom discussions were dominated by a few students. This pattern repeated itself regardless of teaching style—whether the lesson was organized around small-group discussion or teacher-directed talk, or whether the teacher presented information in an engaging or rather dull manner. The sense I had from all these classes was that students view the point of the lesson as essentially a means to identify a correct answer, not to explore ideas and possibilities. The absence of an expectation that they would think for themselves meant that a few students put forward suggestions to test whether any were the right answer, while the rest of the class waited for these students to provide the answer so that the lesson could move along.

Expect Students to Understand Why and How, Not Merely What. Making it clear to students that knowing the right answer is not sufficient is an important first step in building understanding. Students must know why an answer is a good one. And if the answer is not a good one, they need to explain why and suggest revisions to strengthen the answer. Rather than wait for the answer, teachers need to encourage students to consider the range of options suggested by students, the teacher, or found in the textbook. This is an expectation to scrutinize options, not merely to guess the correct answer. Students must be encouraged to judge which suggestions are supported by the evidence and consistent with what is generally known. To reinforce the expectation, it can be helpful to regularly invite students to select the worst idea and explain its weaknesses, and revise the answer to make it more reasonable.

Avoid Giving Answers, When Possible. One way to further support the expectation that learning is about developing sound answers rather than finding correct answers is for the teacher, where possible, to avoid giving a definitive answer. There is a delicate trade-off when responding to student questions. On one hand, answering their questions helps them learn; on the other hand, knowing that the teacher will provide the answer may discourage students from thinking for themselves. Although there are many occasions when student questions should be answered directly, there are also benefits to encouraging students to answer their own questions—to think for themselves. Reinforcing the expectation that the teacher will eventually provide the answer establishes that success in the classroom comes from correct answers rather than thoughtful responses. It encourages many students to wait for the answer rather than invest energy in thinking it through for themselves. There are several ways to support students' individual thinking without providing answers:

- Turn the question back on the student (e.g., Well, what do you think? What is your best suggestion of the answer? How would you respond?).
- Prompt students with clues or hints, or present an example or new situation that might help them see their response as being problematic (e.g., Have you considered . . . ?).
- Suggest tentative answers, including those that many students would see as flawed (e.g., Well, I'm wondering if it could be . . . ? I'm not sure—some people might think . . .).

Create Opportunities to Develop Understanding

To understand what they are learning, students need opportunities to work with facts and concepts as they are introduced, and to see how these ideas fit within a larger context.

Build Daily Instruction Around Invitations to Think. Earlier, we discussed the widespread practice, fueled by a prevailing (but mistaken) interpretation of Bloom's taxonomy, that students must be introduced to content first, and only afterward be invited to think. Teaching for understanding requires that students become involved in thinking about the subject matter on a daily basis. Transmitting content to be memorized as a precursor to meaningful inquiry actually undermines understanding because it conditions students to be passive receptors of information. Teachers can help students understand what they are studying by regularly framing tasks that require students to work with the facts and concepts. Figure 5.1 illustrates how familiar tasks can be revised easily to engender deeper understanding.

Frame Learning Around Overarching Ideas, Questions, or Tasks. Isolated lessons and seemingly unrelated topics impede students' ability to build a coherent picture of what they are studying. Framing learning around a big

Figure 5.1 Refining Common Tasks to Engender Understanding

Invites Factual Retrieval	Revision That Invites Thinking	Engenders Understanding
Compare and contrast life between ancient Greece and ancient China. How is life today similar or different from life in medieval Europe?	Are the similarities/ differences between ancient Greece and ancient China significant? Overall, how similar or different is life today compared to life in medieval Europe?	By going beyond merely listing similarities and differences to consider the significance of the comparisons and to determine the degree of similarity and difference.
List five factors that are contributing to climate change.	Rank order five contributing factors to climate change.	By carefully considering the evidence of impact to determine the relative significance of each factor.
Find three ideas in the text.	List three key ideas from the text.	By considering and then deciding which ideas are most important to understanding the text.
Remember the definition for like terms.	Deduce the attributes of like terms by considering what distinguishes the yes examples from the no examples.	By distinguishing key features of the concept as they test hypotheses drawn from the yes and no examples.

idea, a guiding inquiry question, or an overarching project helps students see how the content learned during a particular lesson builds upon previous ideas, and how together these ideas lead to a bigger point. These structures may assist teachers in eliminating some topics that don't contribute to the overarching concept. The use of unit topics or themes (e.g., diversity or fractions) does not provide the same potential for building coherent understanding. Because themes and topics are so broad, they merely invite students to add more ideas but not to draw conclusions or assess implications. Figure 5.2 offers examples of big ideas and inquiry questions that can be used to frame learning for various topics.

Simply presenting the organizing structure for a unit is insufficient; students need regular opportunities to reflect on and explain in their own words how new learning deepens their understanding of a big idea or to draw emerging conclusions about possible answers to an inquiry question or implications for an overarching project. If the overarching challenge is simply raised at the beginning of a unit and then reintroduced at the end, there is inadequate opportunity for students to make meaningful

Figure 5.2   Framing Units Around Big Ideas

Subject	Topic	Big Idea	Inquiry Question
English	*Romeo and Juliet*	Choices we make shape our destiny.	Fate or free will: Which played a larger role in the deaths of Romeo and Juliet?
Mathematics	Integers	An integer is a number that can be written without a fractional component.	Are integers important in our day-to-day lives or just in classes?
Science	Biodiversity	Earth is a complex and delicate ecosystem.	Are we doing enough to ensure the sustainability of earth as an ecosystem?
Physical Education	Fitness	Appropriate fitness routines can help us maintain good health.	Which routines would be most important for you to maintain good health?
History	Causes of the First World War	Major events have both underlying causes and enduring consequences.	Can an understanding of the causes of conflict help to eradicate war?

connections among the ideas they are learning about each day. Ideally, each lesson would be organized around a smaller idea or question that students would think about, and they would then consider how their answer informs or challenges their emerging thoughts about the larger unit idea, question, or task.

Build Capacity for Deep Understanding

Teachers can provide deliberate instruction for a range of tools that help students build their understanding.

Provide Students With Tools to Construct Understanding. Since understanding involves seeing connections, teachers can help students develop fluency with various thinking strategies that assist them to connect individual facts to broader issues or topics. These include written strategies such as reflective journals, data charts, and anticipation guides.

Figure 5.3 Identifying Relationships

Students most often encounter Euler circles in mathematics classes, but they can also be used to help students explore relationships in other subjects. For example, students might be asked which of the following diagrams best represent the comparison between conditions on earth and outer space. In responding to this question, students would locate key ideas, evidence, or visuals from various sources and determine the implications of their findings for the most likely relationship. Placing the information within the relevant circles helps students consider and explain their conclusion.

Comparing Conditions on Earth and in Space

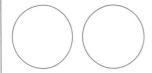		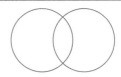
Discrete	**Subsumed Within**	**Some Overlap**
This graphic suggests that the conditions are completely different and that there is no overlap or continuity between earth and outer space.	This graphic suggests that the conditions in one region—either earth or outer space—includes all the conditions found in the other region and that unique conditions exist in one region that are not found in the other.	This graphic suggests that while some conditions are common to both environments, other conditions are unique to each environment. (Students can extend or limit the overlap based on the extent of common conditions.)

Visualization strategies such as concept mapping, graphic organizers, and thinking maps are also helpful. Figure 5.3 describes the use of Euler circles to help students link particular ideas with the bigger picture.

Provide Guidance to Inform Understanding

Informal and formal assessments of understanding provide informative feedback to teachers and students, and signal to students that the goal is to engender understanding.

Always Check for Understanding Before Moving On. Ongoing teacher checks for understanding and student self-assessments are important ingredients of a carefully scaffolded lesson. The goal is to ensure that all students "get it" and not that they simply remember it. This is not achieved by inviting one or two students to provide answers. All students might display their answers by raising the number of fingers that correspond to their chosen response, submit answers on a slip of paper, or share ideas with a peer who would attest to its suitability. The following box suggests the kinds of questions teachers might ask to determine whether students have understood a concept. The most effective strategy is to teach students to reliably determine for themselves whether things make sense to them. Chapter 10, "Nurture Self-Regulated Learners," discusses this in greater depth. The following box lists five strategies to help younger students confirm for themselves and for their teachers that they have understood the concepts taught in a lesson.

Checking for Conceptual Understanding

The following examples use the concepts of a rule and a problem to illustrate five strategies that can be used to confirm conceptual understanding in younger students.

- **Recognize Instances of the Concept:** Provide students with original examples and nonexamples, and ask whether they are instances of the concept. Are the following examples of rules?
  - No one is allowed to use my radio without my permission.
  - Every sentence must end with a period, a question mark, or an exclamation point.
  - Many people vote in presidential elections.
  - I don't like it when people run in the school hallway.
- **Generate Examples:** Ask students to provide their own original examples of the concept.
  - Give two examples of a family rule or a school rule.
  - List two problems that you sometimes encounter at school.
- **Explain Specific Attributes:** Ask students to address questions about specific attributes of the concept.
  - Do all rules forbid action?
  - Are all rules written down?
  - Give an example of a rule that prohibits and a rule that enables.
- **Distinguish Similar Concepts:** Ask students to distinguish between closely related and often-confused concepts.
  - Explain in your own words the difference between a request and a rule. Give an example of each.
  - Explain in your own words the difference between a problem and a question. Give an example of each.
- **Apply the Concept:** Ask students to apply the concept in an assignment.
  - Create a set of class rules to guide how we should treat each other in class.
  - What problems were faced by the character in the story we have just read? Which of these was the most difficult?

Evaluate Understanding Over Recall. Because evaluation signals to students what is important, special effort should be directed to assessing students' understanding and not merely their recall of facts and concepts. There are many ways to do this. Multiple-choice questions may ask students to use their knowledge to draw conclusions (e.g., which of the following statements is least likely given what we know about climate change) or to select the diagram or representation that best reflects a particular body of knowledge (e.g., which diagram best explains what is known about the theory of evolution). The sample questions listed in "Checking for Conceptual Understanding" can be used to create multiple-choice and short-answer questions on a unit test.

Figure 5.4 outlines a rubric that teachers can use to determine primary students' level of understanding of the concepts of problem and solution by evaluating their ability to recognize examples of problems and solutions, match problems with solutions, and provide an example of a solution to a particular problem.

Concluding Thoughts

If students don't actually understand what they are studying, they won't be able to use it to build further learning or to make sense of the world beyond school. To promote subject matter understanding and not merely information recall, teachers must provide students with opportunities to digest the ideas they encounter—to assess, draw conclusions, or rework what they are studying—and to connect these ideas to the larger context of ideas within each subject.

Practices That Nurture Understanding

Shape Climate	• Expect students to understand why and how, not merely what. • Avoid supplying answers, when possible.
Create Opportunities	• Build daily instruction around invitations to think. • Frame learning around overarching ideas, questions, or tasks.
Build Capacity	• Provide students with tools to construct understanding.
Provide Guidance	• Always check for understanding before moving on. • Evaluate understanding over recall.

Figure 5.4 Assessing Understanding of Problems and Solutions

	Sophisticated Understanding	Extended Understanding	Basic Understanding	Partial Recognition	Pre-Recognition
Distinguishes a Problem From a Solution	Correctly identifies problems and solutions, and correctly states in their own words the differences between them.	Correctly identifies problems and solutions, and offers a simple explanation of the differences between them.	Correctly identifies simple examples of problems and solutions but without any explanation.	Understands what is being asked, but has difficulty consistently identifying even very simple examples of problems and solutions.	Does not understand what it means to identify something as a problem or a solution.
Recognizes Matching Problems and Solutions	Correctly recognizes matching problems and solutions when given less obvious examples.	Correctly recognizes matching problems and solutions when given various examples.	Correctly recognizes the matching problems and solutions when given very simple examples.	Understands what is being asked, but has difficulty consistently recognizing the matching problems and solutions when given very simple examples.	Does not understand what it means to match a problem with its solution.
Proposes Possible Solutions	Provides two or more reasonable solutions even with less obvious problems.	Proposes two or more obvious solutions that match a problem.	Proposes a single predictable solution that matches a simple problem.	Proposes a solution that seems unrelated to the problem or is otherwise inappropriate.	Cannot propose a solution when given a simple problem.

The following are selected strategies for educational leaders to use with teachers to promote deep understanding.

Opportunities for Leadership

Pool Strategies That Go Beyond Mere Transmission

Work with teachers in various subject areas to identify instructional strategies that involve students in working thoughtfully with the content and not merely retrieving information from a textbook or teacher presentation.

Encourage Framing of Instruction

Support teachers in organizing their instruction around big ideas, inquiry questions, or overarching projects to help eliminate coverage of unnecessary topics and to provide coherence and focus to individual lessons and larger units of study.

Check That Understanding Matters

Where opportunities arise, confirm that formal and informal assessments of factual and conceptual knowledge consistently require students to demonstrate understanding and do not merely require recall.

Note

1. This attribution is based on a distorted interpretation of Bloom's actual intentions regarding his taxonomy. See Case (2013).

6

From Skill to Real-Life Competency

> This chapter explains the notion of competencies needed for living in the 21st century and how to nurture them. More specifically, it discusses
>
> - the range of competencies that have been suggested as goals and how these differ from skills;
> - the inadequacy of a skills practice approach to building and extending student competency;
> - practices that support the development of real-life competency in a wide range of areas.

As an elementary teacher, I was able to get most of my sixth-grade students to a stage where they could answer word problems such as "What is the cost of a single slice of bread if a loaf costs \$2.00 and there are 25 slices in a loaf?" Despite repeated practice with this kind of problem, they were unprepared when I asked how much each student would need to pay for the box lunch that we planned for an upcoming class outing. None could identify the information we would need, let alone where they might find this information and how they would use it to answer the question.

The rigor that matters most for the 21st century is demonstrated mastery of the core competencies for work, citizenship, and life-long learning. Studying academic content is the means for developing competencies, instead of being the goal, as it has been traditionally. In today's world, it's no longer how much you know that matters; it's what you can do with what you know.

—Tony Wagner, *The Global Achievement Gap* (as cited in West Windsor-Plainsboro Regional School District, n.d.)

I tried a more directive question: "Calculate the cost for each student of two cheese and ham sandwiches, a drink, and an apple." Even then, they struggled to organize the variables and formulate the equations. My students could answer "fake real" problems, but that didn't enable them to tackle real tasks. Most had acquired the pen and paper skill but were not able to solve everyday variations of the problem.

The situation described in this story highlights a major impetus for reform efforts: a concern that students are not adequately prepared to function in the world beyond school. As suggested in the opening chapter, the problem is not that the educational system has completely misidentified the goals that need to be achieved. Students in a digital age must still decide what information they need, where to get it, and how to use it. As well, they must still formulate mathematical problems, even if they use a calculator to crunch the numbers. Rather, the problem resides in how we have interpreted and taught the existing goals.

This move to redefine the existing goals is reflected in the discussions of competencies found in policy documents and educational journals. For example, the Partnership for 21st Century Skills has developed a framework for the competencies that students require to succeed in work and life. These are clustered in three areas: (1) learning and innovation skills (consisting of creativity and innovation, critical thinking and problem solving, and communication and collaboration); (2) information, media, and technology skills (referring to information literacy; media literacy; and information, communications, and technology literacy); and (3) life and career skills (which include flexibility and adaptability, initiative and self-direction, social and cross-cultural skills, productivity and accountability, and leadership and responsibility; Partnership for 21st Century Learning, 2007).

Many individual school districts have their own, often similar, lists. For example, the Washoe County School District in Reno, Nevada, identifies six competencies: collaboration, knowledge construction, real-world problem solving, self-regulation, skilled communication, and use of technology for learning. The list is similar to those identified by the West Windsor-Plainsboro Regional School District in New Jersey. Their list of six student competencies are collaborative team member; effective communicator; globally aware, active, and responsible student/citizen; information-literate researcher; innovative and practical problem solver; and flexible and self-directed learner (see Washoe County School District, n.d.; West Windsor-Plainsboro Regional School District, n.d.).

Although some of these competencies are new additions to or new emphases within the educational agenda, most competencies needed to function in a 21st century world were also required in the last century. In fact, although the terminology may have changed, the majority of competencies have been educational goals for centuries (Pellegrino & Hilton, 2012, p. 53).

If the areas of desired competency are not new, why is there a preoccupation with competencies for a 21st century world? *Competencies* refer to the ability to competently perform a range of tasks. To some educators, *competencies* is simply another word for *skills*. For others, use of the term *competency* signals something different than what was typically understood as skill development (Ananiadou & Claro, 2009). This shift stems from the concern that the skills taught in school do not actually translate into functional ability outside the classroom. In other words, use of the term competencies seeks to capture a richer sense of what it means to nurture meaningful student ability.

What Is Meant by Real-Life Competencies?

To begin, let us consider what kinds of competencies are found in calls for 21st century reform, and then explore what it means to be competent and how competencies differ from skills in nature and development.

What Competencies Are Being Recommended?

As noted earlier, many jurisdictions and educational organizations have their own list of competencies. However, a shared major motivation behind the competency movement is to make schooling more functional—especially in the area of the economy and employment, but also in the areas of personal efficacy, social responsibility, and environmental stewardship. As illustrated in Figure 6.1, these lists can be categorized in terms of student competency in thinking, communicating, and acting.[1]

Figure 6.1   Sampling of Recommended Competencies

Think	Communicate	Act
Explore and generate ideas, assess evidence, and draw conclusions • critical thinking • problem solving • creativity and innovation • collaborative thinking	Access, interpret, assess, and represent oral, written, and visual messages and ideas • traditional literacies (reading, writing, listening, speaking) • media literacy • digital literacy • financial literacy	Consider oneself and others, weigh options, and develop and implement plans for acting responsibly and effectively • global citizenship • environmental stewardship • social responsibility and cooperation • personal responsibility • entrepreneurship

Although helpful for discussion purposes, like any categorization, the competencies do not fit perfectly into the three assigned categories. Some competencies cross over into more than one category. For example, financial literacy (being able to understand and communicate about financial matters) also has an action competency (responsible consumer buying and saving habits). Similarly, digital literacy goes beyond communicative competency to include personal responsibility for appropriate use of digital technologies (e.g., e-mail etiquette, anticyberbullying, Internet safety). This simply means that these competencies span various dimensions.

A significant overlap arises because thinking is required in all three categories of competency. It is somewhat misleading to align thinking with just one category of competency since thinking is needed to communicate effectively and act responsibly. Reading, for example, is a form of thinking, not simply decoding. Therefore, it is helpful to interpret the thinking competency as specifically focused on thinking about ideas, and to see thinking about representations as subsumed within communicative competency and thinking about actions as subsumed within the action competency. The important point about this cross-categorization is to ensure that thinking is seen as an essential aspect of all competencies, not as simply the ability to think about ideas.

What Does It Mean to Be Competent?

Being competent means that an individual has a broad dependable ability to perform a constellation of challenging core tasks across a range of contexts and fields. Let's unpack each of these elements.

- "Broad dependable ability" signals that individuals are proficient in some area of endeavor, and that their ability is not simply a one-off event but persists on an ongoing basis. For example, calling someone a competent artist would mean that the person is reliably effective at producing decent works of art.
- "Constellation of challenging core tasks" signals that there is an array of things that someone must be good at in order to earn the "competent" label. For example, a competent artist would need to be able to prepare materials, execute a design, produce a technically proficient and imaginative product, and so on. If the person was deficient in her or his ability to complete one of the essential tasks, the designation as competent would be challenged. Tasks that are not seen as core are not required for competency. The core tasks that comprise a competency aren't straightforward or easy; rather, they require some skill and thought. This is why we don't use phrases

such as *competent breather, walker* or *eater*, since these are not seen to be challenging tasks for the average person.

- "Range of contexts and fields" refers to the domain in which the individual is competent to perform the core tasks. When we refer to competent artists, we don't necessarily mean that they are proficient in all media or genres. It is more likely that they are a competent painter or sculptor. The discipline, field, or context delineates the more specific tasks that someone is proficient at. For example, someone could be an accomplished writer but only as the author of historical fiction set within the medieval period and not at writing about other historical periods (the Golden Age in Greece) or in other genres (such as poetry). People extend their competency by acquiring knowledge in additional fields and by mastering the conventions and norms used in other contexts.

When we talk about a competent communicator, we must identify the handful of general core tasks that are common to any form of literacy and, within each core task, identify the more specific tasks from the various fields or contexts where competency is desired. For example, educators typically want students to be able to read texts in various subject areas and genres (narrative fiction, nonfiction, poetry). Figure 6.2 provides a sampling of the range of core and specific tasks that we would typically expect of a competent communicator.

How Do Competencies Differ From Skills?

Looking at the lists of competencies and the diagram of core and specific tasks, it is not immediately clear how competencies are any different from the skills that have long been advocated for in education. We believe there are three significant differences between a competency and a skill.

Broader Focus. A competency is the ability to function effectively in a broader scope of activity than that often meant by the term *skill*. Skills typically designate very particular and specific abilities—at the level that we have referred to as specific tasks—whereas competency refers to the ability to perform an interconnected cluster of tasks found within a broad area of human activity (e.g., literacy and numeracy in everyday affairs). This difference is significant because a preoccupation with developing narrowly defined skills has not translated to competency at the broader level. Teaching individual skills, such as writing a five-paragraph essay or creating topic sentences, doesn't achieve the real goal—which is proficiency in expressing oneself when actually communicating in writing with clients

Figure 6.2 Core and Specific Tasks Involved in Communicative Competency

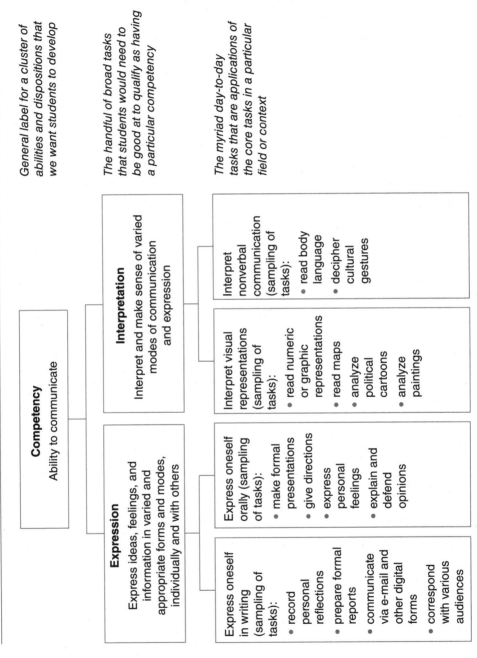

General label for a cluster of abilities and dispositions that we want students to develop

The handful of broad tasks that students would need to be good at to qualify as having a particular competency

The myriad day-to-day tasks that are applications of the core tasks in a particular field or context

Competency
Ability to communicate

Interpretation
Interpret and make sense of varied modes of communication and expression

Expression
Express ideas, feelings, and information in varied and appropriate forms and modes, individually and with others

Interpret nonverbal communication (sampling of tasks):
- read body language
- decipher cultural gestures

Interpret visual representations (sampling of tasks):
- read numeric or graphic representations
- read maps
- analyze political cartoons
- analyze paintings

Express oneself orally (sampling of tasks):
- make formal presentations
- give directions
- express personal feelings
- explain and defend opinions

Express oneself in writing (sampling of tasks):
- record personal reflections
- prepare formal reports
- communicate via e-mail and other digital forms
- correspond with various audiences

or preparing reports for one's employer. Many students cannot or simply do not think how to identify and mobilize all the individual skills they need to complete these real writing tasks effectively. My students encountered this obstacle when they were unable to figure out how to cost the planned lunch.

The limits of a skills approach was the subject of Grant Wiggins's (2015) criticism of efforts to promote independent use of skills. His concern was that teaching individual skills and then expecting students to use them on their own did not prepare students to confront novel situations or to determine which of the various skills they have learned is most appropriate given the particular context. In the real world, there is no sign that flashes "Use this skill here." Students must learn to read a situation and select from a repertoire of potentially relevant tools. Instead of teaching individual skills in isolation, a more holistic competency is best developed by presenting students with increasingly more complex and broader tasks, where they learn to draw upon and integrate a relevant range of abilities. Instead of learning a skill and then looking for a place to use it, the competency approach begins with realistic tasks and helps students identify and master what they need to complete each task.

More Complex Components. Developing competency requires a more complex array of components than is often captured by the term *skill*. In educational circles, it is commonplace to distinguish skills from knowledge and attitudes. This has often resulted in the teaching of generic steps to follow, independent of the content and the attitudes needed to make effective use of skills. For example, students may have learned the skill of drawing inferences from everyday facts provided to them. But the ability to draw inferences about magnets in science and about algebraic expressions in mathematics requires discipline-specific knowledge of the properties of these objects and relationships. Competency is always dependent on relevant knowledge. In addition, genuine competency depends upon attitudes such as persistence, open-mindedness, and attentiveness to detail. Without these mental attitudes, students are unlikely to regularly and conscientiously mobilize their abilities. As we see more clearly in the next section, competency requires a more diverse set of interrelated tools than has been typically associated with skills.

Real-Life Emphasis. The shift to competencies is an attempt to emphasize development of students' real-life ability to complete complex tasks on their own initiative without teacher prompting—because ultimately that is what will be expected in the world beyond school. It is not sufficient to foster pen and paper skills that students can demonstrate when asked to on a test. Genuine problem-solving competency goes beyond students' ability to solve a page of word problems in a mathematics textbook, and extends to their ability to solve comparable problems in the real world where all the variables have not been conveniently packaged for them. The goal of competency development is to empower students to function on their own in realistic situations without the teacher coaching from the sidelines.

Why Are Students Not Better Prepared?

Arguably the most persistent complaint among 21st century reformers is the inadequate equipping of youth for the world outside school. A recent Gallup poll reported that 59 percent of working people between the ages of 18 and 35 said that they acquired most of the skills they use outside of school (Fullan & Langworthy, 2014, p. 1). This shortfall arises because the conventional pedagogy of skill development is not what is needed to develop genuine competency, and this approach does not support the transfer from school-based skills to real-life competencies that many reformers call for.

> Now, more than ever, modern life requires students to take what they learn in school and apply it at home, at work, in their communities, and in future academic pursuits.
>
> —West Windsor-Plainsboro Regional School District (n.d.)

Lack of Genuine Competency

A different pedagogy is needed to develop genuine competency. This shift is signaled in the terms used to describe skill development. It is common to talk about practicing skills and transfer of skills. Yet these terms don't apply when talking about a competency: a person will build and extend their competency, not practice and transfer it. These changes in terminology highlight the difference in how genuine competency is developed.

The dominant pedagogy of individual skill development is to introduce a technique with examples; the teacher models the strategy and then invites students to practice it, initially in easy applications and gradually moving to more difficult applications.[2] To illustrate, consider what a practice pedagogy would look like when developing an athlete's ability to jump. The athlete would receive instructions on proper technique and then start practicing with a training bar set at, say, one foot. After a while, it might be raised to two feet and then to three feet, and so on. The athlete would practice the technique until mastered to a high level of performance.

In actual fact, competency in jumping is not developed to any significant level exclusively by the repeated practice of a single technique.

Athletes need a more diverse set of tools to increase their ability to jump. These would include leg-strengthening exercises for spring enhancement, different jumping techniques such as the scissor kick and the flop, various ways of approaching a jump, knowledge of human physiology, and even mental imaging and coaching about perseverance to enhance performance. Coaches would need to set up tasks across a spectrum of the situations where they wanted to build competency and help their athletes master the diverse mental and physical tools needed to perform the task in each situation.

Despite its inadequacy, repeated practice of a general technique is how many students are taught classroom skills. This approach is reflected in the following box describing a fictional but typical scenario for teaching students to summarize text.[3]

Conventional Practice Approach to Summarizing

Students in Ms. James's class have just completed reading an article. Ms. James asks them to write a summary of the article. She indicates that the summary should be approximately half a page in length and should contain the most important ideas.

Ms. James is aware that the Common Core State Standards require students to "Determine the main idea of a text and explain how it is supported by key details; summarize the text." She wants to prepare students for this outcome, which they will be required to demonstrate on the standardized state assessment they must write this year. She shows them samples of student answers to some of these test questions from previous years.

Several times over the course of the year, she asks them to summarize things they have read and provides comments on their work. She notices that some students respond to her comments and their ability to summarize improves. However, many students are just not getting it. Some rewrite most of what's in the reading, simply changing the wording slightly, and their so-called summaries are far too long. Others tend to write a few lines stating the topic of the article and pick a few points the author makes.

She's not sure how to move them along. She's taught them the definition and elements of a summary, shown them examples, and provided feedback on their work. What else can she do?

Genuine proficiency builds and extends across various contexts by mastering a broader repertoire of relevant tools, not by practicing a prescribed technique or following a set of steps in controlled settings (e.g., preparing a report using a five-paragraph outline). The tools introduced in Chapter 4 are the building blocks of any educational competency. There are some direct parallels with the tools that someone might use to improve physical performance and tools for cognitive performance. For example, mental imaging is a thinking strategy that is useful in both, as is the habit of mind of perseverance. Other tools, such as thinking concepts and criteria for judgment, may be unique to intellectual tasks. The following box contrasts the earlier discussed practice approach to developing students' ability to summarize with a tool development approach. In this example, students think through and work with a diverse set of tools until they "own" them and can use them in varied settings.

Genuine proficiency builds and extends across various contexts by mastering a broader repertoire of relevant tools, not by practicing a prescribed technique or following a set of steps in controlled settings.

Tool Development Approach to Summarizing

Mr. Stavros wants to focus on developing his students' ability to summarize written text. He recognizes that the act of summarizing actually requires significant critical thinking and, therefore, wants to ensure he plans for, explicitly teaches, and assesses his students' use of the intellectual tools they will require to be able to summarize effectively.

First, he frames an authentic task: he informs students that the student council must make a decision about which charity to support this year with their fundraising. There are so many deserving organizations and causes that they have asked Mr. Stavros's class to prepare a concise but informative summary of the various potential organizations to help them make a decision.

Mr. Stavros considers ways to help students uncover the criteria for an effective summary. Knowing that students will be required to summarize on the state assessment they must write this year, he shows them samples of student answers to some of these test questions from previous years.

He asks students working in small groups to rank order the sample summaries from most effective to least effective. He invites them to share what made some samples more effective than others. From this discussion, he draws out the criteria for an effective summary:

- accurately explains the main ideas;
- includes a selection of the most important details;
- effectively connects the details to the main ideas; and
- is appropriate for the purpose and audience.

He realizes that each of these criteria needs to be unpacked. He models the thinking by examining a short text piece and leads the class through an examination of the various ideas and details or examples within the reading. Together, the class builds a set of yes and no examples for the main ideas and important details, and considers why, in this context, they qualify as yes and no examples.

Mr. Stavros invites his students to try their hand at summarizing the article now. He scaffolds the task by first asking them to highlight the main ideas in yellow and the details in green. Then he suggests they trade their article with a partner and examine their partner's highlighting in light of their understanding of the main ideas and significant details. He encourages them to review their own highlighting and decide whether they wish to make changes.

He provides a matrix in which students can gather and organize their ideas before they begin writing their summary. Finally, he invites them to write a "$2.00 summary"—10 cents a word—and he doesn't provide change or give out loans! After this collaboration, students independently write an effective summary in exactly 20 words. Mr. Stavros asks them to consider how they made decisions about what to include and what to leave out. The best of the summaries are forwarded to the student council to assist in its deliberations about which charity to support.

As the year progresses, Mr. Stavros provides many other opportunities for students to summarize ideas presented in texts, oral presentations, videos, and other contexts. Each time, he briefly reminds students of the criteria for an effective summary and includes time in his planning for students to use the criteria to provide feedback to their peers and to assess their own progress.

In subsequent assignments, he encourages them to consider the length and contents of the piece they are reading to help determine how long a summary would be warranted. Later in the year, he regularly asks students whether they think it might be useful to create a summary after reading, viewing, or listening, and encourages them to decide when summarizing might help them—when faced with a situation where it would be helpful to identify and record key ideas.

Lack of Skill Transfer

The assumption behind the practice approach is that a skill once mastered will transfer to other situations. In the case of the athlete who learns to jump high over a bar, this would imply transferring his ability to other challenges, such as jumping hurdles, fences, pommel horses, or skipping ropes. But we know this is unlikely since the other situations each require different considerations and techniques. The demands of actual situations are sufficiently varied that no one technique fits them all. The same is true for intellectual tasks. Even something as simple as note taking is required in varied settings, each requiring specialized proficiencies: recording directions for driving to a physical location, making notes for oneself for a research project, taking notes for someone who has missed class, recording the minutes for a formal meeting, or making speaking notes for a presentation.

The idea of developing a range of tools for each task is helpful in explaining why extending competency is a more apt metaphor than transferring skill. Rather than applying a learned technique in a new context, the metaphor suggests that we broaden the reach of a competency to new areas by adding tools needed to build competency in the new context. Students may be competent in taking notes for themselves but not proficient at preparing notes for others (including taking notes for a friend or minutes for a meeting). This inability arises because different or additional tools are needed in deciding what to record when summarizing for others.

Figure 6.3 compares two situations involving interpretation—one where a presenter interprets the mood of an audience while delivering a talk, and the other where a physician interprets a patient's symptoms. Despite the tools shared in common (e.g., attention to detail, understanding the concept of inference), many more tools are specialized to each of the tasks. Professionals may be proficient at interpretation in their familiar context and poor at it in another's field. Rather than characterize this as a failure to transfer an interpreting skill, it is simply the case that the tools for each task are sufficiently specialized and complex that significant tool development is required to extend competency into these other fields.

Figure 6.3   Comparing Tools for Two Interpretive Competencies

Intellectual Tools	Interpreting an Audience's Mood	Interpreting a Patient's Condition
Background Knowledge	• psychology of human behavior • sociology of the cultural group	• psychology of illness • human anatomy and disease
Criteria for Judgment	• consistency with clues from the audience • plausible	• consistency with patient's symptoms • highly probable
Thinking Strategies	• continually scan the room for signals • look for body language, tone of voice, and explicit comments	• checklist of techniques to try • checklist of symptoms • attend to physical signs and verbal descriptions
Thinking Vocabulary	• inference	• inference
Habits of Mind	• attentive to detail	• attentive to detail • persistent in tracking down cause

To develop genuine competency, educators need to recognize the importance of teaching a more diverse set of intellectual tools organized around realistic tasks, and to understand that the tools will vary depending on the context and field in which each task occurs. The collective challenge over the course of a school career is to ensure that students are exposed to the range of real-life tasks that we want them to be proficient at and that they have opportunities to acquire and learn to draw upon the repertoire of tools suitable for each task. Consider the example of problem solving, a frequently cited competency. There are several core tasks that span the range of problem-solving situations. These include social action, interpersonal problem solving through mediation and negotiation, and practical and mathematical problem solving. Each of these general tasks subsumes many specific tasks, each of them requiring a different repertoire of tools which may be unique to particular disciplines and subject areas.

> The collective challenge over the course of a school career is to ensure that students are exposed to the range of real-life tasks that we want them to be proficient at and that they have opportunities to acquire and learn to draw upon the repertoire of tools suitable for each task.

Figure 6.4 is illustrative of what this requires. The table identifies four specific tasks involved in competently solving a problem through social action (clarify the problem, agree on a solution, plan a course of action, and implement the plan; The Critical Thinking Consortium, 2010, p. 12). For each of these specific tasks, the tools are listed that educators may want to develop in middle school students to build competency. The tools for younger and older students would be modified in complexity to accommodate students' zones of proximal development.[4]

What Practices Nurture Real-Life Competence?

The various competencies needed for the 21st century can best be taught in an integrated manner within the context of realistic tasks that draw upon a shared set of increasingly complex intellectual tools. The practices suggested in the chapter on creating a thinking classroom apply here. What follows are several practices that are particularly directed toward building and extending competencies.

Shape a Climate That Supports Building Competence

Educators can create and reinforce a mindset that supports competency development by attending to the atmosphere established in the classroom.

Figure 6.4 Tools for Social Action Projects

Background Knowledge	Criteria for Judgment	Thinking Vocabulary	Thinking Strategies	Habits of Mind
What do students need to know in order to . . .	By what criteria should students judge attempts to . . .	What concepts will help students . . .	What strategies might help students . . .	What attitudes or values will help students . . .
Clarify the Problem				
What is the problem to be solved? Who are the principal stakeholders? Where is the problem located? When does it arise? Why is the situation problematic? How did the problem come about?	• clear • specific • inclusive • complex	• problem • stakeholder • interests • symptom vs. cause	• information needs • who, what, when, where, why (5Ws) • graphic organizers • causal links • role-play • interests inventory	• tolerance for ambiguity • inquiring attitude
Agree on a Sound Solution				
What has been tried? What could be tried? What might happen? What interests will be affected?	• diversity of proposals • effective • sustainable • feasible • respectful	• short- vs. long-term consequences • intended and unintended consequences	• shortlist • pro/con chart	• persistence • thinking outside the box • open minded
Plan an Effective Course of Action				
What strategies might be used to implement the agreed-upon solution?	• effective • respectful • realistic • comprehensive		• task analysis	• thoroughness

Background Knowledge	Criteria for Judgment	Thinking Vocabulary	Thinking Strategies	Habits of Mind
What resources are available to support each strategy? What obstacles are we likely to face?				
Implement and Evaluate the Action				
What do we need to learn? Has each step in the plan been carried out? What are the effects of the action?	• successful implementation • successful resolution	• intended vs. unintended effects	• implementation checklist • check-backs • periodic reviews	• perseverance • flexibility

Expect Students to Think Through How to Do a Task, Not Just to Get It Done. We have all met students whose mindset is simply to get the work over with. They do not look upon an assignment as an opportunity to learn. This mentality is evident when students say, "Just tell me how to do it." Such responses are most common in situations where students are motivated solely by the need to comply and not out of interest or a perceived value to themselves. To counter this, we must establish an expectation that it is not sufficient to complete a task; rather, students must also think about how to complete it. A first step is to help students appreciate why developing proficiency at the task is useful (e.g., it saves time, eases the difficulty of a task, has applications beyond school). The expectation of "thinking how to do" could be introduced by asking students how they would thoughtfully approach various tasks without actually requiring them to complete the tasks. The expectation can be reinforced by regularly inviting students to explain their approach and indicate what was effective and ineffective. The expectation to think about tasks should include thinking critically, creatively, and collaboratively. For example, in thinking about

> Pedagogy should at its best be about what teachers do that not only helps students to learn but actively strengthens their capacity to learn.
>
> —David Hargreaves (2004, p. 27)

how they might go about framing questions to probe for information, we will want students to consider all three dimensions:

- *critical*: judge relevance and importance of the information sought;
- *creative*: ask questions that are not completely predictable; and
- *collaborative*: consider whether the questions are respectful and build on what others might be asking.

Establish Routines to Encourage Deliberation About the Best Tools to Use. One of the ways in which we undermine the building of competency is by providing students with neatly organized steps to follow. Although my students could solve packaged word problems in mathematics, they were unable to figure out what tools they would need to solve a much more open-ended problem. We must create routines where students are not simply provided with a strategy to follow but are also able to access tools that they can intentionally select and use to achieve a chosen end or objective. We must build the habit, eventually without any teacher coaching, of drawing from a repertoire of tools that students own. Initially, the class may be invited to brainstorm possible tools that might apply and review the purposes and merits of each before deciding on the most appropriate one. Eventually, students would be expected to do this without prompting. After completing a task, students would be asked to explain the various tools they considered and to decide, with hindsight, whether they might do things differently next time.

> One of the ways in which we undermine the building of competence is by providing students with neatly organized steps to follow.

Create Opportunities to Build Genuine Competency

Students will at best develop pen and paper competencies unless they are regularly provided with opportunities to work through real-life tasks.

Structure Competency Development Around Real-Life Tasks. Structuring competency-building around a real-life task challenges students to go beyond canned techniques and is more likely than a practice exercise to engage students. Ideally, the tasks would have a real purpose and actual consequences. Since this is not always possible—although far more possible than many may appreciate—it may be enough that the tasks are realistic in that they are somewhat messy and open ended. Even if my class was not actually going to purchase the materials to make lunch for our field trip, it would have provided the kind of real-life context that the word problems did not. Real-life tasks may be established as the overarching project for a unit of study, and the day-to-day lessons' tasks would require solving smaller challenges leading to the bigger goal. Alternatively, individual lessons can be built around students' own real-life tasks, such as writing a letter to the principal about a school issue, predicting the probability of an upcoming event, or negotiating a solution to an in-class conflict. Figure 6.5 provides suggestions for real-life tasks suitable for varying grade ranges and subject areas.

Figure 6.5 Sample Real-Life Tasks to Build Competency

	Elementary School	Middle School	High School
Science	Build an ideal habitat for the class pet.	Prepare for a "Stop on a Dime" competition in which contestants anticipate momentum and friction in trying to get a rolling object to come to rest on a designated spot.	Prepare for a "Laser the Coin" competition in which contestants anticipate refraction in water by shining a laser on a designated spot at varying depths of water.
Language Arts	Create holiday cards for sale in the school.	Publish an anthology of short stories for a chosen audience.	Publish a historical novel.
Social Studies	Solve real classroom problems.	Research, write, and document the history of an event or person for inclusion in a local museum. Design a campaign to address a community problem.	Rewrite the history textbook from a more inclusive perspective. Prepare a submission to a government agency.
Mathematics	Run a classroom store.	Estimate the number and total cost of items for various events (bagging leaves in the autumn, budgeting annual school supplies).	Create a library of Khan Academy lessons teaching the tools for thinking about mathematical processes.
Fine Arts	Publish a decorative community photo album.	Publish a graphic novel. Publish a picture book.	Create public art or a school mural. Write the lyrics and music for a school anthem.
Health and Physical Education	Design a nutritious snack for the class.	Design and digitally produce a poster to encourage better health and fitness at school.	Design and implement a personal fitness plan to achieve a specified target.

Build Capacity for Competency

The most significant contributor to developing and extending student competency is fluency with a range of tools for the particular tasks we want them to complete.

Help Students Build a Repertoire of Tools for Each Competency. Invariably, when students are unable to perform a task, it is because they lack one or more of the tools required for proficiency. This suggests that significant growth in our collective ability to develop student competency will require systematic tool development across the range of desired competencies. This means identifying a repertoire of tools for each of the desired core competencies that are sufficiently varied to allow for differences among students' abilities and needs, and encompass a diversity of contexts and fields.

Early in this chapter, we suggest the range of tools needed to develop proficiency at undertaking responsible social action. Figure 6.6 outlines the repertoire of tools that thoughtful readers would draw upon when performing five specific tasks that are commonly associated with competent readers (activating prior knowledge, anticipating directions, extracting meaning, challenging ideas, and deliberating about implications; see Abbott, n.d.). These are representative of the spectrum of tools that students will require if they are to develop proficiency in the competencies needed in a 21st century world.

Provide Guidance That Informs Competency-Building

Teachers need to provide students with feedback on their progress in realistic situations, not simply in staged situations.

Capture the Real Thing in Real Time. It is important to collect information about students' competency while they are engaged in actual tasks. Regular in-class behavior and ongoing samples of products (not one-time assignments) are particularly appropriate for assessing student abilities. Extended observation is more likely to provide evidence of student competency and indicate factors that may influence proficiency. These information-gathering strategies may include

- teacher notes during in-class tasks about detectable patterns—for example, the strategies that a particular student uses to solve a problem;
- student–teacher chats to allow students to explain how they approach a task while helping them learn to do it better;

Figure 6.6 Range of Tools to Support Reading

Tasks Involved in Reading	Background Knowledge	Criteria for Judgment	Thinking Vocabulary	Thinking Strategies	Habits of Mind
Activate Draw on personal knowledge and experiences, and information from other sources.	• direct and indirect personal experience • knowledge of a variety of reference sources and merits/limitations of each	• efficient • relevant • useful • credible		• previewing • brainstorming • think of a time • visualizing	• inquiry minded
Anticipate Develop ideas about what might happen next in the text, and more generally about the broader text structure.	• text structures • elements of the text	• can be supported by the text • not obvious	• prediction • evidence • clues • conclusions • inference	• know-wonder • question-answer reading strategy • graphic organizers	• critical minded • attentive to detail
Extract Draw out the details of the text and the overall meaning, both implied and explicit.	• genres • themes • literacy devices (symbols, etc.)	• based on what is known • makes sense in the text	• synthesize • evidence • clues • conclusions • main idea • supporting details	• skim • scan • concept map • reaction codes • think aloud • I think I know • read between/beyond the lines • 5Ws	• persistence • attentive to detail

(Continued)

Figure 6.6 (Continued)

Tasks Involved in Reading	Background Knowledge	Criteria for Judgment	Thinking Vocabulary	Thinking Strategies	Habits of Mind
Challenge Monitor emerging interpretations and understanding of the text, and question the merits of the text given its purpose.	• knowledge of fiction and nonfiction • knowledge of a variety of purposes	• relevant • grounded in the text • fair to author • comprehensive	• evidence • argument • stereotype • bias • point of view • facts • assumptions • argument • counterarguments	• storyboards • survey-question-read-revise-review • character sociogram • evidence charts	• open minded • seeks corroboration • fair minded
Deliberate Explore the ideas and issues presented in the text and their implications beyond the text.	• knowledge of issues/themes in the text	• relevant • beyond the obvious • reflect important considerations	• hypothesis • conclusions • assumptions	• I used to think so what? • discussion circles	• reflective • inquisitive

- checklists or other devices to record the incidence of particular behavior, such as students' ability to participate effectively in group assignments; and

- assessment of peers and oneself that focuses on specific competencies, such as students' ability to reach and defend a position. Figure 6.7 invites students to self-assess their ability to draw on background information to inform a conclusion, their openness to other ideas, and their ability to defend their judgment in light of relevant criteria and available evidence.

Figure 6.7   Self-Assessment of Proficiency in Reaching and Defending a Position

	Exemplary	Good	Satisfactory	Developing	Remedial
Background Knowledge • accurate use of relevant facts	I am able to refer to many relevant facts, always with accuracy.	I am able to refer to relevant facts, most often with accuracy.	I am able to refer to some relevant facts, usually with accuracy.	I am able to refer to a limited number of relevant facts with little accuracy.	I am able to refer to few or no relevant and accurate facts.
Open-Mindedness • open to considering a variety of views • willing to rethink position based on new evidence or arguments	I always carefully consider all viewpoints presented. I am always willing to reconsider my position when evidence or arguments warrant it.	I usually consider most viewpoints presented. I am usually willing to reconsider my position when evidence or arguments warrant it.	I occasionally consider a variety of viewpoints presented. I am sometimes willing to reconsider my position when evidence or arguments warrant it.	I seldom consider other viewpoints. I am rarely willing to reconsider my position, even when evidence or arguments warrant it.	I rarely or never consider other viewpoints. I am always reluctant to reconsider my position when evidence or arguments warrant it.
Reasoned Judgment • uses evidence to reach an informed decision • considers criteria when making a decision	My decisions are always based on available evidence. I always consider the relevant criteria when arriving at a decision.	My decisions are usually based on available evidence. I usually consider most of the relevant criteria when arriving at a decision.	My decisions are sometimes based on available evidence. I sometimes consider relevant criteria when arriving at a decision.	My decisions are seldom based on available evidence. I seldom consider relevant criteria when arriving at a decision.	My decisions are rarely or never based on available evidence. I rarely or never consider any criteria when arriving at a decision.

Concluding Thoughts

Building student ability to function effectively in a wide range of school and beyond-school tasks is arguably the most insistent call among 21st century reformers. Although the range of competencies is similar to the range of skills that have traditionally been promoted in schools, the goals are now more broadly understood, focus on real-world proficiency, and require a more effective, multidimensional pedagogy. The conventional approach to developing proficiency by practicing techniques that hopefully are generalized across contexts has not produced the desired levels and transfer of abilities. In its place, we have described an approach that involves identifying the full range of tasks for each competency where proficiency is desired, articulating the repertoire of intellectual tools needed to build and extend competence in each of these tasks, and supporting students in mastery of these tools in ways that enable flexible and thoughtful use.

Practices That Build Competency

Shape Climate	• Expect students to think through how to do a task, not just to get it done. • Establish routines to encourage deliberation about the best tools to use.
Create Opportunities	• Structure competency development around real-life tasks.
Build Capacity	• Help students build a repertoire of tools for each competency.
Provide Guidance	• Capture the real thing in real time.

The following are selected strategies for educational leaders to use with teachers to encourage competency development.

Opportunities for Leadership

Emphasize a Few Competencies; Reinforce the Rest

Because it can be overwhelming to try to do too much at once, encourage grade-level groups or departments to identify a few competencies that will be systematically supported during a particular year, while remembering to maintain some level of support for the other competencies.

Organize Competency-Building Around Tasks, Not Isolated Skills

Support students in learning to draw upon a repertoire of tools by organizing competency development around open-ended tasks rather than focusing on teaching isolated skills.

Make It Real

Encourage teachers to use realistic, open-ended tasks as the basis for building proficiency in all areas of desired competency wherever possible.

Notes

1. The comprehensive list of competencies commonly associated with 21st century skills assembled on The Glossary of Educational Reform website overlaps extensively with the competencies we suggest. See Great Schools Partnership (n.d.).
2. We recognize that many educators don't exclusively use a practice approach with a single technique; many will draw upon some of the kinds of tools we describe. However, the practice approach continues to play a central role in how abilities are developed in many classrooms, and the range of tools is often incomplete.
3. This example and the one following were developed by Usha James.
4. See guides to social action for primary and secondary students available for free download at The Critical Thinking Consortium (2010).

7

From Attitude to Genuine Commitment

> This chapter explains what is involved in developing students' dispositions to act effectively, responsibly, and thoughtfully. More specifically, it discusses
>
> - the range of personal, social, and intellectual dispositions mentioned in connection with 21st century reform initiatives, and more broadly;
> - the inadequacy of developing students' attitudes that don't translate into dispositions to act upon these values;
> - the importance of more deliberate and systematic efforts to foster student commitments;
> - practices that are likely to foster genuine commitments.

Ron was a student-teacher in my critical thinking course in the faculty of education. He was the best in the class at analyzing arguments and detecting fallacies in articles and editorials. He thoroughly enjoyed doing

> It is not enough to be compassionate. You must also act.
>
> —Tenzin Gyatso,
> Fourteenth Dalai Lama

these critiques and was adept at them. A few weeks after the end of class, he showed me a newspaper article on a topic we had addressed in class. He was excited about its contents and wanted to discuss them with me. But he hadn't thought to apply any of what he had learned a few weeks earlier to critique the article's arguments. It was as though that part of the course hadn't happened. He was to some extent "critically minded"—he was clearly able to critically analyze and he appreciated the importance of scrutinizing arguments for their merits—but he didn't actually carry this ability over when the situation arose outside of class. He had the right attitude, but he wasn't in the habit of using what he knew.

This scenario highlights another challenge facing schools: how to foster the attitudes and dispositions in students so they regularly make use of what they know and can do whenever the situation requires it. This challenge is part of a larger problem with our treatment of attitudes in school—the third dimension of the classic trilogy of educational goals (knowledge, skills, and attitudes). Educators often try to convince students to be critically minded or to persevere, and many students will readily acknowledge the need to think for themselves and try hard. In short, they may believe that these values are important. They have the desired attitudes, but this doesn't consistently translate into the desired behavior.

Our plea for a richer interpretation of attitudinal goals is not because the historically valued attitudes are no longer relevant. They are arguably more necessary than ever: students need to care about the environment, respect diversity, appreciate the importance of personal hygiene, and value critical thinking. The problem, as suggested by the behavior of my best philosophy student, is that in many cases, students' attitudes are simply verbal acknowledgments and not genuine commitments to act. Students may sincerely express their support or appreciation for a value, but students' actions and not merely their words must mirror the traits that are needed for success in the world.

Attitude refers to the disposition or inclination to feel a certain way (e.g., to favor environmental sustainability, support cultural diversity, value the ideas of persevering and working hard, and care about their personal well-being). Schools have seen their role to be instilling appreciation for a list of values. The problem is that a disposition to feel a certain way is not enough: students need to be disposed to carry their feelings through into action. Our choice of the term *commitment* refers to the disposition to act in a certain way (e.g., to do things that support sustainability, act to encourage cultural diversity, consistently persevere in daily pursuits, and actively work to stay fit). The focus on commitment is not on what students are able to do but on what they typically do—how they act or, more specifically, their habits or patterns of action. This adds a new dimension to our explanation of why schools have not adequately prepared students to function effectively in the world. We may not be developing the abilities they need, but it may also be that students haven't acquired the dispositions to apply the competencies that schools have successfully taught them. I know that my best student didn't have the needed disposition to make use of what he knew.

What Do We Mean by Genuine Commitment?

Promoting dispositions to feel in a certain way doesn't go far enough in engendering what our students need if they are to function in the world. Schools must engender genuine commitments, which are the predictable habits or patterns of behavior (not individual actions or verbal affirmations) of a responsible, thoughtful, and functioning individual. I became aware of the gap between attitudes and commitments three decades ago when I surveyed teachers about critical thinking. Ninety-three percent of the respondents stated that critical thinking was a very important goal. If attitude were all that mattered, the results of this survey would have been outstanding. However, it turned out that only about 20 percent of these teachers regularly promoted critical thinking in their classrooms. Their positive attitude toward critical thinking didn't translate into action. The same is true with our attitudinal goals in school. There is little point in encouraging students to appreciate the need for personal hygiene if this doesn't translate into good hygiene habits. Employers may be interested in a prospective employee's attitude toward punctuality, but only if this translates into consistent timely attendance at work. Educators may be pleased that students value the environment, but does this matter if students don't act positively to conserve the environment?

> Genuine commitments are the predictable habits or patterns of behavior of a responsible, thoughtful, and functioning individual.

What Dispositions Are Being Promoted?

There are smatterings of statements found in policy documents that refer to dispositions to feel and act. For example, the Center for Curriculum Redesign in Boston identifies six character traits for the 21st century. These are mindfulness, curiosity, courage, resilience, ethics, and leadership (Bialik, Bogan, Fadel, & Horvathova, 2015). In many cases, dispositions are folded into the discussion of competencies. For example, a previously cited document on 21st century competencies defines the ability to be a collaborative team member to include the dispositions of flexibility, reliability, respectfulness, and open-mindedness. Similarly, being globally aware, active, and responsible subsumes the dispositions to respect rights, feelings, property, and the environment (West Windsor-Plainsboro Regional School District, n.d.). However, for the most part, commitments are not significantly recognized in 21st century educational reform documents, whose main focus has been on building competencies. This omission is unfortunate, since there is no point in students being able to do something if they don't actually do it when the time comes. Fostering dispositions to act is implied in the calls for preparing fully functioning individuals. However, since nurturing dispositions requires different pedagogical practices than building capacity, schools need to devote explicit attention to developing genuine commitments.

> There is no point in students being able to do something if they don't actually do it when the time comes.

We can look at the values and attitudes that have been part of the educational agenda for many decades to get a sense of the commitments that educators wish to foster.[1] The range of desired dispositions can be clustered into three categories:

- **Personal dispositions** are those that individuals exhibit toward themselves, such as self-esteem, integrity, taking personal responsibility for one's actions, and taking pride in one's work.
- **Social dispositions** refer to those that we exhibit toward other individuals and society generally, including national pride, commitment to justice, respect for law, respect for the environment, and a cooperative attitude.
- **Intellectual dispositions** are those patterns of mental behavior that are centrally concerned with how we think and learn, including openness to new ideas, having an inquiring mind, being curious, attending to detail, and tolerating ambiguity. These are the tools mentioned in Chapter 4 that we refer to as habits of mind.

Figure 7.1 presents a representative list of the personal, social, and intellectual dispositions that have been considered as educational goals.[2] Clearly, these lists represent the most important traits needed by every thoughtful, responsible, and effective individual.

What Creates a Disposition to Act?

The psychological literature offers some insight into how to convert attitudes into dispositions to act. Typically, dispositions are seen to involve three components (see Ritchhart, 2002, pp. 36–37):

- **Motivation or Inclination:** A person feels the importance in general of acting or thinking in a certain way. A person's values provide the basic impetus or motivation, but they do not on their own guarantee an appropriate response in any particular situation.
- **Awareness:** People may generally be positively inclined toward something, but they must also see a particular case as an appropriate instance involving their values. This may partially explain my

Figure 7.1   Commonly Identified Dispositions

Personal Dispositions	Social Dispositions	Intellectual Dispositions
• accept oneself, realize one's own worth • integrity, honesty, and frankness with self • hopefulness about the future • willingness to seek adventure, a sense of mission • desire to make a productive contribution to society • love of truth, however disconcerting • respect for work well done • appreciation of beauty in art and the environment • respond with wonderment and awe • pride in family and ethnic background • commitment to personal hygiene and health • self-disciplined and self-directed • manage impulsivity	• respect for the dignity and worth of every human being • commitment to equal opportunity for all • tolerance and kindness • desire for justice for all • acceptance of social responsibilities • commitment to free thought, expression, and worship • commitment to peaceful resolution of problems • respect for privacy • national pride • environmental stewardship • concern for well-being of living things • respect for the rule of law	Thinking for Oneself • inquiring mind (curious) • critically minded • open minded • fair minded • independent minded • persistent • circumspect • empathetic • tolerant of ambiguity • self-reflective • takes initiative • attentive to detail • intellectual flexibility Thinking With Others • respectful • constructive • inclusive • accommodating • consultative

student's failure to apply his critical thinking expertise to the article he read outside of class: he didn't think about or recognize that reading this article was also a situation calling for a critically minded response.

- **Ability:** A person must also be emotionally, physically, and intellectually able to act upon the motivation in a particular situation. If my student had not been proficient at critical analysis, or if he had just received the article moments earlier, he would not have been able to respond in a critically thoughtful manner. Not providing time for students to think through their responses may account for some of the gap between what they value and how they respond.

This three-part explanation of an attitudinal response leaves out an important element needed to understand commitments. We will call the missing component *consciously confirmed resolve.*

Valuing something may produce a disposition to feel in a certain way, but not necessarily to act on these feelings. This gap is what the ancient Greeks called "weakness of the will." It is the failure to align what people feel they should do (what they value) with what they actually do. This is evident when, for example, individuals care about their fitness, are aware that they should do more, have time to work out, but nevertheless do not get around to exercising. There are two ways in which this kind of disjunction is bridged: unconscious habituation and conscious resolve.

- **Unconscious Habituation:** Most of us who regularly nod or say hello to those we greet do not consciously think about doing this; it is simply a matter of habit that was ingrained in us from an early age. Most likely, we acquired this habit because family members praised us when we were particularly polite and reminded or even chastised us each time we failed to comply. In short, we were conditioned or habituated to align our actions (saying hello) with recognition of the value of politeness.
- **Conscious Resolve:** This occurs when individuals intentionally commit to a particular mode of behavior and do not simply fall into the habit of doing it. A personally revealing example of the relationship between unconscious habituation and conscious resolve occurred during my daily walks around a local city park. I noticed that people would frequently look away whenever they approached another person. Since my cue for saying hello to someone was to wait for eye contact, I found myself no longer greeting most of the people I passed. Disturbed by a growing sense of impersonalization, I resolved to greet everyone I met regardless of whether we had established eye contact or not. My disposition to say hello was no longer the result of unconscious habituation; it was now the product of conscious resolve. The majority of people I greeted would look up and smile or nod at me. I carried on my habit of initiating a greeting for several years. Because I walked around the park almost daily, it had an interesting consequence: gradually, the people I approached recognized me and would as often as not initiate a greeting themselves. In other words, my recurring behavior had habituated them into a predictable behavior.

This example illustrates that our disposition to act may initially be the result of unconscious habituation. However, it also points to the importance of eventually consciously affirming these dispositions. As we have discussed in Chapter 1, habits often become hollowed out—they no longer have the meaning or the effect they were initially intended to have. Conscious consideration of our habits allows us to refine and recommit to the intended purpose. This is especially valuable in building habits that will serve youth in ever-changing situations. If the world were predictable, then automatic habits would be adequate. Clearly, conscious and flexible routines are needed. My wife and I are both in the habit of eating breakfast each morning. She has her orange first thing in the morning and only then has coffee, putting the milk in first. On the other hand, I pretty much decide what I'll have each morning based on how I feel and what's available. You can appreciate that I have an easier time coping with breakfast when we travel in remote areas of India. The paradox of dispositions is that they are habits but we need to be flexible when deciding on the appropriateness of particular actions in a given situation.

A second reason for the importance of eventually bringing students to consciously affirm their habits is respect for individual autonomy. Otherwise, educators may be accused of conditioning students without respecting their right eventually to make up their own minds. This criticism has been leveled against some versions of character education that rely on imposition and pressure without giving students opportunities to decide for themselves (K. Kohn, 1997). It is important, especially in our role as educators, to ensure that the habits we inculcate in students are ultimately (even if not initially) the result of conscious resolve. Our choice of the word *commitments* was intended to signal the need to encourage willful dispositions to act.

Why Is Teaching for Genuine Commitment Important?

Over the past 60 years, attitudes and values have been the focus of varied attention in educational circles. In the 1960s, the values clarification and values education movements focused on the teaching of dispositions. Since then, character education, mindfulness education, and citizenship education have provided the impetus to promote personal and social values, and proponents of habits of mind have raised interest in the intellectual dispositions. However, fostering dispositions to act has received far less attention in the 21st century reform literature than the other two core educational goals—developing understanding and building competency. In fact, policy makers seem to acknowledge the need for student commitments without looking seriously into what fostering them might involve. There are three reasons why this core educational goal deserves significantly more effort and attention.

Dispositions Are an Important Part of the School's Mandate

Official rationales for public education typically refer to the need to develop the values of productive citizenship. For example, the California Task Force on K–12 Civic Learning (2014) recommends that state mandated outcomes include the following civic values: concern for the rights and well-being of others, tolerance for different perspectives, and a predisposition to take action to change things for the better (p. 26). The New York K–12 Social Studies Framework contains the civic participation outcome expecting that students "[d]emonstrate respect for the rights of others in discussions and classroom debates; respectfully disagree with other viewpoints" (State Education Department and the University of the State of New York, 2014, p. 20).

Dispositions Are Preconditions for Other Goals

Not only is fostering a range of dispositions an important goal in its own right, but the acquisition of these dispositions is a necessary condition for developing other important educational goals.

Social and Personal Dispositions Are Preconditions for Any Learning. Many of the dispositions identified as personal commitments are essential for success within school. Self-esteem, self-discipline, and respect for work well done are important for any learner. Similarly, many of the social dispositions, including respect for the rights of others and acceptance of responsibility, are also important. Without these kinds of dispositions, any learning within a classroom will be undermined.

Intellectual Dispositions Are Part of Developing Competency and Understanding. The intellectual dispositions or habits of mind are the engines of thinking. Students who aren't at all curious, don't attend to detail, refuse to persist, or are closed minded will not learn to be effective thinkers and will struggle to understand what they are studying. It is not simply that these dispositions are the preconditions to learning; they are the means by which students develop deep understanding and real-life competency.

Intellectual Dispositions Are Essential to Utilizing Acquired Competency and Understanding. The role of dispositions in utilizing one's abilities is the point of the opening story about my student who was able to critically analyze articles but who didn't think to do it after the course ended. Very little is gained by fortifying students with the capacity and understanding needed to function in the world if they don't actually marshal these assets regularly in their personal and working lives.

Fostering Dispositions Is Impossible to Escape

In some respects, the question of whether educators should promote social, personal, and intellectual dispositions in school is resolved. Whether they recognize it or not, educators engender dispositions and, unless they are intentional in their efforts, they are likely to do it poorly. Schools cannot be value free, and teachers cannot avoid promoting one behavior over another. The fact that we praise children for being punctual, asking probing questions, and having an inquiring attitude signals the embedded values in our schools. Every time we permit or prohibit certain behavior, we implicitly promote certain values over others: school rules against fighting or throwing rocks, for example, attest to the value attached to individual well-being and protection of property. Such rules inevitably affect the values that students develop. Such is the case with everything we do (or do not do) in school. The only real choice educators have about promoting values is whether their influence will be largely hidden and inadvertent or explicit and systematic.

It is not simply that educators may miss out on opportunities to foster dispositions. The situation is more disturbing: many classroom practices actually undermine the development of the dispositions that we value and foster dispositions that are not desired. A particularly important influence is what is loosely called the "hidden curriculum"—the implicit norms and values that are promoted, often unintentionally, through the way we run our schools and conduct our classes.[3] The unintended messages we send to students often have a more significant effect on student learning than do our deliberate efforts. For example, we may say to our students that we value perseverance but undermine this message by rarely inviting them to revise their assignments or by rushing students to quickly complete the tasks we assign. The power of unintended effects is affirmed by studies of various educational programs to promote respect for the rights of others (Daniels & Case, 1992). In one study, the climate within the classroom was identified as the determining factor generating increased respect for others, far more than the particular programs and activities that teachers implemented. What mattered was whether or not teachers provided a safe forum for student dialogue, solicited and valued student opinions, and otherwise acted in ways that modeled respect for the feelings and ideas of others. Figure 7.2 illustrates how schools may produce cynicism by establishing administrative practices that contradict the espoused principles of our legal system (Duke, 1978).

Figure 7.2 What Schools Really Teach About the Legal System

Students may inadvertently develop cynical attitudes toward the legal system because the hidden lessons that schools teach about procedural fairness and other civic ideals do not align with the administrative practices that actually operate in many schools. Students will struggle to develop respect for laws if their experiences in school, which is the first and most extensive public institution young citizens encounter, consistently reinforce the opposite.

We tell students . . .	Yet often in schools . . .
• that we live in a society based on democratic principles. • that all people are to be treated equally before the law. • that the punishment should be reasonable and that it should fit the crime. • that society is committed to safeguarding the rights of individuals against abuse by the state. • that no one is above the law.	• school rules tend to be determined by those least subject to their application. • many teachers fail to enforce school rules consistently. • the consequences for disobeying school rules frequently lack logical relationships to the offenses; for example, the punishment for skipping classes is often suspension from school. • students have few options if they disagree with a claim brought against them by school authorities. • teachers frequently fail to adhere to the rules expected of their students.

What Practices Nurture Genuine Commitment?

Despite their importance, one of the reasons why personal, social, and intellectual dispositions do not receive the attention they deserve is that they do not align directly with topics in the curriculum. However, there is room in the curriculum for nurturing self-esteem or open-mindedness in the same way there is for fractions and poetry. In fact, dispositions are more powerfully nurtured by the subtle yet pervasive influences operating within a school environment than they are by any instructional techniques.

The single most important factor in a child's potential success in school . . . is the child's perception that "my teacher likes me."

—Robert Reasoner (as cited in Bluestein, 2001, p. 147)

Shape the Climate to Foster Genuine Commitment

The literature on the hidden curriculum attests to the power of environmental conditions in supporting or inhibiting the acquisition of dispositions.

Create Consistent Reinforcing Environments That Nurture Desired Commitments. In Chapter 4, we introduced five mechanisms for shaping the climate of a thinking classroom. These mechanisms are levers that educators can use to habituate students to any set of desired dispositions.

- **Expectations:** The norms or standards of behavior that educators establish are the first steps in shaping the atmosphere in a school or classroom. These expectations, which can extend to both teachers and students, may include expectations associated with personal values such as hygiene, with social values such as how others are to be treated with respect, and with intellectual values such as the importance of thinking for oneself.
- **Classroom Routines:** It is not sufficient to establish expectations; each must be anchored in routines that support or reinforce them on a consistent and predictable basis. These routines need not be reprimands or consequences for breach of an expectation. In fact, they are more likely to lead to conscious commitment if they are enabling routines, such as setting a few minutes aside each class to discuss student issues or making a habit of discreetly sending notes to students who do something that is especially considerate.
- **Teacher Modeling:** Educators' behavior is especially important in signaling to students what really counts. Teachers who are open minded are more likely to foster this attribute in their students. Similarly, teachers who sincerely demonstrate their empathy for others are more likely to nurture empathetic tendencies in their students.
- **Personal Interactions:** These refer to the day-to-day exchanges and relationships that teachers have with their students and that students have with each other. They are very significant in shaping the tone in a classroom. Strategies to manage interactions range from providing students with respectful language to use when disagreeing with someone to the tone teachers use when speaking to students.
- **Physical Environment:** The look and physical configuration of schools and classrooms influence the atmosphere. Schools where graffiti and garbage are lingering sights send a different message than do schools that are pleasing places to study. The arrangement of desks in classrooms tells students whether or not group discussion is a welcomed and regular part of learning. Even the presence of motivational posters and catchy reminders helps to reinforce a consistent message about what matters in school.

Figure 7.3 illustrates a sampling of the kinds of practices for each mechanism that reinforce three intellectual dispositions: independent-mindedness, critical-mindedness, and respect for others' ideas.

Figure 7.3   Mechanisms to Nurture Intellectual Dispositions

	Independent-Mindedness	Critical-Mindedness	Respect for Others' Ideas
Expectations	Establish a class rule: Everyone thinks for themselves, not by themselves.	Establish a class rule: Don't accept everything you see and read.	Establish a class rule: Everyone is responsible for encouraging each other to think.
Classroom Routines	Use clickers or thumbs up, down, or sideways to enable all students to quickly express their views on questions raised in class.	Regularly hold "fact or fiction?" discussions where students offer their conclusions supported with reasons about the truth of many common beliefs.	Institute the practice by the teacher and students of acknowledging particularly respectful behavior with a note of hidden appreciation.
Teacher Modeling	Make a conscious effort not to be the expert on everything.	Use a think-aloud strategy to model assessing the pros and cons of a class decision.	Ensure that criticism is always constructive and respectful.
Personal Interactions	Respond to students' questions with a question: "What do you think?"	Make clear through the choice of language that all disagreements are about the ideas and not directed at the person holding the ideas.	Train students to use encouraging language when discussing issues with others.
Physical Environment	When possible, configure chairs in a circle to host discussions to reinforce that there is no head, but all have a voice.	Arrange desks during discussions or debates along a continuum or in a U-shape to allow students to see the diversity of positions on an issue.	Post thoughtful sayings by famous people about the importance of treating each other respectfully.

Create Opportunities to Foster Genuine Commitment

As is obvious from the lists provided earlier, there are many personal, social, and intellectual dispositions that educators will want to foster. The encouraging news is that educators who institute the kinds of thoughtful practices mentioned previously will be supporting the development of many desired dispositions concurrently. For example, students who feel that their ideas are valued and who are treated with respect are more likely to develop self-esteem and want to persevere. In addition, once the expectations and routines are established, their maintenance requires less conscious effort. However, there will be occasions when it may be desirable to focus on a few dispositions that seem especially important or in need of attention.

Emphasize a Few Commitments and Do Them Well. Although shaping the classroom and school climate is the most effective strategy for fostering the desired dispositions, educators may want to offer instruction and facilitate evocative experiences to help initiate particularly needed dispositions.

- **Formal Instruction:** Although on its own it will have little impact, there is value in introducing students in a formal way to the dispositions that are especially valued. This would include helping students understand the nature of the disposition—for example, what it means to be open minded or to show respect for others. In addition, there is value in helping students become more aware of the situations that require the disposition. For example, one is most likely to be in need of open-mindedness and respect for others when disagreeing with others. Also useful is helping students increase their capacity to act in ways consistent with the desired disposition. For example, strategies such as pausing before speaking out and trying to see things from another's perspective may help students be open and respectful.
- **Evocative Experiences:** Powerful evocative experiences can motivate students to care about desired dispositions. Unlike a reinforcing atmosphere, whose goal is to gradually habituate students to particular frames of mind, direct experiences present students with opportunities to encounter for themselves, vividly and emphatically, the power and merits of certain ways of being. We have all heard stories of students who were inspired by an encounter with a cherished hero or a life-changing outdoor learning experience. Often, these direct experiences—whether brought about vicariously, through simulation, or in firsthand encounters—will open students' minds and hearts to perspectives and possibilities they would otherwise miss or downplay. The following box suggests how various evocative experiences may encourage students to begin to think and act in desired ways.

> ## Using Evocative Experiences to Motivate Students
>
> - **Vicarious Experiences:** To live vicariously is to encounter life through the experiences of others. Film and literature—both fiction and nonfiction—are especially effective in this regard. Vicarious experiences allow students to live the lives of others and in doing so to experience the power of feeling and caring about matters that may otherwise be foreign or remote. The use of Hollywood films such as *Twelve Years a Slave* (McQueen, 2013) can help to personalize the past by putting a profoundly human face on past discriminations. Similarly, the use of realistic fiction such as *The Fault in Our Stars* (Green, 2014) can help students to understand the challenges faced by others, such as those living with cancer. In fact, Upton Sinclair's 1906 novel *The Jungle* had such a powerful impact on President Theodore Roosevelt that within six months of finishing it, he created the Pure Food and Drug Administration and arranged passage of the Food and Drug Act.
> - **Simulated and Role-Play Experiences:** Drama, role-play, and other simulations allow students to adopt and act out the predicaments of others. One of the most famous examples of a simulated experience was described in the award-winning documentary *The Eye of the Storm* (Peters, 1970). In an effort to help her third-grade students appreciate the consequences of bigotry, Jane Elliott began, without announcing she was going to do so, to discriminate against the blue-eyed children in her class, and the next day discriminated against the brown-eyed children. Students were moved by the unfairness of this contact with prejudice. In a follow-up documentary, *A Class Divided*, filmed almost 15 years after the simulation, the students in Elliot's class described the profound influence the earlier experience had in shaping their values.
> - **Firsthand Experiences:** Powerful, evocative experiences need not be secondhand. Students can encounter situations in real-life contexts through guest speakers, field trips, exchanges, correspondence with pen pals, and social-action projects. A skilled guest speaker can do much to change student attitudes. Personally, many of my early stereotypical attitudes toward ethnic and racial groups were exploded when I first encountered articulate and impassioned individuals from these groups. Social-action projects can also be important value-nurturing experiences. Involvement in environmental and humanitarian projects can counter the global hopelessness prevalent among many students.

Introducing a few dispositions using formal instruction and evocative experiences must be looked upon as a first step. Sustained reinforcement of these dispositions is required by individual teachers or by the staff as a whole. This is especially true if the desired dispositions are significantly at odds with students' current dispositions. In talking about the need for patience and persistence, Ralph Tyler (1969) likens teachers' efforts to the effect of dripping water upon a stone: "In a day or week or a month there is no appreciable change in the stone, but over a period of years definite erosion is noted. Correspondingly, by the cumulation of educational experiences profound changes are brought about in the learner" (p. 83). Clearly, we must take the long view on nurturing student commitments. It requires incremental, collective effort—no one teacher can do it quickly or on their own.

Build Student Capacity for Genuine Commitment

Thus far, the emphasis has been on how educators might habituate students into particular ways of acting and thinking. Over time, students need to be supported in affirming commitments for themselves and in thinking critically about the implications of these commitments in particular situations.

Support Students in Freely Affirming Their Commitments. Respect for the autonomy of individuals requires that educators encourage students to clarify the values they wish to commit to. Rarely will this induce a commitment, and it may not be the best first step in fostering commitments. As suggested previously, it may be more effective to introduce the desired dispositions and allow students to experience them through some level of habituation. However, at some point, students should be encouraged to thoughtfully make up their own minds about their commitment.

This importance of helping students clarify their values has been the focus of the values clarification movement.[4] Its underlying premise is that individuals experience dissonance as a result of being unclear, confused, or uncommitted to their values. Since values are deeply personal, the teacher's role is to help students overcome this dissonance by inviting them to clarify and affirm their own values. This approach identifies three features of a sincerely held value, which are

- **Choosing:** Individuals must ultimately choose their commitments by considering the implications of a range of alternatives, without pressure or influence from others;
- **Prizing:** Once chosen, individuals should be happy with their choices and be willing to publicly affirm these commitments; and
- **Acting:** Individuals should act consistently to reaffirm and strengthen their commitments.

In helping students choose, teachers might ask questions that invite students to identify their commitments, to think about what they mean and their implications for them personally, and to consider the consistency of their words and deeds through the use of clarifying questions such as the following:

- Is this something you value?
- How did you feel when it happened?
- What are some good things about it?
- Have you thought much about it?
- Where does this idea lead? What are its consequences?
- Do you *do* anything about it?

Other clarifying activities include inviting students to rank-order alternatives or locate priorities on a continuum and to reflect on and discuss provocative statements, problems, or issues posed by the teacher. Concurrent with activities to clarify values would be opportunities to publicly affirm and act on them through ongoing routines and through special activities and events.

Support Students in Thoughtfully and Flexibly Acting on Their Commitments. Even where students have consciously resolved to adopt a particular disposition, ongoing critical reflection is required. A commitment to honesty does not imply that a person must be brutally honest all the time. In some contexts, acting on one's commitment may be unreasonable or conflict with other equally important commitments. Aristotle's insights into the golden mean suggest that too much or too little of any virtue is a vice. For example, an excess of courage is foolhardiness, and a deficiency of courage is cowardliness. Particularly in a complex changing world, students should not simply acquire habits that they follow without thinking. Educators must support students in recognizing when their dispositions apply and to consider the wisdom of carrying out these practices in the face of particular circumstances and likely consequences.

Provide Guidance to Inform Commitment

The shift from determining whether students are able to do something toward determining whether they are regularly inclined to do it has important implications for how educators assess student achievement.

Assess for Routine, Not Model, Behavior. If the objective is to promote and assess dispositions to act, then pen and paper measures of students' attitudes are insufficient. Teachers need evidence of students' typical or routine behavior. They need to watch students in authentic situations to see how they perform. Do they actually listen to others? Are they genuinely open to alternative views when talking to their colleagues? Teachers will want to triangulate evidence, using several sources of information to corroborate assessments of student habits. For example, in drawing conclusions about open-mindedness, a teacher may draw on peer and self-assessments of students' willingness to entertain alternative opinions, analyses of revised drafts of work for evidence of changing opinions, and in-class observations about openness to the ideas of others during discussions.

In-class assessments by students of themselves and others are particularly useful in gathering information about dispositions. Not only do peer observation and self-monitoring save teachers time, but they offer useful learning opportunities for students. As well, since students work with their peers extensively, they may have access to information that is not readily available to the teacher. The classroom observation sheet shown in Figure 7.4 is intended for use in peer assessments of collaborative dispositions during group work.

Concluding Thoughts

There is little value in developing understanding and building the competencies we desire if schools do not also foster students' commitments to act on and use what they have learned. In addition, many personal and social dispositions to act are essential for individual and collective well-being. Rather than being largely overlooked, dispositions represent some of the most valued educational goals that schools can aspire toward fostering. School and classroom climate, formal instructions and evocative experiences, and values clarification and critical reflection are the main ways in which educators can foster commitments. However, these dispositions must go beyond affective responses; they must translate into dependable habits of acting and thinking.

Practices That Nurture a Thinking Classroom

Shape Climate	• Create consistently reinforcing environments that nurture desired commitments.
Create Opportunities	• Emphasize a few commitments and do them well.
Build Capacity	• Support students in freely affirming their commitments. • Support students in thoughtfully and flexibly acting on their commitments.
Provide Guidance	• Assess for routine, not model, behavior.

Figure 7.4   Peer Assessment of Collaborative Thinking

Assessing Collaborative Thinking

Your name: _____ Group member's name: _____

1. For each criterion listed below, circle the number that most accurately reflects each person's behavior while carrying out the project.

2. Wherever possible, describe an actual situation or identify a typical behavior that provides supporting evidence for your assessment.

3. Use a separate sheet for each person. Do not show or discuss your assessment with anyone else.

	Consistently in Evidence		In Evidence About Half the Time		Rarely or Never in Evidence	Not Enough Information to Decide
1. *Willingness to reconsider position* Supporting evidence	5	4	3	2	1	NEI
2. *Willingness to defend personal opinion* Supporting evidence	5	4	3	2	1	NEI
3. *Respectful of persons who disagree* Supporting evidence	5	4	3	2	1	NEI
4. *Challenges in responsible ways* Supporting evidence	5	4	3	2	1	NEI
5. *Works toward establishing consensus* Supporting evidence	5	4	3	2	1	NEI

Source: Created by The Critical Thinking Consortium.

Opportunities for Leadership

Create a Strong and Reliable Reinforcing Climate for Teachers

Make a conscious effort to establish routines, interactions, and other mechanisms for shaping a working climate for teachers in schools that nurture the kinds of personal, social, and intellectual dispositions we want in our students.

Remove Hidden Obstacles

Encourage staff to think imaginatively about adjusting any of the ways that their behavior and the practices in place in the school and individual classrooms might unintentionally discourage desired dispositions.

Develop a Concerted Effort

As a staff, identify a few dispositions that would make a significant difference in preparing students for success in school and beyond. Work together to institute common practices that develop and reinforce student commitments in these areas.

Notes

1. Throughout, we use the term *attitudes* to refer to dispositions to feel in a certain way. Valuing something (positively or negatively) is the motivation for the disposition. For example, if I value cultural diversity, I will be positively disposed when presented with it. We reserve the word *commitment* to refer to the disposition to act in a certain way.
2. The lists of personal and social dispositions are based on recommendations proposed seventy years ago by a curriculum committee in New York and cited in Tyler (1969, pp. 92–93). To the list of personal dispositions, we have added habits of mind that are characteristic of the mindful education movement. These are found in the dispositions proposed in Costa and Kallick (2000). The range of intellectual dispositions recommended by prominent educational writers is summarized in Ritchhart (2002, p. 24).
3. The term *hidden curriculum* is thought by some to be misleading in that it suggests a conscious but covert attempt to teach contrary to the formal or official curriculum. Many believe that the so-called hidden curriculum is largely unintentional—that many of us do not deliberately send mixed messages to our students, but in large part we are unaware of the unintended messages that our students draw from their classroom experiences.
4. The classic work on values clarification is Raths, Harmin, and Simon (1966). Many others have espoused it, and it is widely evident in current educational practice.

PART IV
Align With Guiding Principles

*How Teachers
Can Best Support
21st Century Learning*

8

Engage Students

This chapter explores the concept of educational engagement and how educators can engender it in their students. More specifically, it discusses

- a taxonomy that explains different levels and degrees of educational engagement;
- reasons for redirecting efforts away from the lower levels of engagement toward higher levels;
- practices that contribute to increased student engagement with learning.

Chris Good was teaching his eighth-grade social studies class about the War of 1812. This war, which lasted for three years, was between the United States and Canada (then still a colony of Great Britain). It is most notable for the burning down of the White House by British troops in retaliation for an American attack on

> Even if students believe they can succeed in school, they won't exert effort unless they see some reason to do so.
>
> —National Research Council and Institute of Medicine (2004, p. 37)

the city of York (now Toronto) in Ontario. Chris had been teaching about the events and people involved in the war in a rather conventional way until he happened to participate in a writing project where he learned about the power of organizing instruction around a challenging question. Upon returning to his classroom, he decided to implement the strategy by asking his students which of three key historical figures on the Canadian side of the war was the most heroic. Their choices were

- Isaac Brock, a decorated major general in charge of the British troops defending Canada, was knighted for his actions on the battlefield and was eventually killed in action.

- Laura Secord, a heroine of many books, plays, and poetry, was known for her determination in walking 20 miles out of American-occupied territory to warn British forces of an impending attack. Because of the advance warning, the British troops were able to defeat the American forces.
- Tecumseh, a celebrated Shawnee warrior and chief who led a multi-tribal confederacy of Native Indians, joined with the British during the war to defend his traditional land from encroachment. He was killed in action during the war.

After creating criteria for what would constitute a heroic figure, students were given fact sheets about the three candidates. Once the students had decided which of the three was the most heroic according to the criteria and had prepared their arguments, the class was to debate the heroism of the three historical figures. In Chris's words, this is what happened next:[1]

I was not prepared for the lively debate that ensued. Rarely have I seen my students as engaged as they were when they debated the heroism of Brock, Tecumseh, and Secord. My role changed quickly from teacher to referee, as I almost needed to physically restrain some students. As the bell rang, the debate raged into the hallway and on to their next class. I felt very satisfied with the lesson, as this level of engagement is rarely seen at the junior high level. However, it was not until later that night that the impact of that critical challenge really hit home.

I am the school basketball coach and that night we were playing in the city championship. It was a thrilling back-and-forth game that ended with the other team hitting a last second three-point shot to beat us. After the excitement had died down, I was in the gym cleaning up when I heard some players arguing in the hallway. I thought that some of my players were upset about the game so I went to investigate. As I opened the door, the first thing I heard was one of my players yell:

"How can you seriously say Isaac Brock was not the most heroic of the three, when he risked his own life and DIED for what he believed in?"

A smile crept across my face as I realized that the players were not arguing about the championship game they had lost only moments before, but instead were arguing about the topic introduced that morning in social studies. This seemingly simple critical challenge had fostered curricular understanding in a way that was perceived as meaningful and important to my students.

One of the most compelling reasons for adopting thinking as an orientation to teaching and learning is the inherent appeal of getting students to think about their own beliefs and not simply find answers that others have produced. This story is typical of the motivational effect of inviting students to think critically, creatively, and collaboratively about the curriculum.

For the past two decades or more, talk of student engagement has dominated the educational literature. Engagement is central to the educational enterprise. It seems to be a truism that students must in some way be engaged in the activities of schooling if they are to learn what we hope they will. The recent interest in student engagement arises in part because the traditional approaches to engagement are no longer as effective as they may once have been, and there is concern that students are becoming less and less engaged by schooling.[2] Responses to decreasing levels of engagement have been hampered by confusion over the meaning of what one reviewer described as a murky concept. This lack of clarity has, in our view, perpetuated practices aimed at engaging students in ways that are marginally effective and often counterproductive. As one of the core principles of effective schools, it is important that educators clearly understand the concept if they are to align their practices to nurture greater engagement.

What Does Engaging Students Mean?

We begin our quest to define educational engagement by considering four questions about the nature of this elusive concept:

- Can teachers engage students?
- Is being engaged in class the same as being engaged in learning?
- Are all forms of engagement equally desirable?
- How do forms of engagement differ from degrees of engagement?

Can Teachers Engage Students?

The question of whether teachers can engage students seems a silly one; yet the truth is, strictly speaking, they can't. Engagement is not something people cause in others; it is something that people experience—to be engaged is to occupy oneself or to become involved, absorbed, engrossed, or interested. Others may try to induce this state, but they can't do it directly—students must allow it, albeit with lots of support from teachers and others. This distinction parallels the relationship between teaching and learning—an educator may "teach" the lesson, but students may not "learn" it. The success of what the educator does is determined by what students actually experience. This distinction is sometimes missed when people talk about inherently engaging activities, such as allowing for student choice or problem-based learning. Such situations may engage many participants, but the mere use of these strategies is no assurance of student engagement. The importance of defining engagement from the perspective of those who experience is supported by the etymology of the word—coming from the French *engagé*—which means to make a pledge or be committed to something. When a couple announces their engagement, they are indicating their commitment to each other. The key challenge is how to increase students' capacity, likelihood, and willingness to commit to the activities they encounter in school.

Is Being Engaged in Class the Same as Being Engaged in Learning?

Again, this seems to be another silly question, except here too the unexpected answer is "No." Imagine the following situation:

> The teacher asks students to capture all the essential ideas from her presentation in as few words as possible. During the presentation, three of the students are engaged in the following ways:
>
> - Chen is determined, between taking notes, to twirl his pencil between his fingers as quickly as possible in order to best his friend's performance at this task.
> - Emma is fascinated by the movement of the tassels at the end of her pencil, especially the effect created when forming various letters.
> - Lindsay is feverishly rewriting the essential ideas captured thus far because his initial writing is misaligned and unevenly spaced.

While the three students are on task (all are taking notes) and clearly engaged in an activity of some sort, we would be hard-pressed to say that they were engaged in what they were supposed to be learning. The task of deciding what to record and how best to record it was not the source of their engagement. In fact, the focus of their engagement distracted them somewhat from the point of the lesson. This distinction between students who are on task and yet still not engaged by the intended learning is a reason for distinguishing between student engagement (what engages students while at school) and educational engagement (being engaged in the intended learning). This distinction is especially relevant in understanding why students' enthusiasm for using digital technology may not be the panacea for engagement that some advocates would have us believe it is. Students' enthusiasm may have everything to do with the features of the technology and actually distract them from the intended learning. It is notable that a recent international study found that significant implementation of digital technologies in classrooms resulted in no appreciable improvement in student achievement and often had mixed results (Organisation for Economic Co-operation and Development, 2015, p. 4). Educational engagement occurs only when students freely commit to dedicating effort toward the pursuit of the desired educational goals and the performance of intended teaching and learning tasks. This explanation is consistent with Fred Newmann's (1992) definition of engagement: "The student's psychological investment in and effort directed towards learning, understanding, or mastering the knowledge, skill, or craft that academic work is intended to promote" (p. 12).

> Students are engaged in their learning when they personally commit to freely dedicating effort toward the pursuit of desired educational goals and the performance of intended tasks.

Are All Forms of Engagement Equally Desirable?

The previous discussion highlights the need to understand why someone is motivated by something. The varied motives for being engaged in schooling can be organized hierarchically according to their educational desirability.[3] The scale of motives for committing to schoolwork, shown in the textbox, is organized in ascending order of educational payoff. The more educationally desirable reason is at the top of the list and the least desirable at the bottom.

Range of Motives for Educational Engagement

- to achieve a broader, valued result beyond the particular focus;
- to pursue a valued but not easily achieved result;
- to perceive significance or a personal attachment;
- to explore for entertainment, interest, or pleasure;
- to have a desire to secure external rewards or avoid negative consequences.

We can see the justification for this hierarchy by considering the descriptors of each form offered in Figure 8.1. The scale begins with "Not Engaged," then moves to "Compliant," and proceeds all the way across a spectrum to "Transformed." Each form signals a different kind of motivation, ranging from the desire for an external reward to self-enabling desires. Each form can range in intensity from low to high. For example, one student may be highly motivated by marks to complete course assignments, and another student may only be somewhat motivated by the perceived modest value of course assignments. Thus, the hierarchy is not about degrees of intensity but is differentiated by the desirability of the characteristic motive for each form. For purposes of this classification, each form subsumes the level(s) below it but not the level(s) above it. For example, someone who is (merely) "Interested" doesn't see the value of the task and isn't challenged by it. Such students might find the teacher amusing and to possess interesting stories, but they would not feel that what the teacher was saying was of much relevance to them—in other words, they wouldn't see value in what is amusing the teacher. This is not an unusual situation. Many of us may feel this way when watching television: it passes the time and may make us laugh occasionally, but it rarely has any redeeming purpose. Our perception may change, however, when we watch a documentary that is interesting and informative in ways that we find worthwhile.

"Compliance" is the least desirable motive for learning. As mentioned in Chapter 1, students whose motivation for participating in school

Figure 8.1   Hierarchical Forms of Engagement

Not Engaged	Compliant	Interested	Valued	Challenged	Transformed
Noncompliance: Students regularly do not complete assigned tasks.	**Merely complies:** Students perform educational tasks largely because of external rewards or expectations.	**Holds interest:** Students perform educational tasks to the extent that the tasks are enjoyable or pleasing.	**Values experiences:** Students perform educational tasks not solely for their interest but because they appreciate their importance, usefulness, or personal relevance.	**Is challenged:** Students become caught up in their educational tasks because they present appropriate and meaningful challenges.	**Extends to other aspects:** The self-enabling effects of students being excited or caught up by their work are voluntarily extended to other aspects of their personal, work, and academic lives.

is primarily because of external influence (e.g., avoiding punishment or bad grades) are less likely to become engaged beyond a superficial level. Conversely, students who are motivated by a sense of satisfaction or accomplishment are more likely to become involved in their assignment and go beyond the minimal requirements (National Research Council and Institute of Medicine, 2004, p. 32). Students who value their learning appreciate and welcome what occurs in school. If "Challenged," they not only see value in the tasks, but are motivated to more actively pursue the perceived value. Individuals who take up a challenge are committed to acting on what they value in order to bring about a desired result. Merely valuing a task does not imply the determination to promote or pursue the value. The discussion of conscious resolve in the previous chapter on moving from attitude to genuine commitment is the distinction highlighted here.

At the pinnacle of educational desirability is the category "Transformed." This refers to a form of commitment where students voluntarily use and extend the lessons learned in one context to other aspects of their lives. This means that students are motivated to apply their curriculum-based understandings and abilities to inform what they do in other subjects and to enhance their personal and work lives. A school system that has very little transformative impact—where students don't actually use what they learn except to complete school requirements—is a system that is nearly useless to students. Another way of interpreting the concern that schools are not adequately preparing students for the world beyond school is that schools are having insufficient transformative impact on students. The problem is not solely that students have learned too little that is of use to them later; it is also that students have too little commitment to use in their lives outside of school what they have learned in school.

Figure 8.2 offers examples of the motives that define the various forms of engagement in the context of a whimsical account of the reasons for completing Sudoku puzzles.

This taxonomy should not be interpreted, as many have interpreted taxonomies such as Bloom's taxonomy, to direct educators to begin at the lowest level of the hierarchy and work their way in sequence to the highest level. On the contrary, the point of the hierarchy is to direct efforts toward the higher forms of engagement and away from seeking to engage students by appealing to less desirable motives.

How Do Forms of Engagement Differ From Degrees of Engagement?

The forms of engagement are defined by the kinds of reasons people have for getting caught up in an activity. Each form can vary in the degree or intensity to which people get caught up. Someone can be only slightly

Figure 8.2   Forms of Engagement With Sudoku Puzzles

Transformed	In working through the most difficult Sudoku puzzles, I've learned a lot about looking for patterns when approaching a problem. This is causing me to change how I respond to problems in other aspects of my life by looking for underlying patterns.
Challenged	I look forward to the most difficult Sudoku puzzles (I don't bother with the easy ones), and I try to complete them as quickly as possible.
Valued	I enjoy Sudoku and it is good for the brain—keeps me mentally active.
Interested	I enjoy Sudoku puzzles. I know they're trivial, but they are fun to do.
Compliant	I don't really like Sudoku, but it passes the time when I am bored. Besides, my wife doesn't like to see me sitting around doing nothing.

engaged in something, or thoroughly engaged, or somewhere in between. As Figure 8.3 illustrates, each form has its own continuum of intensity, characterized by the kind of feelings that pursuit of the different motives is likely to engender. For example, students who are driven by marks will experience a high degree of eagerness. Similarly, students may be very interested in schoolwork that they don't perceive to be valuable (e.g., coloring maps). Clearly, the ideal is a high degree of intensity at a highly desirable form of engagement. People who become substantially challenged by a task have an experience that Mihaly Csikszentmihalyi has famously described as "flow"—a state of mind brought on by intense involvement in an activity (Csikszentmihalyi, 2002).

It is worth considering how likely it is that someone would be fascinated or passionate about something (experiencing a high degree of intensity) and not in any way be challenged to learn or do more (demonstrating a high level of engagement). In other words, heightened states of intensity

Figure 8.3   Comparing Ranges of Intensity for Levels of Engagement

Forms of Engagement	Low degrees of intensity ⟵―――――――――――――⟶	High degrees of intensity
Transformed	Changed ⟵―――――――――――――⟶	Total conversion
Challenged	Drawn in ⟵―――――――――――――⟶	Engrossed
Cares	Sees value ⟵―――――――――――――⟶	Passionate
Interested	Mildly attracted ⟵―――――――――――――⟶	Fascinated
Willing	Complies/acquiesces ⟵―――――――――――――⟶	Completely eager

may cause people to elevate the form of their engagement. Even if intense feelings do not entirely on their own elevate students to more desirable forms of engagement, we can readily appreciate how much easier it is, relatively speaking, to find ways of challenging students when there are things that fascinate them.

The crux of the challenge to educators, at least as framed by the taxonomy presented here, is to get students to commit to schooling for the right reasons and to achieve a significant measure of intensity. In the next section, we look at why educators should aspire to this goal and, in the final section, what they might do to achieve it.

Why Is It Important to Engage Students Beyond Compliance and Mere Interest?

Engaging students in their learning is one of the main drivers for current reform efforts. We offer it as one of five guiding principles that ought to inform practices in every thinking classroom. The particular point of the discussion thus far has been to highlight the importance of seeking to nurture student commitment to learn beyond mere compliance and interest, and to deepen the intensity of engagement. We can imagine objections such as "It is hard enough to get students to agree to do schoolwork" and "It seems unrealistic to expect to engage many students at the higher levels." Putting the concern another way, these objections can be expressed as "Why does it matter that students learn for the right reasons?" or "What's wrong with a thoroughly entertaining presentation, as long as students are listening?"

The Downside of Appealing to Less Desirable Forms of Engagement

The most significant implication of the taxonomy is the value of directing our efforts to engage students at the higher forms of engagement and away from engaging students in the less desirable forms. It allows us to highlight the implicit objectives and limitations behind popular strategies for motivating students. Consider the notion of setting high expectations, for example. Is this an example

> One of the most well-researched findings in the field of motivational psychology is that the more people are rewarded for doing something, the more they tend to lose interest in whatever they had to do to get the reward.
>
> —Alfie Kohn (1999)

Figure 8.4   Strategies Directed at Each Form of Engagement

Form of Engagement	Strategies to Engage
Transformed (empowered)	• provide an opportunity to feel as though one is making a difference • cause an aha moment to add insight beyond the immediate context • connect with students' passions to lead them in new directions
Challenged (caught up)	• require to think (intellectual challenge) • propose a physical or performance challenge
Valued (motivated)	• connect learning to students' own lives • link to broader issues/topics/narratives that students care about • help to appreciate—not simply learn about—the objective or purpose
Interested (entertained)	• make visually attractive or startling • make humorous or entertaining • embed in a story or narrative • illustrate with a familiar example
Willing (on task)	• offer rewards or inducements (marks) • direct control through classroom management

of challenging students, or simply offering a more demanding external incentive to do schoolwork? Students who are motivated to work harder merely to get a better mark still may not be attaching any value to what they are learning. As Figure 8.4 suggests, educators may undertake different kinds of activities by appealing to different motives in an effort to engage their students.

There are four reasons to worry about the effects of trying to engage students primarily through external incentives and stimulating their interest without worrying whether students find value in what they are doing:

Dubious Effectiveness. Mere willingness and interest without perceived purpose may be highly fickle forms of engagement that are unlikely to have enduring appeal. Sustaining a motivational regimen that appeals to these forms may require more work because they have to be continually stoked. Furthermore, the use of tests as a motivational strategy is ineffective with many students for whom good marks are not a likely reward. The use of gimmicks and reliance on high-interest experiences such as digital technology to hook students may heighten their attention but have little positive connection to educational engagement.

Pressure to "Dumb Down." Dependence on test results to motivate students and attempts to make learning easy and fun often lead to a dumbing down of the work because students won't be less willing to try hard when the tasks get difficult.

Counterproductive. A regimen where students are consistently encouraged to perform well on assignments to gain extrinsic reward has the long-term effect of reducing their interest in the tasks they do in school. In addition, students who "concentrate on getting a good grade are likely to pick the easiest possible assignment if given a choice" (A. Kohn, 1999, "Three Main Effects of Grading," item 2). Thus, we unwittingly encourage students to do the minimum required while progressively decreasing their enjoyment in school. None of the enriched educational goals discussed in Part II of this book (deep understanding, real-life competencies, and genuine commitments) will be well served by students who are simply doing things for marks.

Long-Term Disaffection. It is worth considering the damaging consequences of urging students to regularly do things without seeing a real purpose or value in the tasks. A fundamental human need is to pursue things that matter; otherwise, we lose our sense of integrity, satisfaction, and pride. For students who do not see value in school, the inevitable effect is apathy or disengagement.

The Power of Appealing to More Desirable Forms of Engagement

On a more positive note, efforts to help students see real value and find challenges in their learning are both feasible and potentially powerful.[4]

May Be Easier Than Enforcing Compliance and Trying to Excite Interest. Modest success at higher forms of engagement may well increase the intensity of engagement at lower forms. Or put another way, it may be easier to increase student willingness and interest in undertaking school activities by challenging students.[5] For example, I may not get caught up in completing a puzzle, but it may be more interesting than watching television. The presence of a task to solve makes it more interesting.

Seeing Real Value in Learning Is Compelling. Once students see value in what they are doing, there is a spillover to associated tasks. The power of perceived relevance to dramatically enhance commitment to learning is illustrated by the following example.

In eleventh grade, my humanities co-op students go on a three-week work placement that requires a pre-interview with their employer. The lesson introducing interview skills is one of the easiest ones I teach. Students take notes without any prompting. They ask brilliant questions. If I leave the room while they're rehearsing their interviews with each other, I can expect them to be still at it when I return. They ask each other for feedback and constructively comment on one another's interviews. For the most part, students are motivated to act in these ways because they see why learning this skill matters both in the short term and in the long run.[6]

Students Respond to Challenges. Unlike doing things for marks, many students welcome challenges, provided they are not perceived to be overwhelming. The research is clear that students welcome more authentic or intellectually challenging assignments (Edmunds, Willse, Arshavsky, & Dallas, 2013). In fact, one study concluded that classes that challenged students were rated as more engaging. What is more, 60 percent of students identified the class that made them think the hardest as the most interesting and worthwhile (National Research Council and Institute of Medicine, 2004, p. 50). Another study found that the most engaging math activities were those, to use one student's words, where "you had to work out for yourself what was going on, and you had to use your own ideas."[7] Our experience suggests that finding ways to challenge students may not be as hard to identify and implement as one might think. Consider the opening scenario where students were asked to decide on the most heroic figure of the War of 1812. Here is an explanation provided by Justin, one of the eighth-grade students who was involved in the heated discussion. For someone who was not normally the most motivated student in the class, this simple revision of the lesson presented a particularly motivating challenge:

> Some people may find this story hard to believe, but it is true, because I was the basketball player arguing with one of my classmates after the game. The reason I participated in this class was because the three heroes inspired me. When my teacher told me that we would be debating who we thought was the greatest hero I just felt I had to let him and the class know my opinion. I would not stop letting everyone know who I thought was the most heroic because I needed to make them feel the same way. I wanted to make everyone say, "I think that Isaac Brock is the most heroic." I just wanted everyone to feel the same way I did because I felt so strongly.[8]

What Practices Support
Educational Engagement?

All of the practices introduced in the chapter on creating thinking class-rooms apply to supporting student engagement. The following are additional practices that are especially relevant to this goal.

Shape a Climate to Support Engagement

The research literature (some of it cited in this chapter) is unequivocal about the value of a caring and supportive environment.

Nurture Encouraging Classroom, School, Home, and Virtual Spaces. Countless volumes have been written about the debilitating effects of unsupportive and even hostile learning conditions on students' willingness and ability to make an effort in school. These conditions directly affect student engagement. For example, a recent study identified three factors that correlated highest with student satisfaction in school. These were positive school and teacher relations, good peer relations, and the absence of feeling pressured to achieve (Boyce, 2004, p. 42). A discussion of the practices that nurture supportive real and virtual communities is beyond the scope of this book. Nevertheless, creating environments where students feel safe, valued, and encouraged remains a precondition for all learning.

> [S]chools can take specific actions to increase student engagement such as developing more engaging instruction, improving student-staff relationships, and providing high expectations coupled with support to help students achieve.
>
> —Julie Edmunds et al. (2013, p. 18)

Build Appreciation for School in General and Specific Tasks in Particular. The very act of making a task more purposeful will increase many students' willingness to do it. People are more willing to do arduous tasks if they know they are for good causes, such as digging in the mud in order to prevent a river from overflowing a dike. Yet evidence suggests that high school students are often poorly informed about the value of the general topics and the particular activities they encounter in school (Boyce, 2004, p. 43). It is not enough to tell students that they will need it later or that they have to study it because it's in the curriculum. The goal in helping students see the value of schooling and of specific tasks within school is not served by offering a vague rationale. Four factors are associated with helping students feel the importance of what they are studying:

- The task or topic that is being promoted is actually something worth doing. It is ill-advised to try to sell students on things that may have marginal value for them.
- The teacher must believe in the work and communicate this to students with sincere enthusiasm.
- The reasons for valuing what they are learning should be attached to consequences that students can appreciate, especially when they are linked to the kinds of things students care about (e.g., making things easier, self-esteem, finding adventure, making money, earning respect, impressing others, gaining independence, and self-sufficiency).
- Finally, seeing value is assisted by anchoring the learning to inspiring stories. An example of a compelling story about pushing oneself to achieve is told in the movie *Stand and Deliver* (Menéndez, 1988). It describes the true story of the successful efforts by impoverished students in Los Angeles to pass the Advanced Placement calculus examination because they wanted to prove to themselves and others that they were not losers.

Create Opportunities to Engage Students in Learning

It may be suggested that the earlier-mentioned examples are exceptions rather than the rule—not everything done in school can be modified so easily into activities that motivate students. Obviously, we can't successfully challenge all students in all situations, although our experiences in working with over 175,000 teachers to implement a thinking classroom convinces us that many seemingly rote tasks can be converted to tasks that are more compelling for students.

Provide More Compelling Learning Opportunities. A primary effort to increase educational engagement is to provide rich learning opportunities differentiated by ability and interest that motivate students to freely dedicate effort toward a perceived meaningful educational goal or task. This can be encouraged in various ways:

- **Negotiate Meaningful (Intrinsic) Targets and Plans With Students:** One way to engage students is to involve them in jointly planning their learning. One study reported that only 34 percent of sixth-grade students and 18 percent of tenth-grade students felt they had a say in how class time was used (Boyce, 2004, p. 43). The effect, as another report concluded, is that "students feel that learning is being done 'to them' rather than 'by them'" (Schools Program Division, Manitoba Education, 2010, p. 26). Negotiated decision making may involve setting meaningful personal targets, such as agreeing to work to raise the frequency by which students are challenged in school to at least once a week. Students can be included in decision making in many ways, such as suggesting how to best prepare the class for district examinations or how to use the principles of geometry to figure out the most efficient allocation of desks in the classroom. Negotiated decision making may provide significant opportunities for responsible student choice.

- **Build in Real-Life Implications or Consequences:** There are many ways for educators to turn an assignment into a meaningful task. For example, an assigned essay may become a formal submission that is actually delivered to a local or state agency. Hypothetical discussions actually get translated into action, and presentations are made to real audiences.

- **Problematize the Subject Matter to Be Learned:** This strategy lies at the heart of a thinking classroom and has been the focus of discussions throughout this book. The goal is to problematize what students learn each day so they can't simply remember or find the answer but must reach their own conclusions. Figure 8.5 provides examples of tasks in various subject areas that invite thinking. These examples are organized around six prompts that help convert tasks into a form where students are expected to arrive at a reasoned judgment based on their assessment of options in light of relevant criteria.

- **Remove Obstacles That Discourage Completion:** Much can be done to make school more compelling simply by removing the most tedious aspects of school tasks without impairing their educational value. This may include devoting little or no time to the most marginal topics in the curriculum that students struggle with. It may involve reducing the volume of work without lessening the core learning. For example, note-form answers may sometimes be acceptable, as may a one-page synopsis in lieu of a fully fleshed-out report.

Build Capacity for Engagement

The significant potential to be found by challenging students in compelling ways is lost if the tasks are too demanding for students. As one report

Figure 8.5 Sample Critical Challenges

Prompts	Critique the Piece	Judge the Better or Best	Rework the Piece	Decode the Puzzle	Design to Specs	Perform to Specs
	Students assess the merits or shortcomings of a person, product, or performance.	*Students judge from among two or more options (teacher-provided or student-generated) that best meets the identified criteria.*	*Students transform a product or performance in light of additional information or an assigned focus, perspective, or genre.*	*Students suggest and justify a proposed solution, explanation, or interpretation to a confusing or enigmatic situation.*	*Students develop a product that meets a given set of criteria conditions.*	*Students perform or undertake a course of action that meets a given set of criteria conditions.*
English/ Language Arts	• Determine the appropriate punctuation for this stripped-down version of the song "Galileo." • Is *My Left Foot* an appropriate choice of novel for study in high school?	• In *Hamlet*, who is the more noble character, Laertes or Hamlet? • Is the Wolf in *The True Story of the Three Little Pigs* good or bad?	• Write two editorials, one supporting, another refuting, the view that the Charge of the Light Brigade was "That glorious blunder of which all Englishmen are justifiably proud."	• Deconstruct the message embedded in the ads. • Using corroborating references from elsewhere in the story, explain the author's message in this section.	• Prepare briefing notes for the mayor on today's news that are relevant, comprehensive, and succinct. • Create an antismoking poster using four persuasive techniques.	• Develop and implement a realistic action plan to pursue your writing priorities for this term. • Perform the assigned role expressing at least three feelings.
Science	• Are the results of this experiment to be trusted?	• Who has the greatest mind: da Vinci, Newton, or Einstein?	• Given data on the behavior of an object within earth's gravitational field, reconstruct	• Based on the findings from a simulated dig of dinosaur remains, write a short account	• Build a structure using the materials provided that will achieve the specified results.	• Conduct an experiment with paper airplanes to establish which design variations (nose

| Prompts | Critique the Piece
Students assess the merits or shortcomings of a person, product, or performance. | Judge the Better or Best
Students judge from among two or more options (teacher-provided or student-generated) that best meets the identified criteria. | Rework the Piece
Students transform a product or performance in light of additional information or an assigned focus, perspective, or genre. | Decode the Puzzle
Students suggest and justify a proposed solution, explanation, or interpretation to a confusing or enigmatic situation. | Design to Specs
Students develop a product that meets a given set of criterial conditions. | Perform to Specs
Students perform or undertake a course of action that meets a given set of criterial conditions. |
|---|---|---|---|---|---|---|
| **Science** (continued) | • Is the information on this website credible?
• Are the special effects in the clip from *Armageddon* based on sound physics? | • The earth is overdue to be struck by a heavenly object. Which should we fear the most—being hit by a meteor, an asteroid, or a comet? | the results if this object were on Mars. | explaining what occurred on this site. | • Design a habitat for a classroom pet that meets all of the animal's needs. | weight, paper size, stiffness, shape) result in the farthest flight. |
| **Social Studies** | • How powerful are our proposed questions for the Second World War quest?
• Does the textbook provide a fair and adequate account of what actually happened? | • Which is the more effective form of transportation in the Arctic: the dog sled or the snowmobile?
• Should your family move to Weyburn or Prince George? | • Rewrite a historical account using the "Role-**A**udience-**F**ormat-**T**opic-**S**trong verb" framework.
• Given the information provided, write a letter of reference for Sir Thomas More. | • Find a powerful metaphor that characterizes an aspect of Canadian life.
• Identify and support with evidence the **R-A-F-T-S** framework in a fellow student's writing. | • Create six questions for an end-of-unit exam that are clear, nontrivial, manageable, and require more than mere recall of information. | • Make a lasting contribution to someone else's life.
• Mount an information campaign to boycott products of companies that exploit their workers. |

(Continued)

159

Figure 8.5 (Continued)

Prompts	Critique the Piece *Students assess the merits or shortcomings of a person, product, or performance.*	Judge the Better or Best *Students judge from among two or more options (teacher-provided or student-generated) that best meets the identified criteria.*	Rework the Piece *Students transform a product or performance in light of additional information or an assigned focus, perspective, or genre.*	Decode the Puzzle *Students suggest and justify a proposed solution, explanation, or interpretation to a confusing or enigmatic situation.*	Design to Specs *Students develop a product that meets a given set of criteria/ conditions.*	Perform to Specs *Students perform or undertake a course of action that meets a given set of criteria/ conditions.*
Mathematics	• Are the expert's conclusions about student performance warranted by the data presented in the table?	• Think of three methods of estimating the sum of money in a stack of dollar bills. Which would be the most efficient and yet still be highly accurate?	• Convert the following patterns into an algebraic expression.	• A hemispherical bowl with a radius of 5 inches contains water to a depth of 1 inch. To what angle must the bowl be tilted to spill the water?	• Design a four-panel cartoon that explains in a humorous but effective manner key features of an assigned mathematical concept (e.g., numerator).	• Lead a small group through an activity to help them understand the concept of one million.
Music	• Is Bartok's "Concerto for Orchestra" an appropriate choice for detailed study in Grade 12 music?	• As an *American Idol* judge, create your own persona and performance criteria. Analyze two performances and pronounce your judgment.	• Transform the binary piece you have learned into a ternary piece, keeping the general characteristics of the A section.	• Find a powerful metaphor to describe the period in music history that is currently being studied.	• Build an instrument according to the details and criteria provided.	• Practice the assigned piece, expressing at least four feelings. Choose two feelings to use in your performance for the class.

160

noted bluntly, "Raising standards without providing support is counter-productive" (National Research Council and Institute of Medicine, 2004, p. 58). Concurrent with challenging students is the need to develop their capacity in meeting these challenges.

Develop Tools to Match the Challenges. The discussion in Chapter 4 about developing the intellectual tools to think is especially relevant to increasing students' capacity to be challenged. The challenges we pose—whether to develop powerful questions or analyze a poem—must be within students' zone of proximal development. This is to say that the tasks must be achievable by each student without considerable additional instruction and extensive assistance. The literature is unanimous in the view that students are optimally challenged when there is a good fit between the demands of the task and students' abilities (National Research Council and Institute of Medicine, 2004, p. 44).

Ensuring a match between the tools that students have and the tasks they are expected to complete can be achieved by making the task less demanding by reducing the tools required or by extending the students' repertoire of tools. Rather than believing that some students can't be challenged to think, we believe any thinking task can be made less demanding—so the tools needed to complete it are less onerous—but nevertheless, the task still challenges students to think. For example, instead of asking students to generate an original hypothesis to explain a body of data, we might simplify the task by providing four possible hypotheses for students to judge. If this was still too difficult, we could provide fewer hypotheses and make one of them more obvious as the more plausible interpretation. In other words, rather than reducing the expectation to think, we reduce the amount of background knowledge and other tools that students need in order to complete the task. This does not imply dumbing down—although the task may be easier, it still requires students to think. The other approach to matching ability and challenge is to develop more tools. Significantly, students typically report that the highest levels of engagement occur when they rate both their skill level and the level of challenge as high (National Research Council and Institute of Medicine, 2004, p. 50). Both approaches to matching ability and challenge may occur simultaneously in the same class. For example, the teacher may invite students to tackle the more open-ended task of generating original hypotheses if they wish to and allow others to judge from a list of suggested hypotheses. Both groups would receive instruction on the concept of a hypothesis and on criteria for plausible hypotheses.

Provide Guidance to Support Engagement

Nurturing student engagement in learning requires effective two-way communication. Teachers need to help their students understand how they are doing at every step of the way, and students need opportunities to communicate to their teachers what is and is not working for them.

Provide Timely, Helpful, and Encouraging Feedback. Despite the amount of effort devoted to evaluation and assessment, surprisingly little of it is actually helpful to students. Much of the effort is directed to measuring students' achievement for reporting purposes. But even when assessment is intended to support learning, many efforts may be marginally helpful. Feedback will not be useful unless it is supplied in a timely manner. By timely, we mean at the time students are working on the task. Assignments that are returned two days later are rarely used by students. Furthermore, the information teachers provide doesn't always answer the three key questions that students need answered: "Am I on the right track? (Do I understand the task?)"; "How did I do?" (What have I done well, and what is weak?); and "What do I need to do to improve?" More will be said about providing timely, helpful, and encouraging feedback in Chapter 11, "Create Assessment-Rich Learning," but the important message here is that sustained engagement in learning is aided by reducing students' frustration over not clearly knowing how they are doing and what they need to do to improve at the time that having this information is helpful to them.

Establish Mechanisms to Learn About Student Views. In recent years, considerable attention has been devoted to providing opportunities for students to express their opinions and have their opinions considered. Although they are often discussed in tandem, affording students a voice is not the same as enabling student choice. The latter implies that students are actually involved in making the decisions that affect their lives and learning in school. The call for student voice emerges from a concern that teachers may not always know their students' views and feelings. Even if a teacher continues to decide what goes on in the classroom, it is important that these decisions are informed by an acute awareness of students' opinions and needs. Regularly gathering feedback from students can be very valuable and remarkably simple. It may require little more than collecting exit tickets at the end of class or inviting three-word microblog posts from students to monitor the temperature of the class. The very act of seeking students' opinions is itself a useful gesture in making students feel valued.

Concluding Thoughts

Engaging students in their learning is one of the loudest and most insistent of the calls for school reform, and is arguably one of the most important challenges facing educators. We have argued that conventional reliance on external rewards and on inducements to make learning fun, although well intentioned, may be largely ineffectual with many students and ultimately counterproductive. Instead, we urge educators to place greater emphasis on helping students find value in what they are studying and in challenging them with more compelling learning tasks.

Practices That Engage Students in Learning

Shape Climate	• Nurture encouraging classroom, school, home, and virtual spaces. • Build appreciation for school in general and specific tasks in particular.
Create Opportunities	• Provide more compelling learning opportunities.
Build Capacity	• Develop tools to match the challenges.
Provide Guidance	• Provide timely, helpful, and encouraging feedback. • Establish mechanisms to learn about student views.

What follows are selected strategies for educational leaders to use with teachers to nurture student engagement.

Opportunities for Leadership

Work With All Partners to Nurture the Preconditions for Engagement

Build relationships with home and community to make them active partners in supporting students emotionally and educationally.

Reduce the Reliance on External Inducements

Even while grading remains part of the educational landscape, make efforts to reduce the extent to which it is actively used to pressure student participation and achievement.

Regularly Invite Students to Communicate Their Levels of Engagement

Encourage teachers to solicit and listen to students' views on their levels of engagement and the contributing factors.

Notes

1. This incident was written by Chris Good while vice principal at École St. Gerard School, Alberta.
2. A Health Canada study shows that the number of students who like school a lot declined between 1994 and 2002 (Boyce, 2004, p. 41).
3. Motivation is the precursor, the reason for being engaged, and engagement is the psychological experience or behavior (National Research Council and Institute of Medicine, 2004, p. 31).
4. It is unclear whether "Transformed" is a motivation that can be directly appealed to. It may simply be that seeing the value of something and being challenged to take it up will induce reasons to apply these ideas and lessons in other spheres.
5. Evidence suggests that challenging work promotes interest and enjoyment (National Research Council and Institute of Medicine, 2004, p. 49).
6. An account provided by Stefan Stipp, a teacher in the Surrey School District in British Columbia.
7. A 2002 study by Boaler, cited in National Research Council and Institute of Medicine (2004, p. 50).
8. Provided by Justin's teacher, Chris Good, École St. Gerard School, Alberta.

9

Sustain Inquiry

This chapter explains the principle of sustaining inquiry and its importance in 21st century classrooms. More specifically, it discusses

- why sustained inquiry is best understood as a mindset;
- how sustained inquiry differs from other popular versions of inquiry;
- why sustained inquiry is important;
- practices that support formal and informal inquiry.

When Jenny began the study of the California Gold Rush with her fourth-grade classes, she decided to organize the unit around an over-arching critical challenge: *Was going to the Gold Rush in California worth the risk?*[1] Before being exposed to any material about the Gold Rush, students were asked to anonymously give an answer to the critical thinking question. Their responses were displayed on a large line plot to allow students to track their thinking over the course of the unit. Initially, almost all students felt it might be worth the risk of leaving everything behind in order to make the trek to California.

> To maintain the state of doubt and to carry on systematic and protracted inquiry: these are the essentials of thinking.
>
> —John Dewey (1910, p. 13)

Next, the class established criteria to guide their thinking as they began to learn about the Gold Rush. The agreed-upon criteria were as follows:

- **Little Danger:** Was there little chance of being hurt or killed?
- **High Reward:** Was there a high chance of getting rich?
- **Adequate Comfort:** Were the living conditions (shelter, food, water) comfortable/acceptable?
- **Great Adventure:** Was there a high chance for a great adventure?

These criteria set the focus as the class read various passages on specific topics regarding the California Gold Rush. Using an iterative approach, the children were invited at several intervals to reflect on their new learning to determine whether to revise their response to the critical challenge question.

Students learned first about the different routes to the Gold Rush, all of which were gruesome. At this point, students once again were asked to anonymously record the answer to their question. But this time, almost all responses echoed, "No! It is not worth the risk!" However, when students learned about the possibility of hitting the "mother lode," opinions swiftly transposed.

Throughout the unit, the critical thinking question served as a vehicle for students' metacognition. They were building on what they already knew and were constantly talking to their group members about how the new information swayed their thinking one way or the other. They were excited to read and learn more because they wanted to find out if the Gold Rush was all it was hyped up to be.

Lively and often humorous discussions and debates occurred daily as students adopted a Gold Rush era persona and hilariously addressed one another in their historic roles. The importance of introducing the critical thinking task *ahead* of the unit of study was powerfully demonstrated: students had a clear purpose for their learning, and they knew that the focus on developing a sound answer rather than looking for the correct answer gave them a say in what they were learning. Knowing they would be encouraged to reflect and revise their answer based on extensive exposure to different material and repeated discourse with peers created a safe zone for students. As teacher Jenny Mulligan explained, "This allowed my students to engage with the critical challenge in a manner that led to deep learning for *all, not just some* of the children. It wasn't a matter of being right or wrong but instead a matter of developing a sound answer considering the evidence and criteria. This was a chance for students to speak their mind, make a decision, revise it when appropriate, and defend it when needed."

Over the course of this sustained inquiry, students repeatedly revisited their tentative conclusions and developed an increasingly stronger rationale for their thinking. The teacher was delighted that her students had been so deeply engaged. They had acquired a more sound understanding of the curriculum than had previous classes using a teacher-directed approach or an independent research approach.

Like many educational buzzwords, "inquiry" is much discussed and vaguely understood. For over a century, educators have been encouraging inquiry as an approach to teaching and learning. It is offered as an alternative to didactic instruction where teachers present information to students via lectures or textbooks. One of the areas of confusion concerns the structures offered to support inquiry. Often, inquiry is framed as a sequenced set of steps that teachers and students should follow, without appreciating that there is an important difference between "re-searching" information and critically inquiring into an issue. Conversely, others believe that inquiry must be unstructured, leaving students to reinvent and rediscover everything on their own, with minimal teacher intervention. These kinds of misconceptions obscure the mindset that characterizes genuine inquiry and encourages strategies that have the trappings of inquiry but are poor facsimiles of it.

What Is Sustained Inquiry?

We offer sustained inquiry as one of five core principles for a thinking classroom. At its simplest, to inquire is to pose and try to answer a question whose answer is not directly known to the person or people asking the question. In other words, the answer will require some investigation. Sustained inquiry is best seen as a mindset that seeks to involve students formally and informally in critical, creative, and collaborative investigations at every stage of their studies. To characterize inquiry as a mindset distinguishes it from a specific practice or procedure. Many programs try to encapsulate a spirit of inquiry, but sometimes the practices overshadow the spirit.

> Sustained inquiry is a mindset that seeks to involve students formally and informally in critical, creative, and collaborative investigations at every stage of their studies.

An Inquiring Mindset Versus an Inquiry Model

It is common to translate inquiry into a process or set of steps for teachers and students to follow. Figure 9.1 outlines a widely disseminated inquiry model, inspired by John Dewey's "spiral of learning," that consists of a five-phase framework (Falk & Drayton, 2009, p. 55).

These components may be evident in a very simple inquiry—for example, when family members sitting around the dinner table disagree on which historical person was responsible for a particular event. The daughter may rush to get her iPad and search online for an answer. If all of the information isn't in one place, she might look at a few sites and cross-check ambiguous or contradictory information. She will formulate a conclusion and return to the table to discuss her findings and how she arrived at the

Figure 9.1   Common Inquiry Model

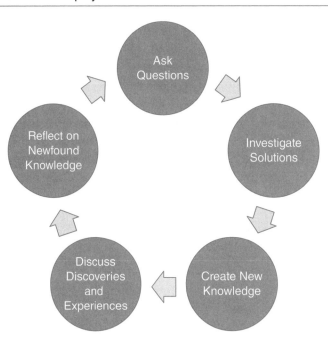

answer. Family members may change their opinions and wonder about the implications of the information.

Alternatively, inquiries can be complicated and lengthy, as is the case when graduate students frame, research, and write book-length dissertations, or when investigative commissions take years to examine matters of public interest or determine the cause of significant events.

Although all of the components will be present in a full inquiry, only some of them may be present in any given case. For example, transportation investigators may not formulate their own guiding questions but be assigned them by the government agency that commissioned an inquiry. As well, the government may decide to shut down the inquiry before a report is created or the findings discussed. The important point is that inquiry need not involve all these phases, nor do the phases need to occur in any predetermined order. It is not the particular procedure but the spirit of investigation that makes something an inquiry. In fact, it is possible to work through the steps of an inquiry model and not adopt an inquiring mindset.

Critical Investigation Versus Research

When faced with the task of covering all that is required in many prescribed curricula, teachers will often assign topics for independent research and ask students to assemble information from a few sources, prepare a presentation usually supported with a digital display or a display board, and then share what they found about their topic with their classmates. Independent research is often referred to as a form of inquiry. We think it important to distinguish between these terms. Although research projects provide opportunities for students to explore topics, they may involve little genuine investigation. They may simply involve "re-searching"— simply finding out what others have discovered and reporting back on their findings. This approach is to be contrasted with the students in the opening story who were expected to draw conclusions from the information they found. Rather than simply gather and present information, students were to weigh evidence to help them decide on the most warranted conclusion about participating in the Gold Rush.

Teacher-Guided Inquiry Versus Student-Directed Inquiry

Students' role in shaping the direction of an inquiry is an area of some debate. As we saw in Chapter 2, "Thinking Is the Key," proponents of a discovery approach believe that students should direct an inquiry based on where their interests take them. We can imagine what it might look like if the Grade 4 students described earlier were engaged in a discovery unit on the California Gold Rush. It is conceivable that no students would be interested in the living conditions or physical dangers, in which case these topics would be ignored. As well, the students could be most interested in the clothing that people wore, even though that might not be a main focus of the curriculum. On the other hand, a thinking classroom approach would encourage student choices so long as the curriculum outcomes could be met. This is consistent with encouraging the Grade 4 students to pursue their own questions and areas of investigation in order to better inform their thinking about the risks and merits of joining the Gold Rush. It seems unrealistic to expect students to direct an inquiry when they neither know much about the topic they are about to inquire into nor the curriculum expectations to be met.

Iterative Inquiries Versus End-of-Unit Inquiries

Use of the qualifying term *sustained* suggests that students will investigate a meaningful challenge over an extended period of time. This is sometimes interpreted to mean that an inquiry question or task will be presented at the beginning of a unit and revisited at the end of the unit, when students are expected to think about what they have learned in the interim and assemble a response. We believe inquiry should drive the entire unit and not simply be the culmination of learning. In other words, the inquiry should be a continuous part of the unit: at every step, the connection should be transparent between what students are learning and the question they are pursuing. Furthermore, each of these steps along the path of learning will present an invitation to inquire into an aspect of an issue or topic, and therefore, thinking critically, creatively, and collaboratively becomes the way students learn. In a sustained inquiry, thinking about an overarching question is iterative because it recurs throughout the unit rather than reappearing at the end.

Embedding Sustained Inquiry Into Various Models

Inquiry learning is an umbrella term that has been operationalized into many different models, including discovery learning, problem-based learning, project-based learning, the research process, and backward design. Each of these approaches has distinguishing features. For example, discovery learning is driven by student interest, while problem-based learning is driven by an agreed-upon problem. However, all these models share the common goal of involving students in exploring issues by framing questions, gathering evidence, and communicating their findings. Despite these features, there is no assurance that they will support sustained, critical investigation. Figure 9.2 illustrates how these various structures can be infused with an inquiry mindset by considering four criteria:

- **Purposeful:** The investigation is focused on meaningful issues and questions that create engaging challenges for students.
- **Prominent and Transparent:** The question that drives the learning is clear from the outset, and the connections between the ongoing learning and the challenge are made obvious.
- **Continuous:** Everything students learn is through inquiry.
- **Genuinely Investigative:** Critical, creative, and collaborative investigation drives the inquiry.

Why Is It Important to Sustain Inquiry?

To ask about the value of inquiry is essentially to ask why it is important to encourage students to think about what they are learning. These reasons have been suggested in earlier chapters. The more useful discussion is on the importance of getting students to think in sustained ways about what they are studying. In many classrooms, there is very little sustained incubation of ideas. Instead, students touch upon one idea after another with little expectation or opportunity to drill down into and to revise their thinking in the face of new information. Providing students with regular opportunities for more sustained investigation is important for several reasons.

Figure 9.2 Infusing Sustained Inquiry Into Common Structures

Common Learning Structures	Opportunities to Embed Sustained Inquiry
Independent Research Students gather information on a particular topic. Information is often organized around topic headings and shared in the form of a report, presentation, or display. *Sample task:* Write a report on common diseases.	**Independent research supports sustained inquiry when . . .** • information is gathered to assist in reaching a reasoned conclusion on an issue, and not largely summarizing ideas found on the Internet; • students are encouraged to consider relevance, credibility, and usefulness of information located. *Sample task:* Rank order common diseases to determine priorities for research funding.
Problem-Based Learning (PBL) PBL uses complex problems encountered in the real world as a stimulus for learning. Students are provided the problem at the start of their learning and are required to integrate and organize learned information in ways that will allow for its application to future problems. *Sample task:* Develop a plan for your home that will help to reduce your family's environmental footprint.	**PBL supports sustained inquiry when . . .** • the problem can't simply be solved by finding information; • the intellectual tools for quality thinking are explicitly taught; • emerging ideas or revisions to the project are considered throughout the unit, and not simply at the end. *Sample task:* Develop a plan for your home that will help to reduce your family's environmental footprint. Your plan should be feasible, make a real difference, and be sustainable over time.
Flipped Classrooms The idea behind the flipped classroom is for students to acquire the content they are expected to learn at home via online reading, recorded lectures, or presentations. Classroom time is then used for activities such as debates, discussions, or simulations. *Sample task:* At home: watch a lecture that outlines the contributions to art of famous Impressionist painters. In class: discuss each artist's work.	**Flipped classrooms support sustained inquiry when . . .** • learning is launched with a meaningful challenge that is addressed through the video; • students are required to select relevant, credible, and important information, even if the task is simply to make notes from a web-based video. *Sample task:* At home: watch a lecture and record all evidence demonstrating the creative contributions and influence of various famous Impressionist painters. In class: discuss and then individually rank the top three Impressionist painters.

(Continued)

Figure 9.2   (Continued)

Common Learning Structures	Opportunities to Embed Sustained Inquiry
Authentic Assessment Tasks Refers to the use of tasks that relate to real-world applications. Students are expected to apply content and competencies to create a product or performance that simulates an application outside of school. *Sample task:* Research an ancient structure and build a model of the structure in sand or snow.	**Authentic assessment tasks support sustained inquiry when . . .** • learning is launched with a meaningful provocation that requires reasoned judgment; • student learning of relevant content and competencies is supported by developing the intellectual tools needed to complete the inquiry. *Sample task:* Select an ancient structure that is representative of an ancient society and create a reproduction in sand or snow. When gathering evidence, consider its credibility, relevance, and importance.
Backward Design Units A method of planning for learning by focusing on big ideas and transferable content and skills. Learning is planned around essential understandings and is launched with students through the use of essential questions. *Sample enduring understanding:* The innovations made by early civilizations influenced the modern world. *Sample essential question:* In what ways do the innovations made by early civilizations continue to influence the modern world?	**Backward design units support sustained inquiry when . . .** • essential questions are framed as invitations to engage in meaningful inquiry; • essential understandings are achieved through active student engagement with the curriculum rather than the transmission of big ideas from the teacher to the student. *Sample essential question:* Which innovations made by early civilizations have had the greatest impact on the modern world? Criteria to consider: • permanence of the impact; • depth or significance of the impact; • breadth or scope of the impact.

Enhances the Quality of Students' Thinking. Good ideas require time to germinate, especially as students learn more about a topic. Living with a problem longer provides time for ideas to percolate and evolve, and leads to better results. Being able to stick with a problem is a key factor in creativity. Although a creative idea may be born from a flash of inspiration, it is much more common for creative ideas that have value to emerge from a period of investigation and experimentation, trial and error, and reflection and revision.

Promotes Deeper Understanding. When students live with a challenge over a period of time, they are more likely to understand the key curricular concepts and ideas. When presented with a series of disconnected inquiries, students often fail to see the meaningful issues that underpin the subject and seldom develop any depth of understanding. The power of sustained inquiry lies not in asking a single question but in the careful sequencing of questions that allow students' learning to deepen over time as they engage with interrelated concepts, ideas, and events.

> The media would also have you believe that science is full of shocking discoveries made by lone geniuses. Not so. The (boring) truth is that it usually advances incrementally, through the steady accretion of data and insights gathered by many people over many years.
>
> —Joel Achenbach (2015)

Nurtures Valuable Dispositions. Sustained inquiry helps to develop many of the dispositions that are so valuable in school and in life beyond school. For example, students learn the value of persevering in pursuit of a sound response to a meaningful challenge. They are more likely to develop the inclination and confidence to take risks as they explore and refine their thinking. Sustained inquiry helps students realize that their first answer is rarely their best answer. Repeated encouragement of students to predict, develop hypotheses, and then revise their thinking based on collaborative discourse develops the kinds of investigative habits that fuel the great advances in society.

What Practices Promote Sustained Inquiry?

Sustained inquiry is a principle to guide teacher decision making. Rather than completely reworking existing lessons, sustained inquiry can be achieved by fine-tuning lessons, reordering the sequence of learning, and building-in support for student thinking. All of the practices discussed in the context of a thinking

> Too many students think effort is only for the inept. Yet sustained effort over time is the key to outstanding achievement.
>
> —Carol Dweck (as cited in Fullan & Langworthy, 2014, p. 17)

classroom apply here. The following are additional practices that are particularly useful in sustaining inquiry.

Shape Climate to Reinforce Sustained Inquiry

Without appreciating it, we may undermine students' development of a disposition toward sustained effort. Rarely do we require a second draft of assignments, and almost never a third or fourth draft. Our rushed time frame leaves little opportunity to delve into topics. Making connections back to previously discussed ideas are usually passing references only. In short, the message that students may draw from these practices is to "do it and move on." A different mindset is required for sustained inquiry.

Create an Expectation of Continuous Investigation. A significant barrier to effective inquiry is student perception that success in school is defined by how well they can recite answers provided by the teacher, a textbook, or another authoritative source. Establishing an iterative process helps students realize they are not trying to find correct answers but are using new knowledge to craft their own reasoned conclusions. All of this requires a rich environment built around rigorous discourse among students and expectations that students will continually rethink, revise, and extend answers as learning unfolds. As well, it involves encouraging tolerance for ambiguity and thoughtful disagreement.

> Establishing an iterative process helps students realize they are not trying to find correct answers but are using new knowledge to craft their own reasoned conclusions.

Create Opportunities to Support Sustained Inquiry

Opportunities for sustained inquiry occur at two levels: on a daily basis as students learn about the new ideas for a particular lesson and on a recurring basis as students use these ideas to respond to an overarching investigation.

Embed Daily Inquiries. Informal inquiries can and should occur frequently (perhaps several times each class). Sustained inquiry seeks to problematize every lesson. Rather than front-end loading concepts and ideas through didactic lessons in which students are the passive receivers of information transferred from teachers, textbooks, or other forms of media, building requisite background knowledge is accomplished through inquiry. These informal inquiries may be student-directed or teacher-framed and individual or collaborative. Just as the example of the family sitting at the dinner table shows, an informal inquiry may grow spontaneously out of a classroom discussion. On the other hand, teachers may also prepare a few inquiry questions that they will pose at various times in the class. For example, prior to reading a piece of literature, the teacher might ask students individually to predict the content of the story using the title and cover as clues. The teacher might also ask students, partway through the story, to use information about the characters and plot as clues to predict what might happen next. Finally, after reading the story, the teacher might ask the class as a whole to use all that they have learned to anticipate how the characters might respond to a new challenge. Figure 9.3 describes various strategies for framing mini-inquiries that illustrate how investigating subject content can become a daily occurrence.

Figure 9.3   Strategies for Problematizing Content

Identify the Attributes of the Concept

Present students with a set of "yes" and "no" examples of a concept, inviting them to identify the attributes shared by the yes examples but not present in the no examples. Then, present a "tester" example and invite students to decide whether or not it is an example of the concept. Alternatively, invite students to create a "yes" and "no" example to add to the data set.

In the example to the right, students use a concept attainment approach to better understand the mathematical concept of "like terms." Students compare each of the matched pairs to determine the difference between them in order to identify the distinguishing features of the concept. After students develop a tentative list of attributes, they check that they all apply to the "tester" example.

Defining "Like Terms"

Compare the paired examples to determine the defining attributes of the concept "like terms."

Yes Examples	No Examples
$2a, 5a$	$2a, 5b$
$-\dfrac{1}{2}ab, +\dfrac{3}{4}ab$	$-\dfrac{1}{2}ab, +\dfrac{1}{3}ac$
$6m^2, 3m^2$	$6m^3, 3m^2$
$4w^3y, -7yw^3$	$4w^3z, 9z^3w$

Do your attributes fit the following tester example?

$$-y4z2x, -\frac{1}{2}x8z2y$$

Select Most Relevant or Important

Provide students with a list of five to seven factual statements on a topic. Invite students to determine, in discussion with their peers, which of the points provided are most relevant or important to the issue being studied. Direct students to eliminate the least relevant piece of information.

The Essentials of Democracy

What can we learn from Athenian democracy to help us create the best democracy possible? Cross out the two least important pieces of information.

1. Ancient Athens was a direct democracy in which all citizens had a vote on all issues.

(Continued)

Figure 9.3 (Continued)

In the example to the right, students must decide which two of the seven facts about Ancient Athens are least important in learning what makes an effective democracy.

2. Only about 15 percent of people living in Athens were citizens.

3. Each year, citizens voted to "ostracize" (send away from the city) one person.

4. Athens was not built around a natural harbor.

5. Women were not considered citizens nor were people who were not born in Athens.

6. Unwanted babies were sometimes left in public squares where others could take them in as slaves.

7. Athenian homes were built around a courtyard and often had a well for collecting water.

Identify the Anomaly

Invite students to use available information to identify the false statement in a list of claims.

In the example to the right, young students anticipate the likely contents of the book The Huge Ceiba Tree *by deciding which one of the provided statements is not supported by details on the cover.*

What Can We Tell From the Cover?

Source: Illustrated by Kirsten Nestor, Corwin.

Which of these statements is least likely to be true considering the evidence on the cover of the book?

1. The story is about a man lost in the jungle.

2. The story is about a man exploring the wondrous sights in the Amazon forest.

3. The story is about a polar bear lost in the jungle.

4. The story is about a man who wants to climb the big tree.

Alter the Perspective

Present students with a brief text or an image and invite them to use clues to infer the perspective that is represented. Encourage students to consider how someone with a different perspective might construct the image or text differently.

In the example to the right, students look for clues in the Trumbull painting and the textbook excerpt on the Battle of Bunker Hill to decipher the perspective represented in each. They then imagine how the painting and account might look if presented from a different perspective.

Whose Perspective Is Represented?

Source: The Death of General Warren at the Battle of Bunker's Hill, June 17, 1775, painted by John Trumbull, 1786. Retrieved from Wikimedia Commons.

Does the following textbook excerpt reflect an American or British perspective? How might a different perspective look?

> "In June 1775, British troops attacked American forces defending Bunker Hill, the heights overlooking the city of Boston. The heroic stand of American patriots inspired the colonists in their struggle for independence" (Beers, 1996, p. 2).

Order Events

Present a list of events without dates or times provided and invite students to determine the correct order of the events based on clues, such as what people are wearing, the weather, or the activities in which people are taking part. Similarly, present a series of images taken over a period of time and invite students to order the images in sequence based on an assigned theme. As an extension, invite students to sketch an image that may lie among, before, or after the images provided.

In the example to the right, young students are asked to sequence selected images on a continuum from "hot" to "cold" depending on the likely temperature depicted in each picture.

What Is the Temperature?

Source: Illustrated by Kirsten Nestor, Corwin.

(Continued)

Figure 9.3   (Continued)

Challenge the Explanation	Does This Explanation Make Sense?
Provide students with a possible explanation to an enigmatic or puzzling situation or phenomenon. Invite students to corroborate or refute the suggested explanation in light of available evidence and their understanding of the topic. *In the example to the right, students are asked to use what they know about gravity to challenge the proposed explanation of the skateboarder's seeming ability to coast uphill.*	 *Source:* Illustrated by Kirsten Nestor, Corwin. The skateboarder is able to coast uphill because the overall force of gravity created by decline of the steeper hill has a greater effect on the mass than the opposing force created by the slight incline of the road on which he is traveling.

Plan for Iterative Structured Inquiries. In addition to embedding multiple informal or mini-inquiries into each lesson, teachers can use an inquiry approach to structure entire units of study. With larger units, formal inquiries are best designed by launching the inquiry with an opening challenge that recurs throughout the unit, establishing transparent long- and short-term goals, and structuring significant time for thinking.

- **Open the Inquiry With a Challenge That Recurs Throughout the Unit:** A key practice in creating opportunities for sustained inquiry is to launch learning by inviting students to offer a prediction or initial position in response to a provocative challenge. We distinguish a launch from a hook. While a hook is often effective at grabbing students' attention by establishing relevance or interest, it is not often used to sustain the inquiry. A launch must establish relevance and interest, but equally important is its use as a recurring focus to help students connect learning throughout the unit. The recursive feature of a teacher-framed inquiry encourages teachers and students to return to and modify conclusions in the face of emerging student interests and insights. Rather than withholding conclusions until the end of a unit, students are invited to reach reasoned judgments at various steps in their learning.

Sample Launches of Recurring Inquiries

A first-grade teacher was planning on having her students create a butterfly garden *after* they learned about living things and soil. It dawned on her that inviting students to begin their learning by sketching a butterfly garden would immediately engage them. Each day, as her students learned more about plants, soil, and butterflies, they were given opportunities to add to their garden plan, make necessary changes, and confirm existing ideas.

A science class was beginning an investigation into the threat posed by climate change. The teacher asked students to set a dial on a dashboard to indicate the degree of threat (from "minimal" to "very serious") that climate change poses and to provide a couple of reasons for their initial assessment. As new information was explored through teacher-led discussions, videos, and readings, students reviewed their dial and made adjustments where warranted by the evidence.

A Grade 11 physics teacher launched an inquiry on motion by asking students to hypothesize from the outset as to why, in baseball, a curveball curves. While learning about Newton's laws of motion, they were invited to affirm, revise, or extend their answers. The quality of their responses improved as students learned and tested their thinking.

- **Establish Transparent Long- and Short-Term Goals:** A common and useful practice is to clearly identify the learning objectives for each day's lesson. However, the need for focus extends beyond day-to-day lessons. If students are to see connections among lessons, they need to understand how individual lessons relate to the broader issue and contribute to their understanding of the big ideas that drive the inquiry. Sustained inquiry can be supported by providing transparent long- and short-term goals. A Cascading Challenges approach, described in the following box, is structured around the sequencing of challenges to provide students with a road map of their learning. The sample Cascading Challenges unit outlined in Figure 9.4 shows the relationships among the overarching challenge and the supporting inquiries, and the individual lessons help students appreciate the relevance of what they are doing each day and how this builds their understanding of the big ideas.

A Cascading Challenges Approach

Cascading Challenges is an approach developed by The Critical Thinking Consortium to support sustained inquiry. The term *cascading* highlights the careful sequencing of questions so that an overarching inquiry is supported by a series of lines of inquiry that are in turn supported by a series of daily lesson challenges. The term *challenges* is used to indicate that at all levels, from the overarching inquiry to the daily lessons, learning is problematized as students are invited to respond to meaningful provocations by reaching a reasoned conclusion based on carefully considered evidence. A Cascading Challenges approach infuses critical, creative, and collaborative thinking through a blending of design-down planning, effective assessment, and sound instruction.

Key Features

- Creates an opportunity for sustained inquiry where every challenge flows from a larger challenge.
- Ensures thinking is at the core of learning by framing the unit, lines of inquiry, and daily lessons around a provocative challenge that invites a reasoned response.
- Creates an invitation to inquire by using a launch. A launch incites student interest by inviting an initial response to a provocation. Depending on the nature of the challenge, the launch may invite a hypothesis, a prediction, a conjecture, or an initial sketch or drafting of ideas.
- Uses a Thoughtbook to encourage continuous incubation of ideas and thoughtful revisions.
- Enriches opportunities for assessment of thinking using the Thoughtbook and rich authentic challenges.
- Allows for the systematic building toward a big idea through the smaller inquiries.
- Ensures a focus on core curriculum goals and key concepts through the development of lines of inquiry while allowing for student voice in the direction of individual lessons and the selection of the unit product or performance.
- Emphasizes explicit development of intellectual tools to support thinking about the issue and not just the product.
- Ensures transparency for students and parents of the flow between the intended learning and the lessons.

Figure 9.4   Partial Cascading Challenges Unit

Newton's Laws of Motion

Overarching Inquiry: Can understanding Newton's laws of motion help to make us better drivers?

Learning Goal: Understand Newton's laws of motion and how they explain movement in everyday life.

Overarching Challenge: Prepare four illustrated pieces of clearly explained and accurate advice on safe driving that apply Newton's laws of motion as if Newton were your driving instructor.

Supporting Inquiry: Gravity	Supporting Inquiry: Inertia	Supporting Inquiry: Force	Supporting Inquiry: Action and Reaction
Learning Goal: Understand the concept of gravity and how it affects everyday movement. **Inquiry:** Does gravity play an important role in driving? **Challenge:** Develop a safe driving tip that takes gravity into consideration.	**Learning Goal:** Understand the concept of inertia and how it affects everyday movement. **Inquiry:** Does inertia play an important role in driving? **Challenge:** Develop a safe driving tip that takes inertia into consideration.	**Learning Goal:** Understand the concept of force and how it affects everyday movement. **Inquiry:** Does force play an important role in driving? **Challenge:** Develop a safe driving tip that takes force into consideration.	**Learning Goal:** Understand the concept of action and reaction, and how they affect everyday movement. **Inquiry:** Does action and reaction play an important role in driving? **Challenge:** Develop a safe driving tip that takes action/reaction into consideration.
Sample Activity on Gravity **Learning Goal:** Understand the role of gravity in an everyday event. **Lesson Challenge:** How did the launch of the car down a ten-story ramp help the toy car jump?	**Sample Activity on Inertia** **Learning Goal:** Understand the role of inertia in an everyday event. **Lesson Challenge:** Why is it difficult for a hovercraft to turn corners?	**Sample Activity on Force** **Learning Goal:** Understand that objects moving uniformly require an unbalanced force to change their motion. **Lesson Challenge:** Why did the cart gain speed as it rolled down the ramp?	**Sample Activity on Action and Reaction** **Learning Goal:** Understand that every action has an equal but opposite reaction. **Lesson Challenge:** Why did the balloon-car move forward?

- **Structure Significant Time for Thinking:** Generating thoughtful solutions to complex problems rarely happens within tight time constraints. Often, the lack of time to think is compounded by front-end loading subject matter content, leaving application of learning toward the end of a unit. Launching learning with a challenge and routinely providing time for students to evaluate their new learning enables them to consider how what they are learning is connected to their prior understanding.

Build Capacity for Sustained Inquiry

Students will most certainly need to develop the range of intellectual tools discussed in Chapter 4 to thoughtfully carry out their inquiries. Notable among these are the ability and inclination for sustained critical, creative, and collaborative reflection.

Support Ongoing Reflection That Is Generative and Constructive. Ongoing student reflection that supports generative and reactive thinking about the challenge can be a powerful way for students to make connections, monitor self-learning, or to generate new possibilities. As students work through an inquiry, their sustained reflections should focus on how effectively their response is meeting the demands of the challenge. By asking themselves "What is working with my response and what is not working?" students can learn to apply learning to either affirm or revise their responses. Reflection about their responses should also help students consider how new learning generates new ideas and possibilities. In this way, reflection serves both reactive thinking (a critique of the work completed) and generative thinking (generating and assessing new options in light of new understandings). The use of a Thoughtbook is one way in which students can connect new concepts and ideas with their existing understanding. The following box explains this strategy and how it supports sustained inquiry.

Supporting Inquiry With Thoughtbooks

A Thoughtbook is a place for students to play with ideas as they engage with a challenge. It might take the form of an artist sketchbook, a small notebook or cahier, or even a digital form in which students can store images of models they are constructing, recordings of performances such as a dance or a reading, or initial drawings or musings. Thoughtbooks allow students to reflect forward to extend and consolidate learning rather than reflecting backward on work completed.

While the label may be new, the concept of a Thoughtbook is not. For centuries, many of history's greatest minds have jotted down their ideas in notebooks, journals, on scraps of paper, and even on the walls of buildings. Great minds throughout history have used variations of Thoughtbooks to initiate their thinking, make revisions, extend ideas, and rethink and reconceptualize ideas that have changed the world. Leonardo da Vinci, Isaac Newton, Charles Darwin, Albert Einstein, Stephen Spielberg, and J. K. Rowling are just a few of history's notables who have used notebooks, journals, or storyboards. Thoughtbooks are also common in many fields of work, including architecture and landscaping, and graphic, car, and fashion design. Moviemakers, choreographers, and video game developers all employ some sort of Thoughtbook to capture initial ideas and to revise them throughout a development process.

Figure 9.5   Da Vinci's Notebook[2]

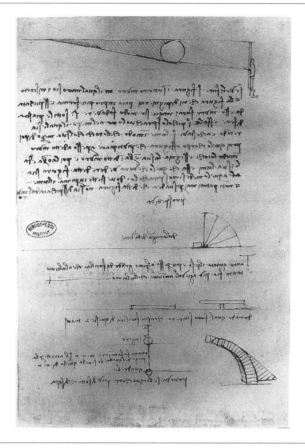

Source: Wellcome Library, London. Wellcome Images (images@wellcome.ac.uk, http://wellcomeimages.org). Manuscript notebooks MS A fol. 42v *Les manuscripts de Leonard de Vinci* (six volumes). Charles Ravaisson-Mollier. Published: 1881. Retrieved from Wikimedia Commons.

Although journaling has long been a part of the educational landscape, journals typically have been used by students to reflect backward on work they have completed. A university education student recalled with dismay having to "reflect on the reflections they had completed during the year." Certainly there is value in reflection, but so too is the value of encouraging students to "think forward" as they test ideas, deepen their understanding, and gather feedback on their ideas and designs. Thoughtbooks assist educators in reframing works in progress as a useful part of learning. As well, they provide multiple supports for effective assessment.

Provide Guidance to Sustain Inquiry

An important component of sustained inquiry is the ongoing supply of feedback that helps students to advance their emerging conclusions.

Offer Continuous and Seamless Peer and Teacher Feedback. Often, assessment takes the form of periodic critiques of student work followed by isolated revisions by students in response to the feedback they receive. In this assessment regimen, students merely implement suggested changes in pursuit of what they believe to be the answer or response the teacher expects. In a continuous and seamless process, students respond to a provocation at the outset of their learning and are provided with multiple opportunities to revise or extend their responses in light of both new learning and feedback from peers and teachers. Making the sharing and critiquing of student responses to mini-challenges presented in daily lessons a routine part of learning provides students with a continual feed of useful new ideas to stimulate ongoing revisions of their work.

Concluding Thoughts

The power of inquiry lies not in asking a single question but in the careful sequencing of questions that leads to sustained inquiry. Through an iterative process, students can develop both a deep understanding of the subject matter and the competencies that are central to a thinking classroom and necessary for success in a rapidly changing world. Rather than being seen as a new idea or another program to implement, sustained inquiry is a principle to guide an evolution that draws together many aspects of effective teaching to create a more coherent and transparent experience for students.

Practices That Sustain Inquiry

Shape Climate	• Create an expectation of continuous investigation.
Create Opportunities	• Embed daily inquiries. • Plan for iterative structured inquiries.
Build Capacity	• Support ongoing reflection that is generative and constructive.
Provide Guidance	• Offer continuous and seamless peer and teacher feedback.

The following are selected strategies for educational leaders to use with teachers to encourage sustained inquiry.

Opportunities for Leadership

Model an Inquiry Mindset With Colleagues and Staff

At every convenient opportunity, frame discussions as questions to investigate in an open and collaborative manner.

Ensure That Major Student Projects Involve Genuine Investigation

Focus on the major projects that students might undertake to ensure that they can't simply re-search for information and report it back to the teacher.

Find Ways to Support Sustained Effort

Encourage colleagues and staff to examine their practices, looking for ways in which students can be encouraged or dissuaded from engaging in sustained effort at school.

Notes

1. Prepared with the assistance of Jenny Mulligan, Grade 4 teacher, Synergy Charter Academy Elementary, Los Angeles.
2. Leonardo da Vinci, Studies of weights and friction ff. 40v-41. http://www.bl.uk/turning-the-pages/?id=cb4c06b9-02f4-49af-80ce-540836464a46&type=book

10

Nurture
Self-Regulated Learners

This chapter explains what it means to support self-regulated learners and the importance of doing so. More specifically, it discusses

- the differences between self-regulated learning and various related concepts;
- reasons why nurturing self-regulated learners is an important guiding principle;
- practices that nurture self-regulated learners.

Each student in Ms. Nielsen's class is expected to know when they understand what is being taught and when they don't. Initially, she provided her students with sets of three colored cards to use in reporting their level of understanding:

- **Green Card:** I totally get it.
- **Yellow Card:** I somewhat get it.
- **Red Card:** I have no clue.

> [T]o promote student self-regulation teachers must assist students to engage flexibly and adaptively in a cycle of cognitive activities (i.e., task analysis, strategy selection and use, self monitoring).
>
> —Deborah Butler (2002)

After explaining a lesson on, for example, how to calculate the area of a rectangle, she would ask students to flash their cards simultaneously on the count of three. Generally, most held up green cards with a few yellows and reds. She would call on a student showing a green card to solve a sample problem and then ask the whole class to flash their cards again, paying particular attention to the yellows and reds from before. She would typically assign five practice problems to allow her time to work with the few students who needed help.

Ms. Nielsen began to reconsider using this strategy to check for understanding when she realized that it was teacher-initiated and not student self-regulated. She, and not her students, was determining when students would assess their level of understanding. Instead of cards, she began using colored stackable cups. Whichever cup was stacked on top (and hence visible) represented the student's perceived level of understanding. Now, students were responsible throughout the lesson for continually adjusting the cups without prompting to reflect their current level of understanding. This modification created an ongoing expectation for students to think about their learning independently. As well, it provided a relatively nonintrusive way for students to signal when they were lost. Quietly placing the red cup on top of one's stack required less courage from students than did raising their hand in the middle of a teacher's explanation to announce that they didn't understand the lesson. This strategy gave students a voice even while Ms. Nielsen was talking, and it encouraged her to listen and adapt her lesson accordingly. Furthermore, the color of the cup became an instant conversation starter whenever Ms. Nielsen started circulating around the room.

This scenario describes Ms. Nielsen's transition from using a familiar strategy that involved students in self-assessment to an enhanced approach that added a dimension of self-regulation. Students were not simply gauging their learning; they were gauging their learning regularly without teacher prompting. Helping students learn to initiate and regulate their learning is a key part of a thinking classroom and has significant implications for student success within school and for preparing them to function in a world where there is not always someone present to tell them what to do.

The fact that it's currently possible to succeed in high school with relatively little self-regulation is shortchanging our students. Those who follow instructions and memorize reams of information carefully assembled by their teachers and managed by their parents may graduate, but then what? Students who lack the intellectual tools and disposition to act independently will struggle, regardless of the knowledge they have accumulated.

Nurturing self-regulated learners is one of five core principles for learning that should inform educators' decisions about almost every aspect of their practice. This includes decisions about how much direction to offer students, how to respond to their questions, what to assess for, what to require during group work, and when to allow students to exercise choice.

So what exactly is implied and not implied by the term *self-regulated learners*?

What Is Self-Regulated Learning?

Self-regulated learning is the ability and inclination to carry out assigned tasks in personally responsible, self-reflective ways, and to exercise reasoned judgment in the pursuit of agreed-upon educational goals. In other words, students will not be sitting in class with their minds turned off, waiting helplessly for their teachers to spoon-feed them with everything they need to know and think about. Rather, students' minds will be turned on as they grapple with and make meaning of what is being learned. Ideally, students would operate this way habitually and without prompting. A completely self-regulated learner can successfully carry out assigned tasks without directive help from others. This doesn't mean that students wouldn't confer with their peers and seek help from their teacher. Instead, it means that students can't expect to be told what to do—they must do some thinking for themselves. The practical implications of this approach are instructively described in the following insert, which lists Grade 11 students' perceptions of self-regulated learning after working for three months to achieve this goal.

> Self-regulated learning is the ability and inclination to carry out assigned tasks in personally responsible, self-reflective ways, and to exercise reasoned judgment in the pursuit of agreed-upon educational goals.

Self-Regulated Learning Is . . .

High school students' perspectives on self-regulated learning:

- Making sure you understand what you learn.
- Thinking about how you can improve your learning.
- Always trying to make your own connections and meaning to what you're learning.
- Being able to take charge of your learning and not have a high dependency on your teachers to spoon-feed you all the time.
- Finding a way that will help you learn.
- Finishing assignments on time.
- Taking the initiative when things aren't clear.
- Using whatever means to comprehend.
- Making your own decisions about how you do things.
- Not having to depend on someone for answers to your questions.
- Finding ways to be interested in your learning even if you're not.

What's Involved in Self-Regulation?

Self-regulated learners possess four attributes (Wolters, 2011). They

- have mastered a repertoire of learning strategies;
- are able to judge which of the particular learning strategies is most appropriate for various learning tasks;
- are able to monitor and, where necessary, modify use of various strategies to suit the particular context; and
- are motivated to regulate their learning and persist at tasks even when not compelled to do so.

Self-regulated learning is easily confused with two related terms: *self-directed learning* and *self-regulation*. Let's consider each.

Self-Regulation Versus Self-Regulated Learning. Self-regulation is a broader notion than self-regulated learning. Self-regulation encompasses several domains, including regulating our body, our emotions, our thinking, and our social behavior (Shanker, 2013, p. xiii). While all of these are important, here we focus exclusively on helping students take greater control over their thinking and actions related to their learning. We do not discuss emotional self-control or control of physical impulses, since our goal is to illuminate the pedagogical principles that should guide teaching and learning in a thinking classroom.

Self-Regulated Learning Versus Self-Directed Learning. Self-directed learning refers to the opportunity to set one's own objectives and learning path. This is often described as personalized or customized learning based on student interest occurring anytime, anyplace, and at any pace, facilitated by learning technologies. Self-directed implies, among other things, that students choose the content and context for learning, whereas self-regulation presumes that these are set by others and that students are working within these parameters to initiate and monitor their thoughtful execution of the directives. It should be clear that effective self-directed learning is not possible without self-regulation of learning. If students can't carry out assigned tasks in personally responsible, self-reflective ways, they are unlikely to competently exercise greater autonomy and responsibility for their learning. Thus, self-regulation is a necessary precondition for self-direction. Lack of students' ability and inclination to self-regulate their learning is a main reason why completion rates in many online learning initiatives are so disappointing.

Self-Regulated Tools Versus Learning Strategies

Another potential confusion arises when teachers equate an instructional strategy with a thinking strategy. We refer to the first as an activity and the latter as a tool. A tool is a device that students intentionally use to achieve a chosen end or objective; an activity is a task that students complete. Students can own a tool—which means they can employ it at will to achieve a strategic purpose. On the other hand, students may get very good at an activity and still never engage in it outside of the assigned context. Consider, for example, the prereading activity "sort and predict" that many teachers use to help activate student thinking about a story or piece of nonfiction. When invited to sort and predict, students are given a selection of words taken from the text. Their task is to organize those words to make sense of and anticipate the content of the text. This is a worthwhile activity, but it is teacher-directed and it is not a prereading strategy that students can use independently since students would already have had to read the text in order to extract the words.

Many strategies, including previewing, creating storyboards, drawing concept and mind maps, and recording evidence on charts, have the potential to be a tool but never become more than an activity that students undertake. Consider, for example, the use of graphic organizers to compare two characters or events in a story. The teacher may model the use of a Venn diagram and guide students in using it with several examples. Many teachers would think that they are teaching a thinking strategy. However, this potentially useful strategy remains an activity unless students add it to their repertoire of self-regulated tools. By self-regulated, we mean tools that are purposeful (i.e., intended to achieve an internalized objective), used independently (not used only upon request), and thoughtfully chosen (selected from an array of possible options). Despite teacher intentions, in many classrooms students would not know or think to use a Venn diagram on their own to make sense of what they are learning.

Distinguishing between strategies that remain activities and those that become tools for self-regulated learning is not intended to diminish the role of instructional activities. Clearly, activities can help students understand the contents of a lesson. However, getting students to complete activities or tasks may contribute little to (and may distract from) helping students learn how to self-regulate their learning. This is because students haven't learned to use a Venn diagram or other such graphic organizer when they (and not the teacher) decide that it is an appropriate strategy. Students acquire tools only as they learn to think for themselves about the purpose or need, consider their options, and choose an effective strategy to assist their learning.

Why Is Self-Regulated Learning Important?

There are several compelling reasons for adopting self-regulated learning as a guiding principle for creating a thinking classroom.

Is Necessary for Competency. Self-regulated learning is an essential component of competency. We've defined a competency as a complex set of tasks requiring various enabling tools. To be considered truly competent, students must demonstrate more than the ability to perform the task; they must learn to select and use the necessary tools without prompting. Genuine competency is possible only with self-regulation. In fact, it makes little sense to talk of someone being competent at anything without a significant degree of self-regulation. Consider what it means to be a reflective thinker. Students may understand the importance of metacognition and be taught how to apply it in various contexts across the curriculum. They may even demonstrate that they are very good at reflecting about their learning. But unless students use this competency without prompting within and beyond the school setting, they can't be considered fully proficient. Moreover, self-regulated learners have the metacognitive awareness to be able to extend their competency to continually more sophisticated levels.

Has Immediate Classroom Benefits. There are immediate classroom advantages when students have the inclination and the strategies to self-regulate their learning. Students who are focused on thinking about their learning are less likely to disrupt the class and are more likely to succeed as learners.

Intensifies Student Confidence and Engagement. Self-regulation presupposes a measure of student engagement, but it also fuels it. Students recognize that the ability to regulate their own learning without being spoon-fed is an important goal of their education. Students also welcome the opportunity to take ownership of their learning and to exercise greater freedom to learn in their own way. After a semester-long program that emphasized self-regulated learning, one student wrote:

> This is the first year that I have enjoyed learning, and I discovered that it wasn't because the material was better but it was because I learned to engage my brain. The minute I engaged my brain the lessons became interesting and I wanted to learn. Through every unit in Social Studies this year I have wanted to suck all the knowledge I can get out of the class. The power tools have been a huge help for me and my attitude towards school has changed tremendously.
>
> —Chelsea Van Randen (eleventh-grade student)

Chelsea's response was representative of many of her classmates. Once students begin to self-regulate, they learn more effectively and improve on their results. For many students, it raises their understanding of how they learn and what they need to improve on as they go about learning. This newfound confidence about learning helps students overcome the disengagement that accompanies chronic lack of success.

What Practices Nurture Self-Regulated Learners?

All of the practices discussed in connection with promoting a thinking classroom apply to nurturing self-regulated learners. There are additional practices that are uniquely suited to developing students' ability and disposition to regulate their learning.

Shape a Climate That Nurtures Self-Regulated Learners

Many students have acquired what we call *learned helplessness*. They have come to expect that if they wait long enough and petition enough people, someone will tell them what they need to do and how they should do it. Educators who wish to nurture self-regulation will need to overcome this often deeply embedded mindset.

Create Expectations and Student Buy-In for Self-Regulated Learning. It is essential that students see the purpose and personal benefits of becoming more self-regulated learners. Creating the expectation that students will self-regulate their learning and helping them see its value is best served by promoting the idea of self-regulation generally and the particular learning strategies they will use.

Seeing the Big Picture. A first step in moving students toward self-regulated learning is to create an expectation and buy-in. Students need an overview to help them make sense of self-regulated learning and to be clear on its purpose and how it can make their lives better in school and beyond. The simple act of introducing students to the concept of self-regulated learning has been shown to motivate them. It is helpful to start with a lesson on what self-regulated learning is and why it's important. An example of this is found in the following box. Continually finding ways to ensure that students see value is essential when supporting self-regulated learning. Students won't bother monitoring their learning if they don't fully appreciate the point of doing it.

Introducing Self-Regulated Learning

Teacher Stefan Stipp has used the following script to introduce the idea of self-regulated learning to his high school students.[1]

> Most teachers are good at spoon-feeding their students. We tell our students what, when, where, how, and with whom to learn. Most students are good at being spoon-fed. You sit passively in class, waiting for the teacher to tell you what to do and often complete your tasks with little thought. The trouble with this is that it leads to little meaningful learning. Far too many of you will leave high school dependent on your teachers to learn. I want to change that by teaching you to become self-regulated learners. As a self-regulated learner, you take charge of your learning. You figure out what you're supposed to learn, how you might learn it, and you notice when you're not learning and know ways to overcome that. You're constantly talking to yourself in your head to make sense of the new stuff entering your brain. This semester, I'm going to teach you some tools that will help you learn better in school and beyond. Using these tools will push you to take ownership of your learning at school and beyond so you have the motivation and the skill to learn just about anything, anywhere and anytime.

Seeing the Value of Self-Regulated Use of Specific Strategies. In addition to seeing the big picture, students need to see the value of the particular learning strategies they are being asked to use in a self-regulated way—whether it is using the colored cups to signal their level of understanding of a lesson or activating prior knowledge to help them read a passage. One approach is to select a cluster of tools that directly relates to an upcoming task, or to propose very general tools that are broadly useful in completing almost any task. Encourage students to identify tools they most want to learn. As well, it is effective in creating buy-in that students see how the strategy works.

The lesson described in the following insert was used to help students see the value of activating prior knowledge before embarking on a task.

Demonstrating the Value of Activating Prior Knowledge

Teacher Stefan Stipp has used the following script to introduce the strategy of activating prior knowledge to his high school students.[2]

> Before you start learning something new, it helps your brain if you get it prepared. Think of your brain as a filing cabinet. If you figure out what you already know about the topic and make predictions, it helps open the right drawer in your brain before the new information arrives, making it easier for your brain to make sense of it and to store it efficiently.

To see how this works, read the stanza and try to make sense of it. You probably found this task challenging. But what if you knew that it describes a bat? If you reread the poem now, you'll find it easier to make sense of. That's because you already have a file in your brain labeled bat, and when you open it everything you already know about bats helps you make sense of phrases like "hangs from beam." Opening the drawer is a metaphor for accessing knowledge you already have about what you'll be learning and awakening curiosity about it.

He hangs from beam in winter upside down

But in the spring he right side up lets go

And flutters here and there zigzagly flown

Till up the chimney of the house quick-slow

He pendulum-spirals out in light low

Of sunset swinging out above the lawns

Gathering sinking insects' sag downflow

Returning as the light on green world dawns

And down the chimney disappears nimble

To the cellar where they catch mice with a thimble.

—James Reaney[3]

Create Opportunities to Nurture Self-Regulated Learning

Students will require many opportunities to develop and apply their emerging ability to self-regulate their learning.

Embed Frequent Opportunities for Self-Regulated Learning. Although most students love the idea of being self-regulated learners, many struggle to achieve self-regulation because they have been habituated into being spoon-fed. It is easier to sit passively in class, waiting for the teacher to tell them what to do, and often complete tasks with little thought. To make matters worse, teachers are often good at spoon-feeding and may be seduced by its apparent efficiency in getting students to complete a task. For example, when explaining the details of an important phenomenon or event using prepared notes, teachers might simply require students to copy the notes verbatim. This approach is simple, and it ensures that the same information is in each student's notebook. However, providing the notes reinforces dependency on the teacher to decide what's sufficiently important to write down, robbing students of the opportunity to make their own decisions. Moreover, copying prepared notes can be done without leading to any learning. Conversely, students who are made to think about what is important must make some sense of the content. Furthermore, encouraging students to learn to make such decisions without explicit prompting increases personal ownership of their learning. Despite the appeal of making it simple for students, meaningful learning and long-term benefits will occur only if teachers use these everyday kinds of opportunities to support students in thinking for themselves and expect that they will do so.

Build Capacity for Self-Regulated Learning

The key to building the capacity and the disposition for self-regulated learning is to help students master a repertoire of learning tools which they select from and thoughtfully use as situations require.

Develop a Repertoire of Learning Strategies, Including Criteria for Their Effective Use. Students require explicit instruction in the use of a repertoire of strategies to help them learn. These strategies may include prelearning tools that help students get ready to learn, on-the-task tools that help them make sense of what they're learning, and confirmation-of-learning tools that help them show and apply what they've learned. Suggestions for teaching self-regulated learning tools include the following:

- **Start with prelearning tools.** Demonstrate how to use each tool and its purpose. For example, when teaching students to annotate assignment sheets, use an interactive whiteboard or digital camera to annotate a handout in front of the class. Use a think-aloud strategy to demonstrate the thinking behind the annotations.

Opportunities to Embed Self-Regulated Learning

**Post Engaging Learning Goals
Before Students Enter the Room**

Providing the objectives for a lesson offers an opportunity for students to develop the habit of prelearning. There is no simple formula for effectively communicating learning intentions: in some lessons, the element of surprise is important, while in others, the best way to clarify learning intentions and criteria for success is to have students infer them through sample work. However, most of the time, it makes sense to display learning intentions in student-friendly language at the beginning of each class.

Big Question

Is our way of electing the president effective?

Figure 10.1   How to Become President of the United States

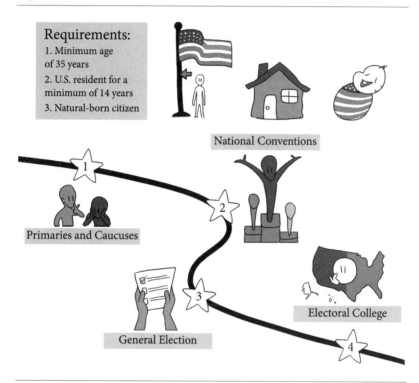

Source: Illustrated by Kirsten Nestor, Corwin.

What Could You Learn?

- What are primaries, and how does someone become a member of a caucus?
- What is the Electoral College?
- Is it possible to be elected president but receive fewer votes than the other candidate?

What You'll Do With Your Learning

Answer the big question in a paragraph.

- Use the acronyms WALT ("We are learning to") and WILF ("What I'm looking for") to frame learning intentions.

(Continued)

(Continued)

- A more labor-intensive but effective way of communicating learning intentions is to create mini-inquiries that invite students to draw inferences based on clues about the contents of the lesson before it starts. The image in Figure 10.1 is from a lesson on American government. The task is to develop a hypothesis about the nature of the day's lesson and, in the process, activate prior knowledge and build new knowledge.

Provide Handouts in Advance

Handouts can be placed on student desks before they arrive or piled by the front door for routine pickup when students enter the room. Alternatively, they can be posted on a class website and be required viewing the night before each lesson. The expectation is that students will formulate an impression of the lesson prior to its commencement. The objective is to create some motivation for the upcoming topic, activate prior knowledge, and clarify learning expectations.

- **Show students how to use each tool in various contexts.** For example, the tool of annotating could be used when reading a novel or a textbook and needs to be modeled again in those contexts.
- **Focus initially on a small number of tools** until students have mastered them in various contexts. Students are easily overwhelmed with too many tools, but they are excited when they master a tool and begin to see its power.
- **Provide students with a menu of tools** by creating a laminated list that is distributed at the beginning of each class or taped to students' desks or binders.
- **Remind students to ask themselves two key questions** while learning:
  - Am I learning optimally right now?
  - If not, which tool would help me learn better?

The tools described in Figure 10.2 have been used with high school students. A guiding question and the defining criterion or purpose is provided for each tool. A teacher may start with a few tools and introduce additional tools as appropriate.

Support Independent Student Use and Ongoing Monitoring. The responsibility to select and effectively use and even adapt appropriate

Figure 10.2   Sample Learning Tools

Prelearning Tools

✻ *Learning purpose*—Look at handouts, textbook, board, screen. *What am I about to learn/do? What will I be able to know or do? What is expected of me?*

Clear Purpose
Clearly understands what they will learn and do.

✻ *Prior knowledge*—Create a hook in your brain. *What do I already know about this topic? What could I consult (previous notes . . .)?*

Meaningful Connections
Meaningfully connects new material to prior knowledge.

✻ *Predict and wonder.* *What do I think I'll learn? What questions do I have?*

Plausible Predictions
Makes plausible predictions and poses genuine questions.

✻ *Think of reasons for learning.* *Why should I bother learning this (interesting, challenging, will improve my life, build connections with others, expand my vista . . .)?*

Strong Motivation
Has genuine reasons for learning.

✻ *Create your own tool.*

On-the-Task Tools

✻ *Write understandings as you read/listen/watch.* Abbreviations will make you more efficient. For example: c. = circa = approximately
+ = and   /h = per hour
pop = population   b/c = because   → = leads to
w/ = with   gov't = government

Meaningful Understandings
Writes understandings in own words, always connecting them to the big picture.

✻ *Visualize what you are learning.* Draw it. What does it look like?

Helpful Visual
Visuals enhance understanding.

✻ *Check your understanding.* *Am I getting this? What am I getting? What am I not getting?*

Accurate Self-Assessment
Uses symbols in ways that clarify understanding.

Use symbols to interact with what you read, hear, or write. For example:
✓ get it   ✓✓ agree
?? confused   X disagree

✻ *Troubleshoot if you don't understand something.* *How could I figure this out?* Reread, look ahead, connect to what you already know, collaborate, ask for help.

Effective Troubleshooting
Troubleshooting steps lead to desired learning.

✻ *Create your own tool.*

(Continued)

Figure 10.2 (Continued)

Confirmation-of-Learning Tools

- ***Write a concise summary***.
  What is the main idea that I learned?

  > **Concise Summary**
  > Briefly and accurately capture main ideas in your own words.

- ***Create a headline*** for your concise summary that packs maximum punch.
  What is the essence of what I've learned?

  > **Powerful Title**
  > Captures the essence.

- ***Create a concept map***.
  How does all this fit together?

  > **Revealing Concept Map**
  > Connections among concepts show relationships and clarify the big picture.

- ***Think about your thinking and learning***.
  How well did I learn? How can I improve the process?

  > **Improved Learning**
  > Thinking about learning leads to better use of tools.

- ***Create your own tool***.

tools needs to be gradually released from the teacher to students. Following explicit instruction in the tools, teachers should slowly encourage greater student responsibility for the use of these tools. Guided and then independent practice using the tool should continue until students are proficient. Increasingly, the teacher withdraws any active support. The following are suggestions for optimizing this process:

- Encourage students to choose from their repertoire the most effective tool for the particular task.
- Invite students to continuously reflect on the effectiveness of their use of various tools. This should lead them to adapt tools and even create their own.
- Hold students individually accountable by randomly calling upon students to identify the tools they have chosen for the task and to explain why and how they are using them. This latter request helps to identify students who may erroneously believe they understand the tool when they are still unclear about its use and purpose.

The following insert describes how one teacher supported her students in gradually developing ownership of a visualization strategy.

Increasing Self-Regulation of a Learning Tool

A seventh-grade math teacher provided students with a chance to practice a visualization strategy during a follow-up lesson on adding fractions with uncommon denominators. After writing the problem "$\frac{1}{2} + \frac{1}{3}$ = ?" on the board, she prompted students by reminding them of a previously introduced visualizing tool. She asked them to work in small groups to try to visually represent the problem. Students individually recorded their ideas onto the visual created by the group and submitted them to the teacher for feedback on how well they used the tool.

Three days later when the class was working on word problems, she again asked students how they might visually represent a problem, but this time they created their visuals independently and she circulated to confirm that they understood how to use the tool. When the teacher was teaching how to multiply fractions two weeks later, she asked students to decide how they might best perform this operation, but she said nothing about using a tool. When 80 percent of her students created visuals of the sample problem, she knew that they had progressed significantly in their self-regulated use of this tool.

At the end of each day, her students reflected on their learning with specific reference to the use of tools in their learning log, a spiral-bound notebook each had with them at all times. As the teacher introduced additional tools, she encouraged students to use them in different subjects. Over time, they adapted the tools to suit their own needs, and students customized a personal toolkit of the learning strategies they found most effective.

Provide Guidance to Inform Self-Regulated Learning

Teacher and student assessment of self-regulated learning should be ongoing and include frequent feedback.

Assess Situation-Specific and General Levels of Self-Regulated Learning. It is helpful to regularly gather feedback on students' ability to self-regulate in specific learning situations and also to gauge their confidence and ability overall.

- **Assess Specific Use of Self-Regulating Strategies:** The habit of self-assessing in light of well-understood criteria is an essential attribute of a self-regulated learner. This should happen throughout the learning process in a learning log and be submitted occasionally for feedback. It should also be a routine part of the completion of all major assignments, and in these cases, a more formal process is helpful.

The self-assessment strategy outlined in Figure 10.3 can be used with almost any assignment. Students complete the first three rows before they begin the task, as soon as the teacher has explained an assignment. The point is to ensure students are aware of the task, its purpose, and what success looks like. Students complete the lower three rows after a first draft of the assignment. Ideally, the assignment is then returned to students so they can make their suggested improvements and resubmit a final version. The most important feature is the self-check of their explanation for each of the six questions. The point is to confirm that students recognize when they know what is being asked of them and when they don't. Students who explain the requirements of the task poorly but recognize their weakness in doing so are better able to self-regulate than are students who either don't realize they don't know what the task requires or erroneously think they don't understand the task when in fact their explanations of the requirements are sound.

- **Assess General Levels of Self-Regulated Learning.** Students should continuously self-assess by reflecting informally on their learning. In addition, more formal periodic self-assessment of students' overall ability to regulate their learning with teacher feedback is helpful in gauging students' progress and in improving their use of learning strategies. Regularly setting time aside for such self-assessments reminds all students of the importance of self-regulation.

The self-assessment checklist outlined in Figure 10.4 has proved effective with high school students in nurturing the ability and disposition for self-regulated learning. Periodic use of this checklist allows teachers an opportunity to offer feedback and to encourage students further along the self-regulation continuum. Students demonstrating consistent levels of self-regulated learning based on this self-assessment could be given increased freedoms when exercising choice about how, with whom, and where to learn.

Concluding Thoughts

The ability and inclination to carry out assigned tasks in personally responsible, self-reflective ways is vital for success in a thinking classroom and in the world beyond school. In addition, self-regulating one's learning is a necessary condition for more independent self-directed learning. Self-regulation requires mastery of a repertoire of learning tools that

Figure 10.3 Self-Assessment of Understanding and Performance

Helping Students Recognize What They Don't Know

Self-assessment for: _____ Name: _____

	Explain in My Own Words	Self-Check
What am I supposed to do for this assignment?		How clearly do I understand what is required? ☐ very clear ☐ fairly clear ☐ so-so ☐ very confused
What's the point of this assignment?		How clearly do I understand the purpose? ☐ very clear ☐ fairly clear ☐ so-so ☐ very confused
What are the criteria of quality for this assignment?		How clearly do I understand the criteria? ☐ very clear ☐ fairly clear ☐ so-so ☐ very confused
What have I done well in light of the criteria? What do I understand well?		How well have I done? ☐ very well ☐ fairly well ☐ so-so ☐ very poorly
What needs improvement in light of the criteria? What don't I understand?		How well have I assessed what I need to do to improve? ☐ very clear ☐ fairly clear ☐ so-so ☐ very confused ☐ N/A
What will I do to improve this?		How clearly do I understand what is required? ☐ very useful ☐ fairly useful ☐ so-so ☐ not useful at all ☐ N/A

Source: Created by The Critical Thinking Consortium.

Figure 10.4   Self-Assessment of Self-Regulation

Assessing Overall Level of Self-Regulation

How self-regulated am I as a learner?	Always	Most of the Time	Some of the Time
I get ready to learn by getting the right stuff out, checking what I know, wondering, and setting a purpose for learning.			
Explanation:			
I keep myself focused and on task in class. When my teacher is talking, I use tools to make sure I'm listening and getting it. For example: writing stuff down, annotating handouts.			
Explanation:			
I am motivated to learn and I know how to motivate myself when I'm not.			
Explanation:			
If I don't get something, I know how to get unstuck and make it happen.			
Explanation:			
I show grit when things get difficult, boring, overwhelming, confusing.			
Explanation:			

Improvement Plan

How self-regulated am I as a learner?	Always	Most of the Time	Some of the Time	Improvement Plan
I use an effective system to get my homework and assignments done well and on time.				
Explanation:				
I use results of assessments (teacher comments/criteria) to improve my learning. I go back and fix/redo work with a focus on learning.				
Explanation:				

Circle your level of self-regulation in the rubric below.

Completely Self-Regulated

I am fully aware of what I need to do, why I'm doing it, and how to make sure I'm succeeding. I take complete charge of the task at hand.

Almost Self-Regulated

I am mostly aware of what I need to do, why I'm doing it, and how to make sure I'm succeeding. I usually take charge of the task at hand.

Some Self-Control

I'm sometimes aware of what I need to do, why I'm doing it, and how to make sure I succeed. At times I take charge of the task at hand.

Minimal Self-Control

I'm rarely aware of what to do, why I'm doing it, or how to make sure I succeed. I rarely take charge of the task at hand.

Completely Dependent

I'm not aware of what to do, why I'm doing it, or how to make sure I succeed. The teacher is in charge of my learning.

Source: Created by The Critical Thinking Consortium.

students select from and apply thoughtfully in appropriate situations without prompting from others.

Practices That Support Self-Regulated Learners

Shape Climate	• Create expectations and student buy-in for self-regulated learning.
Create Opportunities	• Embed frequent opportunities for self-regulated learning.
Build Capacity	• Develop a repertoire of learning strategies, including criteria for effective use. • Support independent student use and ongoing monitoring.
Provide Guidance	• Assess situation-specific and general levels of self-regulated learning.

The following box contains selected strategies for educational leaders to use with teachers to encourage self-regulated learning.

Opportunities for Leadership

Clear Up Confusions About Self-Regulated Learning

Because of the potential to conflate self-directed learning with self-regulated learning, or to confuse instructional strategies with learning tools, ensure that staff members are clear about the nature and purpose of nurturing self-regulated learners.

Make Self-Regulated Learning a Schoolwide Student Expectation

Encourage the entire staff to adopt and reinforce the expectation that students will learn to be more self-regulated. Over time, monitor the general level of self-regulated learning for the entire student population.

Develop a Common Set of Core Learning Tools

Work with teachers in grade-level or subject-area groups to identify a common repertoire of learning tools that all might use with their students. Create resources to support teachers in introducing the tools to students and monitoring their use.

Notes

1. An account provided by Stefan Stipp, a teacher in the Surrey School District in British Columbia.
2. An account provided by Stefan Stipp, a teacher in the Surrey School District in British Columbia.
3. This is the fifth stanza of "February Eclogue," a poem by James Reaney (2010, p. 18).

11

Create Assessment-Rich Learning

This chapter explains what it means to create an assessment-rich learning environment and the importance of doing so. More specifically, it discusses

- six ways in which assessment-rich learning builds on and extends the work done by other scholars on effective assessment;
- the importance of assessment-rich learning in helping to improve student achievement;
- practices that create assessment-rich learning.

As it was the last assignment in eleventh grade, Mathew worked especially hard on an English paper comparing the novel and movie versions of *Les Miserables*. He was disappointed in the B+ mark he received, thinking he had written a better paper than was reflected in the teacher's assigned mark. When asked what the teacher had to say about the paper, Mathew responded, "I don't know." Asked to retrieve the paper,

[W]e need to ensure that feedback causes a cognitive rather than an emotional reaction—in other words, feedback should cause thinking.... Indeed, the whole purpose of feedback should be to increase the extent to which students are owners of their own learning.

—Dylan Wiliam (2011, p. 132)

he dug into his bag and produced the assessed work. Every page of the essay had insightful and potentially helpful comments, and yet Mathew hadn't looked at them. The effort the teacher had put into critiquing the essay was wasted time.

This scenario is not uncommon and highlights a persistent issue in school assessment practices. Even the most clearly written rubric and the most insightful comments by a teacher will have no impact on student learning if they are not seen as a dialogue between the assessor and the assessed. Mathew, like so many other teens, had looked at the mark on the front of his paper, took the disappointment in stride, and moved on. The opportunity to nurture perseverance was missed and, more important, so was the opportunity for him to grow as a writer from his teacher's insightful feedback. Considering that Mathew was 1 of 30 students in the class, the teacher effectively wasted approximately thirty hours providing comments that did little more than justify a mark and had no impact on her students' learning. Imagine the potential for learning had Mathew been supported with meaningful and ongoing discussions with his peers and teacher as he shaped the preliminary ideas that would frame his paper and as he moved through subsequent revisions.

Despite significant progress made over the past couple of decades, assessment in schools too often remains periodic critiques of products or performances that may provide some feedback and be used to assign grades, but often doesn't enhance learning to the extent that it should. Mathew saw so little value in assessment as a vehicle for his learning that he didn't bother to look at the feedback he received. If we hope to create assessment-rich learning, then assessment must become a useful and routine aspect of instruction.

What's Wrong With the Current Assessment Landscape?

Two competing tensions have long plagued education: the desire to support student learning and the desire to hold students, teachers, schools, and school systems accountable. An accountability focus and the use of grades and standardized assessments as gatekeepers to higher education have created evaluation-driven regimens. Working with thousands of teachers across North America, we have often heard teachers lament, "I really agree with the critical thinking work you do, but I have to get my students ready for the standardized test."

Standardized assessments will likely remain a dominant feature on the educational landscape, and grading will continue to be a contentious issue. High-stakes tests often bear the brunt of the criticism that assessment is failing to align with our stated educational goals. This singular focus can detract from another problem that often inhibits our success at establishing assessment-rich learning. Too often, classroom-based assessments are periodic interruptions rather than central components of learning,

Furthermore, they focus almost exclusively on the products students submit, and little attention is devoted to the thinking that led to the product. In assessment-rich learning, the goal is to make assessment one of the more powerful tools in a teacher's instructional toolkit. This is not to ignore the presence of standardized assessments in education but rather to recognize that if we use assessment opportunities properly, then student success on standardized measures is likely to follow.

Prior to the work begun in the 1990s by Paul Black and Dylan Wiliam in the United Kingdom, Alfie Kohn and Rick Stiggins in the United States, and Ken O'Connor and Anne Davies in Canada, assessment was used primarily to gather evidence of student success at meeting curricular goals. These educators have helped to enhance assessment practices in three ways:

- **More Diverse Assessment Tools:** In many classrooms, assessment has evolved from being a collection of largely pen and paper tests, essays, and projects supplemented with quizzes, homework checks, and marks awarded for various behaviors. Assessment now draws increasingly on a richer variety of assessment tools that guide learning and determine grades that more accurately reflect student success at meeting curricular outcomes.
- **More Authentic Measures:** The shift to a wider variety of assessments has been accompanied by a move to more authentic assessments that more closely reflect the kind of everyday tasks that are found outside of schools.
- **Greater Emphasis on Formative Assessment:** Perhaps most significantly, educators have come to realize that the power of assessment does not lie in the mere collection of evidence (assessment of learning) upon which to base a grade. Assessment is now valued for the opportunities it provides to guide students in their learning (assessment for learning).

These contributions to assessment have led to broader uses of assessment, with a greater emphasis on providing feedback to guide student learning. Assessment-rich learning proposes a further shift, one that elevates assessment so that it becomes as integral to learning as any form of instruction.

What Is Assessment-Rich Learning?

We use the term *assessment-rich learning* to draw attention to the use of student and teacher assessment as an integral, continuous, and genuinely helpful aspect of all student learning. By integral, we mean that assessment becomes a seamless and essential aspect of instruction; by continuous, that it happens throughout the lesson; and by genuinely helpful, that students welcome assessment as an opportunity to inform and advance their learning. By contrast, assessment-poor learning exists when assessment is relatively infrequent and is dreaded by students, who resist or avoid seeking feedback and see assessment as an occasion where their peers and teachers pass judgment on their work rather than as an opportunity to support their learning.

Assessment-rich learning positions student and teacher assessment as an integral, continuous, and genuinely helpful aspect of all student learning.

There are various ways in which assessment-rich learning builds on and extends effective assessment practices:

- integrating assessment more seamlessly with instruction and increasing its frequency;
- enhancing the perceived value and utilization of feedback;
- viewing all work as "in progress";
- improving the rigor of student critiques; and
- emphasizing learning over task completion.

Assessment Is Seamless With Instruction and Timely, Rather Than Disruptive and Delayed

Typically, formative assessment has been limited to periodic checks on student progress. A key element of assessment-rich learning is the integral and continuous role of self-, peer, and teacher assessment in supporting student learning. By making timely and useful guidance a routine element of daily instruction, teachers can help students come to see assessment as a vital component of learning. By timely, we mean that comments are offered in time for students to make use of them. Mathew's disregard for his teacher's extensive comments are understandable considering they came some time after he had completed his paper, and he wasn't thinking about storing ideas for next time. The next box describes a ninth-grade English teacher's efforts to advance her students' thinking by inviting them to regularly reassess their previous conclusions in light of new information.

Students Recognize Value in Feedback

Only when students realize that assessment can significantly improve their learning are they likely to seek out feedback and to use the guidance they receive. We will know we have fully achieved an assessment-rich classroom when students stop fearing assessment and instead eagerly seek more feedback to help improve and further their learning.

Reassessing Previous Conclusions

The ninth-grade students were asked "Which shapes our lives more, fate or free will?" Students were presented with a dial ranging from "Fate" to "Free Will" and asked to reflect on their initial responses. The class then began a study of *Romeo and Juliet*. As the study of the play unfolded, students continually reassessed their rating in light of new evidence and insights from the play. A large dial in the classroom acted as the collaborative space for gathering evidence, and students used their own smaller version to record their own emerging thinking.

Fate or Free Will—Which Contributed More to the Deaths of Romeo and Juliet?

Criteria for fate as dominant factor:

- Romeo and Juliet had little control over the events that directed their lives.
- Events directly leading to the deaths of Romeo and Juliet resulted from actions and decisions beyond their control.
- Decisions made by Romeo and Juliet did not directly lead to their deaths.

Figure 11.1   Rating Scale on Extent of Free Will

Fate or Free Will	Supporting Evidence
More free will than fate More fate than free will Free will Fate	**Initial View**
More free will than fate More fate than free will Free will Fate	**Act I**

Almost Everything in School Is a Work in Progress

Assessment-rich learning helps students to recognize that learning is an iterative learning journey rather than a product-driven destination. Multiple iterative responses to a challenge should not only be allowed, but they should be an expectation. Consider the following example.

In a fifth-grade class, students were asked, as a launch to learning about energy conservation, to select and rank order three out of five actions that families could take to reduce energy use. The students were provided with three criteria (would make a significant difference, could be sustained over time, would have no harmful effects). Students selected and justified their initial choices. Over time, as the class explored issues relating to energy and energy conservation, each day students discussed actions that would make a difference. As they did, students reviewed their ranking ladder and made adjustments if necessary. All students, even those who had decided to make no changes, were required to provide reasons for their decisions. Ultimately, students came to see that the task required them to create increasingly sound answers by adding more evidence to support their positions but also that there was no one correct answer. Their answers were a work in progress that allowed them to develop a deep understanding and encouraged them to maintain an open mind.

In an iterative approach, the product or performance is simply the vehicle through which learning occurs. A unit might be launched with a challenge that provides diagnostic evidence to inform teachers' planning; each lesson provides opportunities to integrate new ideas and concepts as the response to the opening challenge evolves. Self, peer, and teacher critiques are timely and encourage modifications to thinking. "Failures" become opportunities for reflection and further insights. In short, rather than focusing assessment on a particular end result, the primary focus is on the process of learning.

Students Are as Rigorous as Their Teachers in Their Assessments

Most students don't take self-assessments or those of their peers seriously for two reasons. One reason is that student assessments aren't nearly as competent as those of their teachers. If students are incapable of judging how well they have understood a concept or mastered a task, then we must question the depth of their understanding and the level of their competency. Knowing when you have or haven't done a good job and why are part of mastering the material. Assessment-rich learning means that students are confident and rigorous in their assessments of themselves and of others. The example in the next box describes efforts to nurture this goal with teachers in a graduate class.

A second reason why students don't take self- and peer assessment seriously is that their assessments don't count for much. Assessment-rich learning means that students attach value to critiques because they understand how they can help them learn. It may help to signal their importance if teachers assign marks on the quality of student assessments and emphasize that "knowing when we know and knowing when we don't know" is one of the important abilities that anyone can learn in school.

Teaching Self-Assessment Rigorously

Recently, I had some success in dissipating the unhealthy and counterproductive assessment environment in university classes by convincing teachers in a graduate class of the value of knowing their marks before I did. I explained that they would practice assessing ungraded interim assignments using the rubric that I planned to use on their final draft. I arranged for multiple opportunities for self- and peer assessment—not of the assignment per se but on their assessment of the assignment. In other words, the focus was on students' ability to accurately and insightfully assess the strengths and weaknesses of their work. We needed repeated opportunities to build their confidence so that they could determine when and why an assignment was good or very good. They appreciated that repeated opportunities to assess similar assignments was a powerful way to get better at the task—and hence they appreciated that their grade was likely to improve with the practice. In addition, they felt somewhat less vulnerable to the whims of the instructor. Students understood that they could do repeated drafts of their graded assignments until they judged their performance to be at a level that would result in the grade they felt they needed. Students were in control of their grades to a degree they had not previously experienced.

Learning Is Emphasized Over Task Completion

When educators focus their assessments exclusively on submitted assignments, students come to believe that what counts in school is producing an acceptable end product or performance. If educators hope to create assessment-rich classrooms, they must signal to students that every task in school is seen as an opportunity to learn. Completing the task is not the objective; it is the means to achieving the objective. The use of the term *learning opportunities* rather than *assignments* represents an important distinction. Assessment-rich learning supports students in improving their performance by ensuring they are mindful in how they approach a challenge and have carefully assembled and weighed evidence. This may include reflecting on what additional information might be helpful to make a more sound argument, whether or not the criteria has been satisfied, or which of several possible thinking strategies would be most useful in helping them to reach a decision. Assessment-rich learning helps students focus on what they need to think about and do to improve rather than exclusively on what they have done well or poorly (Wiliam, 2007).

Assessment Is a Conversation, Not an Inquisition

Given a choice between being perceived to be lazy or stupid, most students opt for lazy. Rather than admitting they don't understand, many students choose to fail with dignity by opting not to complete work or not to make an effort. There is greater dignity in failure caused by lack of effort than from failure after making an effort. The focus of assessment on a specific product or performance makes assessment an inquisition of student work rather than a collaboration between teacher and student. In assessment-rich learning, the growth in students' thinking over time, their ability to provide feedback to others, and their openness to receive and integrate feedback to improve their own work are as important as the end product or performance.

A collaborative discussion is more likely if students look upon their teachers as coaches rather than umpires. While both umpires and coaches make judgments, umpires do so to enforce the rules of the game, while coaches' judgments are intended to advise their players on how best to improve their game. When students perceive teachers as umpires, they submit work to be judged; but when they see teachers as learning coaches, they seek guidance on how to improve.

Why Is Assessment-Rich Learning Important?

Despite the significant improvements, many current evaluation and assessment practices continue to impede learning. We discuss two obstacles to learning that assessment-rich learning seeks to overcome.

Misuse of Grades to Secure Compliance and Motivate Effort

Despite well-intentioned assessment practices, confusion over the primary purpose of assessment often inhibits its effectiveness. While it is common for educational authorities to proclaim that the primary purpose of assessment is to support student learning, many policies and practices in schools are designed to measure students' success at meeting curriculum goals, control student behavior, or sort students into various streams. Too often, fear of poor grades is used to pressure students to complete work or meet deadlines.

These uses of grades have created a mindset that Robert Pirsig (1999) in *Zen and the Art of Motorcycle Maintenance* characterized as "grade motivated," not "knowledge motivated." There is evidence that this mindset undermines student achievement:

- In one experiment, those students who were told they'd be graded on how well they learned a lesson had more trouble understanding the main point of the text than did the students who were told that no grades would be involved. Even on a measure of rote recall, the graded group remembered fewer facts a week later (Grolnick & Ryan, 1987).
- Another study found that students who were provided marks with no comments showed no gains in their learning, while students who were given comments but not marks showed on average an increase of 30 percent in their learning. Interestingly, those who were provided with marks and comments, as Mathew had been by his English teacher, also showed no gains in their learning. The presence of marks overshadowed the comments, making the effort to add comments to graded work a waste of the teacher's time (Wiliam, 2007).

Compounding this sense of a need to perform rather than to learn is the belief prevalent among university students (and likely more broadly among all students) that grades on assignments depend heavily on putting forth the ideas and opinions that are held by the course instructor (Wolcott, 1997).

Marginally Useful Teacher and Student Feedback

While students may be invited to undertake self- and peer assessments, our experiences show that most students are not particularly good at doing them. In fact, there is evidence to suggest that many teachers may not be adept at offering helpful feedback. For example, while teaching an online course to teachers a few years ago, I was frustrated by the poor quality of peer feedback the teachers provided to each other. When each other's work was posted for critique, most teachers simply wrote how useful and interesting they found their colleagues' work. Few were comfortable or skilled in providing specific and constructive feedback. Research suggests that praise offered to students that is not genuine and that is not accompanied by clear directions for further work can actually undermine student learning (Karpinski & D'Agostino, 2013, p. 203). The study also indicated that teachers who were rated as most effective offered praise slightly less often than other teachers and instead focused their comments on providing credible, specific, and honest feedback on how to improve. As well, students who became stuck on a problem and were given a completed solution showed little progress when provided with a new problem to work on. When given only as much help as they needed to get unstuck, students learned more and retained the learning longer.

What Practices Support Assessment-Rich Learning?

The shift from periodic feedback to routinely embedded comments can be enhanced by changing the way students and teachers look upon assessment, altering how it is structured and delivered, improving students' ability to provide and utilize assessment feedback, and making assessment more effective in supporting learning.

Shape Climate to Support Assessment-Rich Learning

The pursuit of assessment-rich learning begins by cultivating a climate in which students value thoughtful reflection and assessment. The goal is to help students see significant value in assessment. Various strategies can help students appreciate that self-review and commentary from others are two of their most valued learning supports.

Make the Experience Constructive. Students are likely to continue to dread assessments as long as they accentuate students' shortcomings. If teachers treat formative assessment simply as a prelude to summative assessment, they are more inclined to judge the work in light of a desired standard and to focus on its shortcomings. This need not be the case. Instead, teachers can focus on the strengths of a student's work and on a few manageable suggestions for improvement in areas that would be most productive. Offering more appreciative and useful commentaries helps students overcome their dread of formative assessment.

Create Rich Learning Tasks. Engaging students in peer and self-assessment is more likely when students are working on rich learning tasks that challenge them to think and allow them to deepen their understanding over a period of time. In addition, it helps that the task requires thinking. The opportunities for assessment-rich learning are limited when students believe that the objective is to find a correct answer or remember ideas provided by the teacher.

Promote the Value of Peer and Self-Assessment. It is important that students perceive peer and self-assessment as a way to bolster their own thinking—to make themselves "smarter" than they would be entirely on their own. A story told by comedian John Cleese explains this point. He observed that a colleague of his from the Monty Python troupe was naturally more talented than he was but that he routinely created better skits than the colleague. He explained that his colleague would hit upon an idea and that would be the idea he would run with. Cleese explained that he would work for several hours to revise, extend, and rework his initial idea, and in the end, because he had "lived with the problem longer," his skits were better (Cleese, n.d.). The important lesson for students from Cleese's experiences is that often their first answer will not be the best answer, and even if it is, by living with the problem, they will be able to test the idea.

One way to help students appreciate that they can improve their performance through trial and error, reflection, and revision is awarding marks for the quality of ongoing thinking that leads to a final product. This may include, for example, asking students for evidence that they tried more than one approach or developed more than one theory, that they considered the merits of various options, and that they were able to incorporate suggestions from others to improve their work.

Create Opportunities for Assessment-Rich Learning

Assessment-rich learning occurs where there are ever-present opportunities to benefit from self-review and comments from others. While there is value in setting aside designated times for so-called self-, peer, and teacher assessments where one individual is charged with providing feedback to another, there are many more opportunities for less formal ways to give and receive ideas to help rethink one's learning.

Create Timely Teacher–Student Exchanges. The commendable efforts by Mathew's English teacher to supply thoughtful, detailed comments on every student's paper bore little fruit because her feedback was not offered in a timely manner. As well, the volume of comments would likely overwhelm most students. Helpful comments should come throughout the learning, at a time when students can actually make use of the help and receive it packaged in manageable doses. This suggests redirecting assessment efforts to less formal and less intensive teacher–student exchanges such as quick checks, one-minute conversations, and exit tickets. While many teachers frequently employ assessments for learning strategies, all such checks are not necessarily effective. For example, orally asking a class for a definition of a word and receiving a good answer from the first student who raises a hand is not a reliable indicator that the class understands the concept. Wiggins and McTighe (2005) offer an ironic caution in this regard: "Students should be assumed innocent of understanding until proven guilty" (p. 247). Instead, teachers need to collect evidence of individual students' progress with the intent of helping them master the learning outcomes before they are graded. Assessment-rich learning is about finding unobtrusive, timely ways to determine who needs what kind of help and making sure they get it. And that includes helping students figure it out for themselves.

Broaden the Uses of Peer and Self-Assessment. In some circles, peer and self-assessment consist of a somewhat formal review of a person's own work or the work of another with the objective of rating and explaining the person's level of achievement. Often, this rating is aided by use of a rubric. Reducing the formality and diminishing the expectation of offering ratings can help reduce student resistance to peer and self-assessments and make it easier to embed them routinely into day-to-day teaching. Teachers will be more successful in embedding frequent peer and self-assessments into the routines of the classroom if they adopt a broader view of the forms in which self- and peer review may occur:

- **Critiques:** They are somewhat formal assessments where one person will enumerate the pros and cons of the work of another without necessarily offering any rating of the product or performance. Removing the tendency to link assessment with ratings diminishes the impression that it is only the final product or the final mark that matters.
- **Commentaries:** They involve less formal assessments than critiques. They include observations and insights as well as comments about merits and shortcomings. They tend to be collegial and do not normally involve the assignment of ratings. Commentaries can be reciprocal, where two or more individuals concurrently exchange views on their respective ideas. This two-way dialogue has the advantage of being easier to embed into daily lessons because it is more spontaneous than a critique that is offered by one person to another. For example, the commonly used strategy of think-pair-share can simply involve a sharing of ideas, or it can be framed as a reciprocal commentary where students comment on each other's thinking and receive immediate reactions from their peers.
- **Self-Reviews:** These are relatively informal assessments in which an individual or a group reflects on ideas and reassesses their thinking and behavior. The use of reflective learning logs and the more forward-looking Thoughtbooks described in Chapter 9 are useful strategies to help students reconsider and make ongoing revisions to their thinking.

Build Students' Capacity for Assessment-Rich Learning

The benefits of assessment-rich learning will not be realized unless students are able to provide helpful comments and are disposed to use the comments they receive.

Help Students Become Proficient at Self- and Peer Assessment. Students will not become effective self- and peer assessors without significant support. This means developing their ability to generate helpful observations and to frame them appropriately when sharing with others. One approach is to give students feedback on their feedback. This begins with helping students understand the criteria for productive peer commentary—that it should be respectful, warranted, specific, and constructive. Students will need guided opportunities to practice commenting on others' work. Students might then be able to use the criteria for the learning task to be critiqued as guidelines to generate useful ideas to share. In a practice session, students might then share their comments with the students who created the work, and a third group may be charged with observing how effectively the comments were provided. This process can be repeated until all students have commented on the work of others and critiqued the feedback provided by others.

Help Students Learn to Benefit From Feedback. The potential usefulness of assessments does not depend solely on the quality of the comments offered. Also important is students' willingness to receive suggestions and their ability to make use of them. If feedback is perceived as a criticism rather than as a critique, students will be less receptive and may simply ignore any advice. Clearly, the ability to benefit from commentary depends on the tone and quality of the feedback, but it also depends on the receptivity of the individual receiving it.

- **Recast Setbacks as Opportunities to Fail Forward:** One way to increase student receptivity is to encourage them to view failure as a learning opportunity. Students can learn to *fail forward* if they reframe setbacks as opportunities to become even better rather than to feel defeated. This mindset is needed when writing a book: an author wants to receive all of the feedback prior to going to print. Negative comments received after publication are too late and not helpful. Creating this mindset involves nurturing open-mindedness and perseverance. These habits are undermined when students consistently have one opportunity to complete a task and then are expected to move on to the next assignment. Assessment-rich learning requires that students regularly be given opportunities for revising and editing their work and their thinking based on helpful comments from the teacher, their peers, or their own self-assessment.
- **Encourage Active Listening:** Another strategy to increase receptivity is to encourage students (or groups of students) to assume an active listening role when receiving comments from others. This

involves limiting their responses to asking for clarification or elaboration, and confirming that the ideas offered by individual commentators are widely held. It helps to encourage recipients not to be defensive and not to feel that they should justify what they have done. Their primary role is to hear what others have to say, and after the critique is over, to decide for themselves which, if any, of the comments are worth acting upon.

- **Practice Making Use of Advice:** It is presumptuous to expect that all students, if given good advice, will be able to make effective use of it. One strategy to assist students in making good use of the comments they receive is to ask them to revise a piece of work that they have completed based on a set of comments provided by the teacher. Students can compare their attempts at revision with their peers to see how each of them profited or not from the teacher's commentary.

Provide Guidance That Informs Assessment-Rich Learning

Effective teacher comments should guide students in thoughtfully reflecting on the merits of their work and considering how they can advance their thinking. Feedback that appears merely to justify an assigned grade or that provides little direction for improvement may inhibit learning. In fact, Dylan Wiliam (2011) reports that poorly framed formative feedback actually impeded student learning in 40 percent of cases studied (p. 132).

Ensure That Teacher Comments Advance Student Learning. Ensuring that the comments provided to students are helpful is not only central to assessment-rich learning, but it ensures that teachers' investment of time and energy is not wasted.

A common dilemma teachers face is how to provide guidance that prompts students' thinking about their work and does not simply provide the answer. If students submit a draft paragraph with a weak topic sentence, the teacher may draw their attention to the inadequate topic sentence. If students respond by saying they have no idea how to improve the topic sentence, teachers often feel stymied. Telling students to "think harder" will do little to help them, and showing them how to fix the topic sentence will contribute to learned helplessness.

Teacher comments are often best framed as guiding questions and, when appropriate, should offer alternatives for students to consider. Offering three or four options can prompt thinking without providing the answer. It is also helpful to provide models to review as long as students can't simply copy the approach in their own work. Teacher comments must be genuine, address issues of substance, and include both praise and constructive comments. Pointing out deficiencies in student work without offering guidance can undermine student confidence and achievement. Similarly, praise that is unwarranted or that addresses a clearly insignificant aspect of the work will be dismissed as insincere. As illustrated by the enhanced versions of the original comments listed in Figure 11.2, teacher feedback should be honest, respectful, specific, manageable, and constructive.

Figure 11.2   Reworking Teacher Comments to Enhance Effectiveness

Original Comment	Enhanced Comment	Rationale for Revision
Your understanding of the key ideas is deficient.	Can you think of how you might make your understanding of (X) clearer? Perhaps you might review (Y), then revise it, trying for greater clarity.	Revised comments identify the nature of the deficiency and the area where the deficiency occurs.
Effective use of visuals to capture attention; however, the insights into the issue reflected by the text is weak.	The use of the table to organize ideas in section (X) is very effective. I wonder if something similar could be used in section (Y) to clarify the important ideas.	Original comment explained why the grade was assigned but provided little support for how the student might work toward a stronger response.
You present some very interesting ideas, but the organization of your ideas is somewhat confusing.	I was interested by the ideas you presented. What was the central point you were trying to make? Perhaps you could map out what you see as the central point, the key arguments, and the supporting evidence for each argument. This might help you to restructure your response with greater clarity.	Revised comments offer students clear direction for next steps.

Concluding Thoughts

Assessment can undermine students' confidence and impede their learning or it can potentially be one of the most powerful tools in teachers' instructional repertoire. Used thoughtfully, assessment can inspire and empower students and greatly improve their learning. But this requires that assessments be viewed with a different mindset, that they be embedded more seamlessly into classroom routines, and that teachers and students are more adept at providing helpful comments that will actually be used by students to inform their learning.

Practices That Support Assessment-Rich Learning

Shape Climate	• Help students find significant value in assessment.
Create Opportunities	• Create timely teacher–student exchanges. • Broaden the uses of peer and self-assessment.
Build Capacity	• Help students become proficient at peer and self-assessment. • Help students learn to benefit from feedback.
Provide Guidance	• Ensure that teacher comments advance student learning.

The following box contains selected strategies for educational leaders to use with teachers to encourage assessment-rich learning.

Opportunities for Leadership

Create a Tone of "Opportunity to Learn" When Presented With Teacher Shortcomings

Resist the natural tendency to focus on what is deficient and instead look upon shortcomings as a learning opportunity.

Model the Qualities of Helpful Critique in Your Own Dealings

When situations arise involving educators' work, be deliberate about offering comments that are honest, respectful, specific, manageable, and constructive.

12

Enhance Learning Through Digital Technology

This chapter explains what is involved in digitally enhanced learning and how technology offers unprecedented educational opportunities and efficiencies—but only if used well. More specifically, the chapter discusses

- what it means to digitally enhance learning;
- how many well-meaning efforts to integrate digital technology into classrooms are failing to have a **significant** impact;
- why it matters that educators find powerful ways to enhance learning through the use of digital technology;
- practices that support the use of digital technology to amplify student learning.

When interactive whiteboards were gaining popularity across North America, a large school district in the eastern United States invested in over 10,000 boards and planned an ambitious rollout for every school in the district. The district wisely realized that training in using the technology by itself would be insufficient to effect significant gains in student achievement. Our consortium was invited to support teams of teachers across grades and subjects in a multiyear project to embed thinking as the

> To succeed in our struggle to build technology and new media to support learning, we must move far beyond the traditional view of teaching as delivery of information.
>
> —John Seely Brown (n.d.)

cornerstone of learning in their schools, using interactive technologies to assist with this goal.

In working with these teachers, we helped them use their interactive boards as hubs to access other digital resources, including videos and digital content that expanded the scope of the ideas that students considered. Teachers learned to empower students as image detectives using spotlight tools to isolate and magnify sections of images for closer examination. We helped teachers nurture collaborative student problem solving in mathematics. Student teams used the interactive board to share provisional solutions to an assigned open-ended problem; subsequent groups built upon previous groups' efforts, which had been saved for display and modification. Students compared different solutions to identify criteria for a sound answer.

Grade by grade and subject by subject, we helped teachers see the potential of interactive whiteboards to support a thinking classroom. One of the middle schools involved in this project was located in an impoverished area with traditionally poor test results. Students had failed to meet the state standards in the previous two years, and the school was under review when we began our work. In the year following the schoolwide adoption of our thinking approach, the school soared past state standards and was removed from the under-review list. The school reported results on multiple-unit tests administered to four sixth-grade mathematics classes that showed a 32 percent increase in the number of students successfully meeting the expected unit indicators (from 34 to 45 percent of students) and a 167 percent increase in the number of students exceeding the expected unit indicators (from 15 to 40 percent of students). After working with our team, the school progressed from a situation where 51 percent of sixth-grade students were performing below the standard in mathematics to one where only 15 percent of students were performing below the standard.

This experience illustrates how valuable it can be to harness digital technology, including the use of 3-D printers, interactive whiteboards, tablets, and the myriad of available apps as well as digitally accessed content and other emerging technologies, in support of a thinking classroom. Digital technology should be an indispensable component of every classroom, both because of the need to prepare digitally literate students who will contribute to a world that is increasingly digital and also because specific technologies can amplify and extend the learning opportunities available to students. But technology has a seductive appeal because it is cutting edge and impressive. This has led to its use simply for its own sake. Not only is this a waste of time and money, but it distracts educators from pursuing the goals that need to underpin learning in the 21st century. Ensuring that digital technology use enhances learning is one of five core principles for learning that should inform educators' decisions about almost every aspect of their practice.

What Is Digitally Enhanced Learning?

There is no doubt that digital technology has significantly impacted many facets of our daily lives, from banking to telecommunications and from how we book travel to how we shop. Some would argue that a similar revolution is happening in our schools with cloud-based apps, tablets, and bring your own device (BYOD) policies. Certainly, the environment in which learning takes place is changing—but are these changes enhancing learning? A quick survey of the Internet will reveal extensive recommendations about ways to infuse digital technology into classrooms but very limited discussions about the use of digital technology to enhance learning.[1] The push toward virtual classrooms has proceeded despite research that suggests this may not improve results. A study of thousands of virtual charter-school students in eighteen states found that these students "performed dramatically worse on standardized tests relative to similar students in traditional schools" (Barnum, 2017). It is unclear whether the decline in achievement is a result of less intensive face-to-face teacher and student interactions or whether we have not learned how to effectively integrate digital technologies with existing classroom practices. Regardless, a more robust pedagogy is needed in order to realize the potential of new technologies.

Our focus in this chapter is on the use of digital technology to ensure that the competencies, understanding, and commitments discussed in earlier chapters are advanced directly or indirectly through the use of technology. The term *digitally enhanced learning* refers to the use of a variety of digital technologies within virtual and face-to-face classrooms to enrich learning environments and experiences beyond what was possible through nondigital means. In other words, if educators could achieve similar or better results without the inclusion of digital technology, then the infusion of the technology has not enhanced learning.

> Digitally enhanced learning is the use of digital technologies within virtual and face-to-face classrooms to enrich learning environments and experiences beyond what was possible through nondigital means.

Distinguishing Digitally Enhanced From Digitally Infused Learning

If schools are going to invest in digital technology, they must find the value added to their students' learning by considering how the technology allows for greater interaction with and enhanced students' understanding of the material. Too often, scarce education dollars are spent on infusing digital technology into classrooms, but it does little to strengthen student learning by stimulating deeper understanding and innovation, increasing the ability to use information in productive ways, or enabling more effective collaboration among students. Digitally enhanced learning is about seizing the opportunities afforded by new technology for nurturing understanding, competency, and commitment in a thinking classroom. Figure 12.1 illustrates how educators can enhance common practices that merely infuse technology to add real value to learning.

Figure 12.1   Distinguishing Digitally Enhanced and Digitally Infused Learning

Infused but Not Enhanced	Opportunities for Digitally Enhanced Learning
Providing Students With Tablets	
Students use a variety of apps instead of hard-copy resources to access similar or the same information (which may be even more dangerous than in the past if students do not know how to filter information, because online materials often have fewer filters than materials prepared for educational uses). Students independently learn from apps that reinforce rote learning.	• Apps are carefully selected to support critical, creative, and collaborative thinking, and are organized on the tablet around three broad phases of inquiry: inputs, processing, and outputs. • Students use the tablets to access materials otherwise unavailable or in modes (e.g., video, visuals, artifacts, audio) that would not be otherwise available. • Students use apps to create polished forms of media productions, or they use apps to record practice or final performances for immediate feedback from themselves or others.
Installing Interactive Whiteboards in Classrooms	
Interactive whiteboards are used in a way that reinforces a teacher-centric classroom involving delivery of content. They are used to create more entertaining lessons with visuals and sound, but students are still passive recipients of information.	• Interactive whiteboards are used to reinforce a community of thinkers by providing a medium in which students can share their thinking with their classmates. • Use of interactive whiteboards creates greater efficiencies, and therefore more learning time, in the delivery of a multimodal lesson.
Purchasing 3-D Printers for the School	
Students are able to watch the creation of the pieces required to build a predesigned bridge. Students assemble a variety of catapults and test out each of the designs to see which launches the projectile the farthest.	• Students design, print, assemble, test, and revise their design of a bridge until it meets the specifications required. • Students design, print, assemble and test, and revise an antisiege machine.

Infused but Not Enhanced	Opportunities for Digitally Enhanced Learning
Adopting BYOD Policies	
Students use their personal devices to quickly access content but apply no filters in selecting what to believe and record. Students use their personal devices to take notes, complete calculations, and take pictures, but rarely think about the information they are recording or the answers they have calculated.	• Personal devices are used as curiosity amplifiers by encouraging students to confirm or add to ideas, or to find relevant information to solve a problem. • Instant access to an almost endless body of information is used as an opportunity to create a climate of healthy skepticism. • Personal devices are used to help students organize and store a more varied body of information than has been possible in the past, including storing and organizing videos, drawings, audio recordings, and written notes using information-gathering software.
Using File Hosting Services to Share and Cocreate Materials	
Students access and contribute to material anywhere/anytime but do not collaborate in a way that deepens each other's thinking or improves the quality of their work. Students post their work to compile a common document, but the online environment does not involve actual collaboration in the forming of ideas or responses to a challenge. Students read online content rather than hard copy, but otherwise, their interactions with the materials are no different than with hard-copy materials.	• Students are routinely expected to use the online platform to critique and offer feedback to their peers. • The online platform is used as a space for collaborative "genius" to flourish as students share and build on the ideas of others. • Students learn to collaboratively read materials by adding annotations that provide clarity, raise questions, and make connections to the big ideas that frame the learning. • The features of the file hosting service are used to support sustained inquiry by allowing students to assemble, revise, and test ideas collaboratively as learning progresses.
Replacing or Supplementing Hard-Copy Textbooks With Digital Textbooks	
Students have access to textbook materials anywhere and in a more convenient (lighter) format with more interesting features such as embedded video. However, the interactions with the materials don't go beyond passive consumption of information.	• Digital technology allows for a rethinking of the role textbooks play in classrooms. They become sources of information that present a variety of perspectives and ideas through a variety of media that are used to support students as they engage with authentic challenges. • The contents of textbooks should be problematized (e.g., select the most useful information to respond to a challenge) and not presented as a body of information to be accepted without scrutiny.

Recognizing a Digitally Enhanced Classroom

At first glance, using nondigital and digital technologies in classrooms may appear to create very different learning environments. Consider the following examples.

Using Technology Before the Digital Age. Delivering a multimodal lesson to students in the 1960s would have been quite challenging. Teachers would have had to book and set up a film projector to play a film they would have ordered weeks in advance from the board office media library, find music on a tape and arrange for a tape player, set up an overhead or slide projector, and perhaps arrange to have markers and chart paper on hand. Even after all of this effort to assemble the "technology" needed for multimodal learning, the content would still have been limited to what could be gleaned from textbooks or the few other resources that teachers may have been able to assemble.

Figure 12.2   A 20th Century Classroom

Source: Library and Archives Canada. Credit: Gar Lunney/National Film Board Fonds/e010975628.

Using Technology in the Digital Age. Flash forward to the present. That same multimodal lesson can now be delivered through an interactive whiteboard or with a laptop and a projector with all the required technology centralized and available when needed. In addition, with access to the Internet, the available resources are boundless—websites, guest experts brought in by videophone, image banks from major museums and art galleries, and videos from online repositories.

Is the learning really that different in these two classrooms? The answer depends on how the technology is being used. Are students passively listening to a virtual or face-to-face guest speaker, or are they posing powerful questions to the guest that are designed to elicit information to inform their inquiry? Are students unquestioningly accepting information presented to them, or are they scrutinizing sources and considering the relevance and credibility of the information they find? When students use technology to connect with others around the world, are they merely posting information to share their research, or are they genuinely collaborating by integrating new ideas into their own responses, providing productive feedback, and considering a variety of perspectives? Unless the answers to these questions suggest that the new technologies are being used to support deeper thinking, then, at heart, learning in the classrooms of the 21st century may not differ much from that of the 20th century.

Figure 12.3   A 21st Century Classroom

Identifying Criteria for Digitally Enhanced Learning

[I]t is not whether technology is used (or not) which makes the difference, but how well the technology is used to support teaching and learning.... It is therefore the pedagogy of the application of technology in the classroom which is important: the how rather than the what.

—Michael Fullan and
Maria Langworthy (2014, p. 30)

Creating digitally enhanced learning requires more than the integration of new digital technologies into classroom practices. Digitally enhanced learning occurs only if the integration of these technologies leads to deeper understanding and greater competency. Eight criteria are helpful in guiding the use of digital technology to ensure that it actually enhances learning. These criteria are explained and exemplified in Figure 12.4.

Figure 12.4   Criteria to Guide Digitally Enhanced Learning

Criteria	Applications
Increase Authentic Learning Opportunities Digital technologies provide meaningful real-life learning tasks that would not be as easily available or as effective without the infusion of technology.	• Students use archival records to assemble evidence from the past; students use safe online student communities to connect with children around the world to learn about life in different countries. • Students use microlending sites to participate in worthy development projects and student enterprises around the world. • Students use video editing software to create high-quality media products that support a local or global cause.
Promote Rigorous Engagement With the Curriculum Digital technologies allow for careful examination of evidence and access to evidence and artifacts that would either not be available or would be more difficult to examine without technology.	• Students virtually handle digital copies of rare artifacts that have been scanned, allowing students to closely inspect them and zoom in and turn them over, in order to determine composition and purpose.
Enhance Creativity Digital technologies encourage students to generate and test ideas with immediate results, and easily revise them at little or no cost in time or money.	• Using three-dimensional digital sculpting and painting software, students sculpt in virtual clay to create creatures, vehicles, or other artifacts to populate a graphic novel.

Criteria	Applications
	• Word processing programs allow for quick movement of materials, easy editing, and quick reformatting, making reworking of writing spawned by new ideas easy to do.
Increase Collaboration Digital technologies create opportunities and platforms for more students to work together to solve complex problems and to share ideas while ensuring accountability of all students.	• Using an online platform, students across a province or state or even around the world can share ideas and insights. • Collaborative writing tools allow students to write collaboratively while tracking each student's contribution to the work.
Expand the Range of Perspectives Digital technologies provide greater ease of access to a wider range of resources, reflecting a broader spectrum of views across a wide range of media.	• Interactive news-sharing sites provide daily access to newspapers around the world, allowing just-in-time examination of reactions to world events from multiple perspectives. • Access to experts via videophone and web-based collections of the great museums of the world provide materials never before available to students.
Foster Efficient Delivery of Lessons Digital technologies provide multimodal lessons in a more efficient manner than could be achieved without the technology.	• Embedding videos, songs, and other forms of media into presentation software allows for easy and efficient use. • The ability to assemble materials digitally reduces the time needed to order materials from a central board location or dependence on signing out various pieces of equipment from the school media center.
Differentiate Learning Digital technologies increase diversity in the ways teachers present lesson materials and offer students a broader range of ways to develop and demonstrate their learning than would be possible without the use of technology.	• Embedding visuals, graphical representations, and audio using presentation software helps all students to engage with a lesson. • Students can choose to demonstrate their learning in many media, including songs created in music recording software, films made in video editing tools, or posters assembled in graphic design software.
Empower Self-Regulation Digital technologies increase students' ability to complete tasks in personally responsible, self-reflective ways without relying on others to tell them what to do.	• Using mathematics sites, students can enter their answer to an algebra question and within seconds see a graph of their answer, allowing them to check for reasonableness.

Why Is Digitally Enhanced Learning Important?

Providing teachers and students with access to current technology is a widespread ongoing challenge for schools. And yet the investment in digital technology often does little to improve students' learning and can actually undermine the very goals that are central to 21st century learning. There are three reasons why the use of digital technology needs to enhance teaching and learning.

> One thing is clear, technology can amplify great teaching, but great technology will never replace poor teaching.
>
> —Andreas Schleicher (2016)

The World Is Going Digital

Use of digital technology is necessary if schools are to be relevant in the 21st century. The world is being transformed by digital technologies. Virtually every aspect of our daily lives has been impacted by digital technology:

- **Shopping:** The number of online shoppers worldwide is expected to surpass two billion by 2021, and the value of goods and services sold online is expected to exceed $4 trillion (Statista, 2017).
- **Banking:** In 2013, 51 percent of American adults used online banking (Fox, 2013).
- **Access to Information:** Digital technology is transforming the way people receive and share information, communicate with friends and family, navigate our way to unfamiliar destinations, or even feed our curiosity.
- **Work:** The flow of economic reports and employment results attest to the increasing digitization of work environments and of the products and services that companies offer.

The role of teaching must be to prepare children for a world beyond school that is changing in unpredictable ways. To do so, the use of digital technology must become more than an occasional visit to a lab, and we must ensure that the integration of digital technology enhances the core competencies students will need to succeed in a rapidly changing world. Ineffective integration of technology wastes billions of dollars in scarce educational funds and inadequately prepares students for a digital economy. Evidence shows poor technology use becomes a distraction that contributes to underperforming students. A 2015 Organisation for Economic Co-operation and Development report concludes:

The reality in our schools lags considerably behind the promise of technology. . . . And even where computers are used in the class-room, their impact on student performance is mixed at best. Students who use computers moderately at school tend to have somewhat better learning outcomes than students who use computers rarely. But students who use computers very frequently at school do a lot worse in most learning outcomes, even after accounting for social background and student demographics. (p. 3)

Effective Use of Digital Technologies Must Be Taught

Learning how to operate digital technologies is insufficient. Students need to be taught how to use them purposefully and thoughtfully. An important role of schools in a digital environment is to show students how to effectively use technology as a tool for learning and thinking. In the past, students primarily consumed information that had been assembled into a coherent narrative and was subject to a number of filters, including those exercised by reviewers, editors, and in some cases, state regulatory bodies. Today, information readily accessible on the Internet has few or no filters, making it imperative that students learn to view information skeptically and apply criteria for assessing the credibility of sources. As well, the Internet is a highly visual medium, and students are increasingly becoming visual learners—but they are not necessarily visually literate. If they are to become competent users of the Internet, students need to be taught to scrutinize images, question sources, and navigate websites beyond merely clicking on the boldface words.

Without guidance, students may simply use inferior digital resources to replace superior-quality nondigital resources. For example, students may forego using a printed textbook that is controlled for reading level and quality for a digital text with little or no value added to the content. Students need to be taught to recognize the inherent merits and limitations in each technology so that they thoughtfully select and properly use the most appropriate one for their needs. Teaching students to consider the purpose and audience for their work helps them learn to choose the best digital tool and to effectively utilize its features.

Learning Can Be Greatly Enhanced

Digital technologies have the potential to add great value to learning. Educators can make use of this potential in many ways:

Expanding the Variety and Breadth of Voices That Students Encounter in Their Learning. In the past, students were often limited to the printed materials that were available in the classroom and local libraries, or to the individuals encountered on a daily basis. Today's students may have access to a broad range of written, audio, and visual sources, and can bring virtual guests like astronaut Commander Peggy Whitson into their classrooms from as far away as the International Space Station.

Ensuring Students Benefit From Increased Interactions With Others. The use of file-sharing platforms and cloud-based apps enable students to exchange ideas and co-construct responses to challenges with peers who may be in their class or possibly somewhere else in a province, state, country, or the world.

Broadening the Means by Which Students Communicate Their Learning and Contribute to Knowledge Construction. The range of tools available that allow students to show what they have learned has exploded in the past few years. Students can now create professional-looking flyers, digital posters, or polished video presentations, and can share their work through numerous social media sites.

What Practices Support Digitally Enhanced Learning?

While passing through security in the Dubai airport, I was fascinated to see airport avatars instructing travelers on what they were allowed to take on board in their carry-on luggage. These avatars are reliable and inexpensive relative to the yearly salaries paid to humans. So why not place an avatar at the front of every classroom? The reason, as Steve Jobs noted, is because effective teaching and learning requires a thoughtful teacher who can choreograph learning to meet students' needs. Used effectively by a skilled teacher, digital technology can enhance learning by ensuring it serves as a curiosity amplifier and a means to share ideas, and enables students to challenge each other, reach new understandings, and create innovative products.

All of the practices discussed in the chapter on a thinking classroom apply equally to digital technology. Here are additional practices that are especially relevant when using digital technology to enhance learning in a thinking classroom.

Shape Climate to Support Digitally Enhanced Learning

The tone in the classroom that teachers set regarding the use of digital technologies is a first step in helping students use them as learning tools and not simply for entertainment.

Expect Students to Use Digital Technologies as Learning Tools. Initially, students are often more impressed with the features of digital technologies than they are with their contents and learning potential. There are various strategies that teachers can use to signal to students that support for learning is the primary role for digital technology use in classrooms.

- Support students in seeing the potential for deep learning that can result from effective use of digital technology, but ensure that they know that deeper learning does not occur merely from using the technology.
- Help students learn to make thoughtful selections and use technology effectively to meet intended purposes by making sure they understand the biases inherent in all technology. For example, while online social networking messages may be effective for sharing links or drawing attention to issues, the brevity of the messages prevents them from being an effective tool for discussing serious social issues.
- Maximize the utility of the digital technologies selected by exploring with students the various features and considering which of the features are most suited to a given task. For example, presentation software can be an interesting way to organize information, but zooming in and out too often can make a presentation nauseating.
- Foster open-mindedness by encouraging students to rethink their assumptions as they encounter different views or new information (e.g., newspaper-sharing websites provide instant access to news from around the world every day). Access to multiple perspectives on global events can feed curiosity and challenge assumptions, and encourage open-mindedness as students explore diverse views.

Create Opportunities for Digitally Enhanced Learning

There are countless ways in which technology can be infused into classrooms; the key is to ensure that these opportunities actually enhance learning.

Use Diverse Forms of Technology to Amplify Learning Opportunities and Perspectives. As suggested earlier, technology enhances learning when it creates conditions and opportunities that could not be as easily achieved using nondigital technology. Digital technology can achieve this by enabling authentic learning situations that draw upon a broad range of perspectives and resources, engaging students more effectively in critical and creative thinking, and supporting differentiation and self-regulated learning.

- Embed the use of a wide variety of technologies to support various phases of inquiry.
  - **Inputs:** Tools to support access to credible information;
  - **Processing:** Tools to support discussion, organization, and manipulation of ideas;
  - **Outputs:** Tools to enable creation and sharing of conclusions and insights.

  All three phases of inquiry can be opportunities for digitally enhanced learning. For example, students might access digital content through websites, virtual guests, and social media as they assemble evidence for consideration. They then might use digital tools that help organize information graphically. Finally, students could use presentation software to create a dynamic presentation, video editing software to create a documentary, or a 3-D printer to create reproductions of artifacts.
- Ensure that the selected digital technology enhances the intended learning targets. A high school biology student was frustrated by having to use inappropriate software to create a cartoon that explained the concept of genetic drift. Having to learn the software without support did nothing to advance her understanding of the science that was the focus of the learning and required a much greater investment of time than did learning the science. Other digital tools would have been better aligned to the intended learning and been far more efficient with this student's time.
- Routinely use diverse sources of information that introduce multiple perspectives and competing narratives that consider a range of possibilities. For example, create an inquiry lesson using a format that invites students to consider information hosted by various groups to help students select relevant and credible information.

Build Capacity for Digitally Enhanced Learning

Simply because students can use many of the technologies that they encounter does not mean that they can use them well, and it certainly doesn't mean they can use them to maximal effect as learning tools.

Teach Students to Skillfully Select and Use Digital Technology. We wouldn't expose students to a buzz saw without careful instruction on how to use it responsibly, nor should we expose students to digital tools without teaching them about responsible and effective use.

- Introduce students to several digital tools and require them to select the most appropriate tools to construct, test, revise, and integrate their ideas.
- Encourage collaborative sense-making where students make connections between lessons and among key ideas, events, and concepts. There are sites that connect students from around the world, and other sites that enable collaboration and allow use of various modalities through which students can share their thoughts on a topic or issue.
- Present all information as an opportunity for thoughtful scrutiny rather than blind consumption. This is more important than ever. Traditionally, most resources had filters controlling what students read or saw. Many current information sources that students encounter have few, if any, filters. Instead of using the lack of filters as a reason to ban students from unregulated online encyclopedia sites, use the questionable credibility to provoke students' interest in assessing their sources.
- Download authentic examples from digital media to model exemplary and nonexemplary work.

Provide Guidance to Inform Digitally Enhanced Learning

The technology focus in classrooms is typically used as a teaching and learning tool. It can also be profitably used as an assessment tool.

Encourage Teacher and Student Use of Technology to Provide Timely and Useful Feedback. Teachers and students can use technology to enhance assessment by capturing demonstrations of students' learning, providing constructive feedback, and fostering iterative revision.

- Use digital tools to offer and receive just-in-time feedback to deepen students' understanding and improve teacher–student communication. These tools include
  - online tools that facilitate peer-to-peer critiques of written assignments;
  - apps that record a performance that can be played back in slow motion, allowing for self- or peer critiques; or
  - cloud-based tools that allow collaboration and feedback through multiple media.
- Create a digital Thoughtbook, using software in which various forms of media can be organized and stored, that allows students to try a performance or draft a product, then revise it as learning deepens. This may involve using software to record a piece of choreography

in a dance class, a piece of music, or while practicing layups in bas-ketball; or using a smartphone to capture and store an image for future reference of a pencil and paper sketch of a model utopia.

- In place of pen and paper quizzes, use digital tools such as response devices (clickers) or mobile response apps for immediate assessment of student understanding and the opportunity for teachers to adjust instruction in a timely manner.

Concluding Thoughts

The vision for powerful learning transcends eras and fads. Technology will continue to change at an increasingly rapid pace. Today's tablets will be replaced by as yet uninvented technologies. Using digital technology to support 21st century learners requires finding ways in which that technology creates conditions and opportunities that enhance learning. Educators must resist the lure of short bursts of interest gained from introducing students to novel technologies and seek thoughtful integration of technology in the support of a thinking classroom. Despite the considerable challenges presented by the advent of the digital age, educators should embrace the opportunities made available through classroom use of digital technologies.

Practices That Support Digitally Enhanced Learning

Shape Climate	• Expect students to use digital technologies as learning tools.
Create Opportunities	• Use diverse forms of technology to amplify learning opportunities and perspectives.
Build Capacity	• Teach students to skillfully select and use digital technology.
Provide Guidance	• Encourage teacher and student use of technology to provide timely and useful feedback.

The next box contains selected strategies for educational leaders to use with teachers to build their support for digitally enhanced learning.

Opportunities for Leadership

Invest in Technologies That Hold the Greatest Potential

Not all technologies are equally powerful. As a staff, select digital technologies that use education dollars wisely to provide the biggest impact on achievement of 21st century goals.

Focus Professional Learning on the Educational Use of Digital Technologies

Implementing new technologies without sufficient pedagogical training leads to poor implementation. Ensure that professional learning support for teachers on the use of digital technology focuses on ways to enhance the goals of 21st century learning and not primarily on how to operate a tool.

Help Educators Recognize the Limits of and Opportunities Offered by Various Technologies

Not unlike their students, educators must be helped to recognize how the particular features of each technology biases it to serve some purposes but not others (e.g., microphones assist with audibility but may limit mobility and shared discussion).

Note

1. One of the few exceptions is discussion about digitally enhanced learning from the California Council on Science and Technology (2011).

PART V

Support
Teacher Growth

13

Leading a Renovation, Not a Revolution

This chapter explores the idea of renovation as a guiding metaphor for school and districtwide reform. More specifically, it discusses

- why renovation is a more helpful mindset than revolution when leading educational change;
- the importance of framing reform efforts as professional inquiries that are supported in coherent, comprehensive, and continuous ways;
- practices that educational leaders can adopt to guide and support change in their school or district.

Our team began to offer professional learning support to various schools across India in 2003, but particularly at Vivek High School in Chandigarh, which was led by a visionary principal, Mrs. P. K. Singh. Our inaugural three-week visit consisted of presentations to the entire school staff, smaller grade and subject meetings,

> New teaching practices need to be discussed face-to-face in ways that make clear how their use fits with one's current practices and professional identity.
>
> —David Johnson and Roger Johnson (1994)

and planning time with individual teachers. Near the end of the first visit, several influential teachers on staff made a point of thanking me for my efforts but explained that while this "thinking approach" might work in Canada, it was not the Indian way. They cited several illustrative differences; one that stands out was that what I had called *group work* was in India called *cheating*.

In taking stock of the level of staff receptivity at the end of this first visit, we judged that 3 of the staff of over 100 teachers appreciated the ideas and were highly motivated to continue, largely because the approach closely matched their own philosophical orientation to teaching. The majority of teachers were still unsure what all of this meant, and the sizable old guard was strongly opposed to the idea of a thinking approach. Their view was that the current system was working—this was an elite school after all—and besides, this new approach seemed to require a lot of work.

On subsequent trips, we continued to work with the entire staff, encouraging every teacher to try one thinking lesson each month. And we made sure to provide extra support to the most committed teachers. We raised their profiles by bringing them with us when we offered sessions to other schools. We encouraged them and others to develop lessons that we would share more broadly. Gradually, the number of teachers who wanted to learn and do more grew to fifteen. This core group started off as a writing team but soon became school leaders, acting as a primary line of support for other teachers in their grade or subject groups. One of the great advantages of teacher interactions in Indian schools is considerable shared lesson planning. Typically, one of the three or four teachers in a grade level would prepare a lesson that the others would use with their students. Another positive factor was growing teacher recognition of the difference in student reactions. Teachers started to notice that students from across the hall were emerging with uncharacteristic excitement after participating in a "thinking" lesson. One of the memorable turning points occurred when we modeled teaching the same topic using the didactic discovery and thinking approaches. For many teachers, this was the first time they really saw the differences we had been talking about.

After two and a half years of semiannual visits, we had effected some change. In a poll of 550 fifth- to eleventh-grade students, 72 percent reported that the thinking approach was more interesting than conventional activities, and 86 percent said it had helped them learn. The school climate had shifted toward supporting the approach. Many of the old guard had had a change of heart or had moved on either to retirement or other placements. Twenty-five teachers had earned certificates for meeting agreed-upon criteria for notable effort. The staff had assembled a substantial bank of lessons that were used regularly and revised. Most teachers implemented thinking lessons at least periodically, but even then, not everyone understood what they were doing. Despite the successes, the level of adoption was not where we thought it should be. We were frustrated by the impediments that are familiar to educators in every country, including ever-changing staff, conflicting school priorities, changes in administration, long gaps in professional support, and teacher fatigue. But the school was a different place than it was when we first encountered it, and many hundreds of students have since benefited from an enhanced environment where, among other changes, group work is no longer seen to be cheating.

Our experiences in India helped us realize that educational reform is never a destination; it is always a work in progress. We never achieved our targets, and even as we got close, other issues arose that required us to deviate or pause. In this respect, educational reform is like life itself—both are journeys. And there are no silver bullets that once put in place will fix everything.

These insights are helpful when contemplating the current calls for a revolution in education. Citing the system's perceived failure to effectively prepare students for the real world, vocal advocates push for sweeping and substantive changes. The scale of these demands is overwhelming. The totality of the practices described in this book is overwhelming if educators see them as things to be achieved all at once. In this respect, the talk of revolutionary change is potentially counterproductive and certainly fear inducing. Just as in life, we must take one day at a time, doing what we can do to make things a bit better than the day before. If we do this faithfully, and remember to look back periodically to see the distance we've traveled, we will likely surprise ourselves with what we have achieved. In this chapter, we explore how educational leaders might work with teachers to thoughtfully shepherd them through the potentially daunting tasks we have described. The metaphor of *renovation* provides an empowering and prudent mindset to guide this important and necessary journey at the classroom, school, or jurisdictional level.

Why Think Renovation?

To begin, it is worth considering how the metaphor of renovation orients educational leaders with a different and more promising mindset than does the metaphor of revolutionary change.

What Distinguishes Revolution and Renovation Mindsets?

In an educational change context, there are three features that distinguish remodeling from starting over.

Building on What Is There Versus Seeking to Make a Clean Sweep. Leading an educational renovation is premised on the belief that it is preferable to revise existing structures, whereas educational revolution invites wholesale replacement because current practices are obsolete, headed in the wrong direction, or otherwise not worth salvaging. Revolutionary change seeks to quickly remove (not modify) existing practices and implement a significantly different alternative. This may require system-wide changes such as redesigning school structures or redrafting gradu-ation requirements. Changes may be more contained but nevertheless revolutionary—for example, imple-menting a new approach to unit planning or prohibiting use of text-books to precipitate changes in teach-ing practices.

> When you improve a little each day, eventually big things occur . . . [D]on't look for the quick, big improvement. Seek the small improvement one day at a time. That's the only way it happens—and when it happens it lasts.
>
> —John Wooden, highly successful basketball coach (Nater & Gallimore, 2010, p. 52)

Working Gradually, Possibly Toward Transformation, Versus Working Rapidly Toward Transformation. A renovation mindset believes that change must be ongoing and incremental. Over time, it can be transforma-tive, but not in the short term. Advocates of revolutionary change operate from the assumption that anything less than transformation will be inad-equate, and the best way to bring this about is to get things done while there is momentum, popular interest, and resources.

Adapting Based on What Is Uncovered Versus Fixing a Course Based on Predetermined Problems and Solutions. Renovation-oriented change begins with a general idea of the focus but anticipates that the specific directions will need to be adjusted as new issues and problems are uncov-ered. A revolutionary change begins with a decision that things need to be improved in specific ways for reasons that are understood before the changes are embarked upon.

Why Adopt a Renovation Mindset?

Educational leaders are often pressured to seek immediate, predetermined changes to the school system. The bleak history of large-scale educational innovations suggests that pressing for wholesale changes isn't a very robust approach. Rather, we believe for several reasons that making small but continual adjustments will ultimately lead to greater and more sustain-able improvement.

Builds on Existing Strengths and Practices. The tendency in education when something isn't working well is to replace it. There are several con-cerns with this orientation. It unwittingly eliminates many good practices that aren't accommodated by the new initiative. It operates on the dubious assumption that all of the benefits from present practices will be included in the new regimen. Typically, this results in the proverbial throwing the baby out with the bathwater. The tendency to replace rather than enrich practice explains in part why the history of planned educational change has had such modest results. For example, teachers may feel that they "did" critical thinking last year and now they are being asked to do problem-based learning—in which case, previous years' efforts are shunted aside to make room for this year's innovations. A preferable approach is to treat existing practices as platforms to build upon. In our shoulder-to-shoulder work with teachers, we have noticed that encouraging them to revise existing lesson plans leads to small, but not insignificant, changes to their practice.

Allows for More Individual Self-Direction and Less Mass Imposition. If the educational system were monolithic, it might be feasible to implement a common fix across all settings. Initiatives such as project-based learning are potentially powerful approaches to learning. But it is unrealistic to expect that any single approach will be the best method in every subject area and that it will fit with all teaching styles and strengths.

Not only are individuals different, but so are the needs for change. The extent of educational reform will depend entirely on the state of individual schools and teacher practices. Very few ideas for educational reform are brand new. Many have been around for a decade or more, others for centuries. This means that they are already present to greatly varying degrees in every school and classroom. For some, the renovations required to meet the called-for expectations will be relatively modest; others will require substantial refurbishing. It should not be presumed that the same approach will serve these diverse situations. For example, addressing a need for greater student engagement may be done effectively through project-based learning in some classes; in other classrooms, it might be through the greater individualization of topics. Just as homeowners focus on renovations that address their most pressing needs, so too should educators be able to prioritize their needs. A wholesale approach does not accommodate this need for flexibility.

Is Impractical to Expect of Educators. It is not feasible, even if it were desirable, to require educators to dismantle aspects of their practice while simultaneously expecting that successful teaching and learning would continue. Classrooms must remain livable during reform efforts. For good or bad, the education system—or a teacher's practice—is not a tabula rasa. Teachers' foundational beliefs and instructional approaches are constructed over time with careful thought, practice, and refinement. Practices are not easily interchanged and swapped; they are deeply ingrained habits and, even more profoundly, as Parker Palmer (2007) suggests, "[G]ood teaching comes from the identity and integrity of the teacher" (p. 10). A renovation mindset is a constructivist mindset that respects the need to affirm the effective aspects of teacher practice while seeking to refine areas that require improvement. And while it may seem counterintuitive to begin change conversations by affirming existing practices, even when a leader is delivering a message of change or correction, "the message needs to dignify those who hear it" (Tomlinson, 2015).

Is Counterproductive to Mandate Change. Most efforts at revolutionary change are mandated in an effort to mobilize reluctant teachers. The paradox of mandating change is that it makes change harder to achieve. The mere act of requiring teachers to adopt a practice invokes latent tendencies to resist. It shifts the emphasis from helping teachers perceive the need for themselves; otherwise, why the need to mandate it? Just as with students, creating a climate where decisions are made for teachers diminishes personal responsibility and encourages a mentality of minimal compliance.

Comparing Approaches to One-to-One Mobile Device Policies

Many jurisdictions have spent millions of dollars ensuring that students have their own personal tablets or computers at school. Initial reports on the impact of such initiatives highlighted decreased problems with student discipline and reduced spending on textbooks, paper, and other conventional resources. Despite these early gains, long-term studies now reveal that most one-to-one initiatives in the United States had marginal positive impact on student learning and achievement (Goodwin, 2011). Why has an initiative with such promise and good intentions floundered so?

Let's contrast a renovation and revolution approach to the introduction of one-to-one mobile devices. Rather than undertaking the wholesale purchase of technology or crafting a districtwide policy to support the initiative, a jurisdiction possessing a renovation mindset would start by probing the underlying needs or concerns that are prompting the initiative. What is the problem that individual access to a mobile device will solve? Did policy makers simply want greater teacher use of technology? If so, why? Is the point to improve student fluency in technology (aren't many students already fluent?), or is the point to enhance learning experiences by broadening the access and use of powerful learning tools? In either case, to what extent is the deficiency largely a result of lack of availability? These may be problems in some classes but not in all. Perhaps the greater impediments are lack of teacher understanding on how to use technology and lack of time to retool their lessons to accommodate the technology. In this case, is the solution to put a mobile device in every student's hands, expecting that this will provide the impetus for teachers to learn to make use of this opportunity? Would it not be better to investigate the range of reasons why teachers aren't making greater use of technology? Is it lack of availability and access, pedagogical knowledge, time constraints, or philosophical orientation? As it turns out, a determining impediment to the success of one-to-one initiatives was the absence of a clear focus related to instructional and learning goals, not just the successful logistical implementation of the initiative.

The renovation-focused administrator would identify what aspects of technology used to support learning are currently working and with whom. Rather than mandating an across-the-board policy, teachers with high interest would be encouraged to adopt the policy immediately. These early adopters might then assist other teachers who are open to the idea but not fluent in the pedagogical uses of technology before raising the expectation that they use it every day with their students. Collectively, they might develop resources and lesson materials to ease the stress on those who can't find the time to develop their own materials. And finally, efforts would be made with those who were opposed, in principle, to the idea of one-to-one devices so they could witness firsthand the successes of those who were currently using the technology effectively. Without a change of heart, there is no point in insisting on a practice that is doomed to fail given these teachers' current frame of mind.

How to Lead an Educational Renovation

As anyone who has embarked on a renovation project can attest, renovations often include many surprises, take longer than anticipated, and cost more than expected. Similarly, any renovation in education must begin with a carefully considered but tentative and flexible plan. We propose three key elements of an effective and responsive plan:

- identify a focus for the renovation;
- launch the initiative around a series of interrelated inquiries; and
- establish a plan for professional learning that supports educators in their inquiries in a coherent, comprehensive, and continuous manner.

Decide on a Promising Focus to Explore

When operating from the premise of an opportunity or a problem to identify and solve, rather than a blanket initiative to implement, leading an educational renovation starts by identifying the most productive or promising place to explore. Ideally, this will be the product of collaborative decision making by school and community partners, but even if determined by those in authority, two criteria are especially important considerations.

Look for the Area of Greatest Need or Frustration Around Educational Goals. Just as we saw with the implementation of one-to-one policies, there is no point in adopting any practice without clarity about the ultimate educational goals. This means, for example, not setting increased frequency of computer use or higher test scores as a focus, since these are merely proxies for the achievement of other goals such as deeper understanding of content or increased literacy and numeracy. Targeting higher frequency levels simply encourages technology use for its own sake, and higher test scores legitimizes "teaching for the test"—both of which deleteriously affect genuine achievement.

Get to the Source of the Problem. This criterion is a plea to move beyond the symptoms to get at the root causes of a problem or area of frustration. As we saw with implementation of one-to-one policies, often there are multiple causes, and they won't apply equally to everyone in the system. A reason for distinguishing the various components is to ensure that change efforts target the most appropriate aspects of the system. Is the perceived state of ill-prepared graduates largely a result of pursuing the wrong educational goals in some or most subjects, or partially a result of certain teaching practices that aren't effective in promoting the current goals? Similarly, what are the sources of low student engagement in various classes? To what extent is it a result of teaching topics that aren't particularly valuable (hence, change the curriculum) and/or inadequate efforts to make the potential value of current topics known (if so, help teachers develop ideas to promote the curriculum to students), or that the way the curriculum is taught is not appealing or challenging to students (if so, help teachers develop more compelling lessons)?

The focus for an educational renovation is best viewed as an area to investigate and not the final answer. For this reason, it is helpful to frame the focus as an inquiry, as suggested by the following examples:

- Which practices would most enrich our ability to make learning more meaningful and engaging to students?
- How can we better align our practices with sustained inquiry (or one of the other guiding pedagogical principles for a thinking classroom)?

Identify Professional Inquiries to Investigate

With a general common focus, educators can begin to generate the many more specific questions that must be answered in order to translate the initiative into a meaningful and effective modification of their practices.

The approach we encourage is of sense making—navigating the myriad of changes whirling through education by identifying the ranges of issues that are best pursued. Individually or as a staff, educators need to unpack the agreed-upon focus by asking how they will align this focus with the other elements of their teaching. For example, if student engagement is the focus, educators may ask: "What practices might support this?" "What opportunities are there for students to be engaged?" "Do any of my practices conflict with this?" "Are my educational goals supportive (are they meaningful for students)?"

These questions are not a blueprint but starting points for investigation. Educators will add to these questions and revise them as they continue in their journey. The point, however, is to agree on some initial questions that might guide decisions about the kind and nature of professional learning support that would be useful.

Provide Coherent, Comprehensive, and Continuous Support

Developing the collective understandings and abilities of educators—the "social capital"—is a key factor in successful education change (Fullan, 2012). The individual and collective capacity of teachers is best developed when support is coherent, comprehensive, and continuous.

Coherent Support. The desire for coherence is an attempt to "connect the dots"—to ensure all elements are in alignment in two ways: internal coherence within a teacher's practice so that the various aspects of the practice are working in harmony, and external coherence so that the other initiatives emanating from the school or district are congruent with each other and with the teacher's practice. A number of factors conspire to undermine coherent support. First, the strategies and structures supported by previous professional learning cycles are often not carried forward. New initiatives are often disconnected, particularly because they arise from diverse sources, including trends in education research, changes in school or jurisdiction leadership, or changes in governments. In other words, last year's efforts and initiatives are often left behind to make room for this year's innovations, contributing to disjointed and compartmentalized attempts at professional learning. As a result, educators may view the predictable yearly array of new initiatives as being unrelated and, as a result, receive them with skepticism and reluctance. Professional learning must be structured to articulate and foster coherence by using previous initiatives as platforms to build upon or as lenses to inform how the current innovation will be supported.

Comprehensive Support. Despite significant investment, the necessary supports that teachers require for successful implementation are often missing. For example, new curriculum might be launched, but the required instructional resources may not be available in time to support implementation. Teachers are then expected to create exemplary resources at the same time as they are learning about the changes and the related implications for their classrooms. On a different scale, teachers may be asked to infuse digital learning outcomes into classes even though reliable technology and Internet service are unavailable. Comprehensive support anticipates the range of resources needed for successful education renovation: learning and teaching materials, human resources, funding, and various forms of infrastructure.

> The episodic and piecemeal nature of typical professional development (i.e., scattered in-service days) dooms any attempt to sustain intellectual community.
>
> —Pamela Grossman, Samuel Wineburg, and Stephen Woolworth (2000)

Continuous Support. Despite efforts to change how teachers are supported, the one-off workshop remains the most common form of professional learning. A summary of studies on effective professional development for teachers confirms a number of findings (Gulamhussein, 2013):

- short-term, one-shot, and pull-out programs are not effective in improving teacher practice;
- even though this shortcoming is well known, more than 90 percent of teachers report that this is the most common form of professional learning that they attend—with a majority also indicating that it was ineffective;
- professional learning sessions or programs of less than fourteen hours in length do not typically lead to increased student achievement or changed teaching practices.

The shortcomings of many professional learning models extend beyond the limited time that may be devoted to any topic or initiative. The assumption behind short-term professional learning opportunities is that by attending a session, a teacher would then possess the knowledge to effectively implement a new strategy, or that by merely hearing about a new strategy, a teacher would be ready to use it in class. According to this view, professional development is something that happens to teachers: districts workshop their teachers and the teachers are then expected to apply the ideas in their classrooms. Unfortunately, this does not recognize that "changing teacher practice is difficult, because it involves changing long established habits" (Wiliam, 2010). Not only does changing habits take time—approximately twenty repetitions by some accounts—many teachers are reluctant to change their beliefs about new practices until they are assured that students will be successful (Guskey, 2002). Rather than relying upon sporadic and short-lived forms of professional learning, teachers require continuous support that extends beyond workshop sessions.

What Practices Support Coherent, Comprehensive, and Continuous Professional Inquiry?

As suggested by the diagram in Figure 13.1, the same framework used to nurture a thinking classroom can be adapted to guide coherent, comprehensive, and continuous professional learning support. If educators are to understand an initiative, they must have opportunities to investigate what it means for their practice. School and jurisdictional teams must become professional learning communities where all participants feel safe and supported to question, try out, and even fail with new ideas. And just as

Figure 13.1   Promoting Professional Growth

Source: Created by The Critical Thinking Consortium.

students must possess the intellectual tools needed for thoughtful inquiry, teachers must be supported confidently and effectively to acquire and use the requisite tools to make sense of the initiatives they are intending to adopt. Feedback related to progress toward specific desired outcomes is one of the five most powerful factors supporting learning (Hattie & Timperley, 2007). This guidance may come from a variety of sources, including other colleagues, education leaders, students, and parents.

Shape a Climate of Collaborative Professional Inquiry

Educators readily recognize the important role that the classroom climate plays in student learning. Likewise, a key facet of improving teacher practice is the climate of collaborative professional inquiry. Among the many powerful practices for building this type of climate, we suggest two that can serve as effective starting points.

Establish a Renovation Mindset. Many teachers feel that professional learning is something that is done to them. Instead, teachers need to see professional learning as an ongoing self-enabled renovation of their own practice. As discussed in Chapter 12, "Enhance Learning Through Digital Technology," modifying technology use by infusing the criteria for digitally enhanced learning and refining common inquiry structures by infusing the criteria for sustained inquiry discussed in Chapter 9, "Sustain Inquiry," are examples of how the guiding principles described in this book can help teachers renovate existing practices without requiring wholesale replacement of them.

An orientation of "affirm, refine, and aspire" can be effective in supporting a spirit of professional renovation:

- **Affirm:** What am I currently doing regarding . . . (e.g., climate) that effectively supports the feature I wish to renovate (e.g., student choice)?
- **Refine:** What can I easily refine in what I currently do regarding . . . that will more effectively support the aspect I wish to renovate?
- **Aspire:** What more substantial changes might I aspire to undertake regarding . . . that would effectively support the feature I wish to renovate?

Nurture a Professional Learning Community. The most effective learning support includes creating communities of inquiry (Sergiovanni, 1994) in which educators work with their peers to inquire into and reflect on shared goals, practices, and experiences. Principals and other education leaders must commit to establishing learning communities founded upon collegial internal accountability (Elmore & City, 2007) rather than punitive account-ability (Fullan, 2012). The levers for shaping the climate in a thinking classroom discussed in Chapter 4 apply to the nurturing of a professional learning community. Facilitating an atmosphere that supports safe and rigorous collective inquiry among teachers involves establishing appro-priate expectations, creating helpful routines, modeling desired behavior, monitoring professional interactions, and arranging the physical space to accommodate open and productive discussion.

Encourage Opportunities to Investigate Practice

In addition to a climate that supports professional inquiry, teachers need frequent opportunities to investigate their practice.

Continually Pose and Pursue Inquiry Questions. Within the context of a professional learning community, opportunities to investigate practice might take the form of inquiry questions designed to prompt deeper inves-tigation. These inquiry questions would invite educators to engage in an action-based investigation of a theory, possible solutions, or various prac-tices. Teachers might pursue the question "Realistically, what aspects of the four facets of a thinking classroom can I affirm, refine, and aspire to in my own teaching to effectively support critical, creative, and collaborative thinking?" All of the questions should be framed from the perspective of "What do I, as a self-enabling educator, need to know and do to thought-fully adapt an innovation" rather than from the perspective of an other-directed educator asking "What do I have to do to be in compliance with an initiative that I must implement."

Explore Alternative Explanations and Solutions. In pursuing inquiry questions, teachers should be exposed to and assess the merits of alterna-tive strategies and possibilities. Otherwise, they may simply revise their practice within the parameters of what is already known to them. The power of effective professional support lies not in explaining to teachers how things can be done but in awakening them to new possibilities of how they might choose to do things. The professional literature is a good source of alternative ideas. The practices discussed in this book and summarized in Figure 13.2 are examples of the kinds of possibilities that teachers may want to entertain as part of their professional learning.

Build Capacity for Professional Learning

Supporting effective professional growth also means ensuring that the requisite tools and resources are in place. Unless the majority of teachers

Figure 13.2 Summary of Suggested Practices

	Shape Climate	Create Opportunities	Build Capacity	Provide Guidance
Thinking Classroom	Create a physical environment conducive to thinking. Set clear expectations for thinking. Establish routines that support thinking. Foster teacher–student interactions that nurture thinking. Model the traits of a good thinker.	Problematize learning through curriculum-embedded critical challenges.	Teach the range of intellectual tools needed for each task.	Assess thinking and performance. Involve everyone in providing effective feedback.
Deep Understanding	Expect students to understand why and how, not merely what. Avoid supplying answers, when possible.	Build daily instruction around invitations to think. Frame learning around overarching ideas, questions, or tasks.	Provide students with tools to construct understanding.	Always check for understanding before moving on. Evaluate understanding over recall.
Real-Life Competency	Expect students to think through how to do a task, not just to get it done. Establish routines to encourage deliberation about the best tools to use.	Structure competency development around real-life tasks.	Help students build a repertoire of tools for each competency.	Capture the real thing in real time.
Genuine Commitment	Create consistently reinforcing environments that nurture desired commitments.	Emphasize a few commitments and do them well.	Support students in freely affirming their commitments. Support students in thoughtfully and flexibly acting on their commitments.	Assess for routine, not model, behavior.

	Shape Climate	Create Opportunities	Build Capacity	Provide Guidance
Engagement	Nurture encouraging classroom, school, home, and virtual spaces. Build appreciation for school in general and specific tasks in particular.	Provide more compelling learning opportunities.	Develop tools to match the challenges.	Provide timely, helpful, and encouraging feedback.
Sustained Inquiry	Create an expectation of continuous investigation.	Embed daily inquiries. Plan for iterative structured inquiries.	Support ongoing reflection that is generative and constructive.	Offer continuous and seamless peer and teacher feedback.
Self-Regulation	Create expectations and student buy-in for self-regulated learning.	Embed frequent opportunities for self-regulated learning.	Develop a repertoire of learning strategies, including criteria for effective use. Support independent student use and ongoing monitoring.	Assess situation-specific and general levels of self-regulated learning.
Assessment-Rich Learning	Help students find significant value in assessment.	Create timely teacher–student exchanges. Broaden the uses of peer and self-assessment.	Help students become proficient at self- and peer assessment. Help students learn to benefit from feedback.	Ensure that teacher comments advance student learning.
Technology-Enhanced Learning	Expect students to use digital technologies as learning tools.	Use diverse forms of technology to amplify learning opportunities and perspectives.	Teach students to skillfully select and use digital technology.	Encourage teacher and student use of technology to provide timely and useful feedback.

have what they need—whether in the form of supplied resources or time to complete and assemble resources—we cannot expect their change efforts to progress very far.

Scaffold Extended Professional Learning Support. Effective professional learning involves a variety of learning activities, opportunities for practice, feedback coaching, and access to quality professional and student resources. In our work, we use the metaphor of a comet to emphasize the relationship between formal sessions and the support provided between these sessions. The head of the comet may consist of provocative workshops and presentations intended to introduce key ideas and to stimulate teachers' interest. However, these sessions, like the head of the comet, create interest and shed some light on a topic. Although they may be exciting, typically their effects are short-lived. The tail of the comet is that prolonged period where teachers develop themselves professionally. The building blocks of sustained growth include conversations with colleagues, creation of learning and assessment activities, access to professional resources, and classroom modeling. The goal in our professional learning programs is to sustain teacher conversation once a week or more for three years or longer.

The cascading approach to inquiry described in Chapter 9, "Sustain Inquiry," can be used as a structure for planning professional learning support. As an integral part of continuous inquiry, the overarching inquiry and critical challenge serve as the unifying focus for successive years of professional learning and initiatives. Most important, the cascading approach assists teachers and leaders in seeing how various initiatives and professional learning work in concert toward the identified focus. A school might consider the overarching question of "How can we coherently, comprehensively, and continuously nurture a thinking classroom while also effectively implementing other school, district, and provincial education initiatives?" This would then be supported by any number of related lines of professional inquiry, each designed to support teacher learning in more particular areas. A sample template for a cascading challenges approach to professional learning is detailed in Figure 13.3.

Ensure That Needed Tools and Resources Are in Place. Comprehensive support includes ensuring that the necessary tangible resources (e.g., textbooks that support the changes, time to learn) and the intellectual tools to pursue a thoughtful inquiry are both in place. Identifying a comprehensive list of the resources needed to support successful education renovation involves seeking advice from multiple sources about the tangible and less tangible supports that teachers require. The most obvious tangible resources include teaching and learning resources related to new

Figure 13.3 Cascading Challenges Approach to Professional Learning

Overarching inquiry question: How can we coherently, comprehensively, and continuously nurture and support a thinking classroom while also effectively implementing other school, district, and provincial education initiatives?

Overarching critical challenge: Using the four facets of implementation and the five core principles of a thinking classroom as guides, identify which practices might be affirmed, refined, or aspired to in order to nurture a thinking classroom and effectively implement other school, district, and provincial education initiatives.

Strand A (Year one)	Strand B (Year two)	Strand C (Year three)
Developing teacher effectiveness in nurturing critical, creative, and collaborative learners	**Developing teaching effectiveness in supporting student competencies**	**Creating competent learners through deep learning**
Embedding the *four facets*[1] *of a thinking classroom* to support students' competence in thinking *critically, creatively, and collaboratively* (C3 thinking).	Nurturing the *five guiding principles*[2] *of a thinking classroom* to support students' competency at . . . (district/school educational goal [e.g., literacy, communicative competence, social responsibility]).	Infusing the principles and practices of a thinking classroom into the implementation of *(district/school pedagogical initiative [e.g., problem-based learning, instructional excellence, school redesign])* to support students' competency at . . . *(district/school educational goal).*
Inquiry question: Realistically, what aspects of the four facets of a thinking classroom can I affirm, refine, and aspire to in my own teaching to effectively support C3 thinking?	**Inquiry question:** Realistically, what aspects of the five enabling conditions of a thinking classroom can I affirm, refine, and aspire to in my own teaching to effectively support student competency at . . . (district/school educational goal)?	**Inquiry question:** Realistically, what aspects of . . . (district/school pedagogical initiative) can I affirm, refine, and aspire to in my own teaching to effectively support student competency through deep learning?
Critical challenge: Share what you have learned about using the four facets of a thinking classroom in your own teaching to support C3 thinking in a presentation/portfolio with supporting student samples built on a range of minilessons that you adapted, taught, and revised.	**Critical challenge:** Share what you have learned about using the four facets of a thinking classroom in your own teaching to support . . . (district/school educational goal) in a presentation/portfolio with supporting student samples built on a range of lesson sequences that you adapted/designed, taught, and revised.	**Critical challenge:** Share what you have learned about using . . . (district/school pedagogical initiative) in your own teaching to support . . . (district/school educational goal) in a presentation/portfolio with supporting student samples built on a unit/course that you adapted/designed, taught, and revised.

(Continued)

Figure 13.3 (Continued)

Educational goal: Build student competency in critical, creative, and collaborative thinking by making rigorous thinking that is not only reactive but also imaginative and carried out alone and with others as the prime means by which learning occurs in our classrooms.

Pedagogical focus: We can enhance a thinking classroom/school by engaging students in rigorous critical, creative, and collaborative inquiry.

Possible line of inquiry (Year one)

1. Understand C3 thinking and the power of a thinking classroom.

2. Embed effective opportunities for C3 thinking into daily teaching.

3. Build student capacity by teaching the tools for C3 thinking.

4. Ensure timely and effective guidance about performance and thinking.

5. Nurture a home and school environment that supports C3 thinking.

Educational goal: Build student competency in . . . (district/school educational goal) by making critical, creative, and collaborative thinking the prime means by which that competency is mastered.

Pedagogical focus: We can enhance a thinking classroom/school by engaging students in sustained inquiry that is self-regulated and digitally enhanced in an assessment-rich environment.

Possible line of inquiry (Year two)

1. Understand (district/school educational goal) and the importance of the guiding principles for a thinking classroom.

2. Sow the seeds of student engagement.

3. Plan for sustained student inquiry.

4. Ensure self-regulated tool development.

5. Create an assessment-rich learning environment.

6. Use digital technology to enhance teaching and learning.

Educational goal: Build student competency in . . . (district/school educational goal) by making critical, creative, and collaborative thinking the prime means by which that competency is mastered.

Pedagogical focus: We can enrich a thinking classroom/school by infusing . . . (district/school pedagogical initiative) into our teaching using the four facets and five guiding principles of a thinking classroom/school.

Possible line of inquiry (Year three)

1. Understand how (district/school educational goal) and (district/school pedagogical initiative) work within a thinking classroom.

2. Embed aspect or dimension A of (district/school pedagogical initiative).

3. Embed aspect or dimension B of (district/school pedagogical initiative).

4. Embed aspect or dimension C of (district/school pedagogical initiative).

5. Embed aspect or dimension D of (district/school pedagogical initiative).

initiatives, administrative policies, and time for teachers to collaborate. We were reminded recently of the importance of providing teaching and learning resources and not presuming that teachers can easily create them on their own. Upon seeing the comprehensive resources our group had developed to support a new social studies curriculum, one conscientious beginning teacher burst into tears. She had been feeling overwhelmed by the daunting task of implementing it and the vast number of after-school hours she anticipated having to spend trying to make sense of the curriculum, plan her lessons, and assemble the materials needed to do justice to the new expectations. Feeling a sense of relief with this resource, she saw that teaching the new curriculum was no longer a Herculean task.

Less obvious but equally important are the intellectual tools required for success within any change effort. An important role of workshops and other formal presentations is to introduce teachers to the range of tools they might need to inquire into various initiatives and to think through how they might adopt aspects of these initiatives by modifying their own practices. The kinds of tools that teachers require are suggested in Figure 13.4.

Figure 13.4   Intellectual Tools Required for Professional Inquiry

Background Knowledge	Knowledge of the various reform initiatives and their pros and cons.
Criteria for Judgment	Knowledge of the criteria for effective use of various initiatives (e.g., the criteria for digitally enhanced learning).
Thinking Vocabulary	Understanding key concepts to help inquire into professional practice.
Thinking Strategies	Use of planning templates, idea generation strategies, action research approaches, and so on.
Habits of Mind	Possession of professional dispositions such as open-mindedness, attention to detail, and perseverance.

Provide Guidance on Educational Practices and Student Achievement

Guidance is required for effective progress. Providing data and information directly related to the intended goals are "critical for motivating and encouraging educators to persist in the challenging work of improvement" (Elmore & City, 2007, p. 2).

Create Mechanisms for Ongoing Collegial Feedback. An important source of guidance is feedback from colleagues within the context of collaborative professional learning. This may involve peer review of lessons, collegial observation of teaching, and ongoing discussion. In recent years, research has affirmed the importance of the leadership provided by school principals through instructional rounds and other forms of feedback and mentoring.

Create Mechanisms for Regular Student and Parent Feedback. Students and parents are another valuable source of guidance. The acknowledged importance of student voice has heightened attention paid to the need for and value of formal and informal student feedback and direction. Action research is one way to collect this information, as is analysis of the results of formative and summative assessments. Consultation with parent advisory groups is useful, as are data from local, state, or national surveys of parents and students.

Concluding Thoughts

The challenge of making sense of the diverse calls for school reform is itself a daunting task but is nothing compared to the enormity of the task of supporting teachers in accommodating these proposed changes in their practices. Conventional approaches that mandate across-the-board changes that teachers must implement by displacing their current practices have not proven to be successful and are likely counterproductive. We offer the metaphor of a renovation mindset to signal an approach that invites teachers to adopt modifications to their practice based on thoughtful inquiry and with the aid of coherent, comprehensive, and continuous support.

Practices That Support Teacher Professional Growth

Shape Climate of Collaborative Professional Inquiry	• Establish a renovation mindset. • Nurture a professional learning community.
Encourage Opportunities to Investigate Practice	• Continually pose and pursue inquiry questions. • Explore alternative explanations and solutions.
Build Capacity for Professional Learning	• Scaffold extended professional learning support. • Ensure that needed tools and resources are in place.
Provide Guidance on Educational Practices and Student Achievement	• Create mechanisms for ongoing collegial feedback. • Create mechanisms for regular student and parent feedback.

Notes

1. The four facets of a thinking classroom are shape climate, create opportunities, build capacity, and provide guidance.
2. The five guiding principles are engage students, sustain inquiry, nurture self-regulated learners, create assessment-rich learning, and enhance learning through digital technology.

References

800ceoread blog. (2013, March 5). Thinker in residence: Bruce Nussbaum, author of *Creative Intelligence*. Retrieved August 11, 2017, from http://inthebooks.800ceoread.com/news/articles/thinker-in-residence-bruce-nussbaum-author-of-creative-intelligence

Abbott, M. (n.d.). Reading as thinking: "Critically" constructing meaning of text. *Critical Discussions*. Vancouver, BC, Canada: The Critical Thinking Consortium. Retrieved from http://tc2.ca/cd.php

Achenbach, J. (2015, March). The age of disbelief. *National Geographic, 227*, 30–47.

Ananiadou, K., & Claro, M. (2009). *21st century skills and competences for new millennium learners in OECD countries* [OECD Education Working Papers, No. 41]. Paris, France: OECD Publishing. doi:10.1787/218525261154

Antonelli, F. (2004). *From applied to applause*. Toronto, ON, Canada: Ontario Secondary School Teachers' Federation.

Barnum, M. (2017, June 12). Are virtual schools the future? Retrieved July 2, 2017, from https://www.theatlantic.com/education/archive/2017/06/are-virtual-schools-the-future/529170

Beers, B. F. (1996). *Patterns of civilization* (Vol. 2). Upper Saddle River, NJ: Prentice Hall.

Beyer, B. (2001). Putting it all together to improve student thinking. In A. Costa (Ed.), *Developing minds: A resource book for teaching thinking* (3rd ed., pp. 417–424). Alexandria, VA: Association for Supervision and Curriculum Development.

Bialik, M., Bogan, M., Fadel, C., & Horvathova, M. (2015). *Character education for the 21st century: What should students learn?* Boston, MA: Center for Curriculum Redesign.

Bluestein, J. (2001). *Creating emotionally safe schools: A guide for educators and parents*. Deerfield, FL: Health Communications.

Boaler, J. (2002). *Experiencing school mathematics*. Mahwah, NJ: Erlbaum.

Boyce, W. (2004). *Young people in Canada: Their health and well-being*. Ottawa, ON, Canada: Health Canada.

Bridgeland, J., Dilulio, J., Jr., & Morison, K. (2006). The silent epidemic: Perspectives of high school dropouts. Retrieved from https://docs.gatesfoundation.org/Documents/thesilentepidemic3-06final.pdf

Busteed, B. (2013, January 7). The school cliff: Student engagement drops with each school year. Retrieved from http://www.gallup.com/opinion/gallup/170525/school-cliff-student-engagement-drops-school-year.aspx

Butler, D. (2002). Individualizing instruction in self-regulated learning. *Theory Into Practice, 41*(2), 82.

California Council on Science and Technology. (2011). *Digitally enhanced education in California*. Sacramento, CA: Author. Retrieved April 6, 2015, from http://www.ccst.us/publications/2011/2011digital.pdf

California Task Force on K–12 Civic Learning. (2014). *Revitalizing K–12 civic learning in California: A blueprint for action*. Retrieved from http://www.cde.ca.gov/eo/in/documents/cltffinalreport.pdf

Case, R. (2013). The unfortunate consequence of Bloom's taxonomy. *Social Education, 77*(4), 196–200.

Case, R., Gini-Newman, G., Gini-Newman, L., James, U., & Taylor, S. (2015, December). The "basics" and inquiry teaching: Can they be reconciled? *Education Canada, 55*(4), 40–43.

Case, R., Harper, K., Tilley, S., & Wiens, J. (1994). Stewart on teaching versus facilitating: A misconstrued dichotomy. *Canadian Journal of Education, 19*(3), 287–298.

CBS News. (2011, June 14). Ulysses S. who? US history stumps students. Retrieved from http://www.cbsnews.com/news/ulysses-s-who-us-history-test-stumps-students

Cleese, J. (n.d.). Lecture on creativity. Retrieved August 11, 2017, from http://genius.com/John-cleese-lecture-on-creativity-annotated

Costa, A., & Kallick, B. (2000). *Discovering and exploring habits of mind*. Alexandria, VA: Association for Supervision and Curriculum Development.

The Critical Thinking Consortium. (2010). *ImagineAction: Making a difference—Grades 5–8*. Ottawa, ON, Canada: Canadian Teachers' Federation.

Crockett, L. W. (2016, August 2). The 21st century skills every student needs and why. Retrieved from https://globaldigitalcitizen.org/21st-century-skills-every-student-needs

Csikszentmihalyi, M. (2002). *Thoughts about education*. Retrieved from http://www-bcf.usc.edu/~genzuk/Thoughts_About_Education_Mihaly_Csikszentmihalyi.pdf

Cuban, L. (2010, July 21). How history is taught in schools. Retrieved from https://larrycuban.wordpress.com/2010/07/21/how-history-is-taught-in-schools/

Daniels, L., & Case, R. (1992). *Charter literacy and the administration of justice in Canada*. Ottawa, ON, Canada: Department of Justice.

Darling-Hammond, L., & Bransford, J. (Eds.). (2005). *Preparing teachers for a changing world*. San Francisco, CA: Jossey-Bass.

Dewey, J. (1910). *How we think*. New York, NY: D.C. Heath.

Dewey, J. (1938). *The experience of education*. New York, NY: Simon & Schuster.

Duke, D. (1978). Looking at the school as a rule-governed organization. *Journal of Research and Development in Education, 11*(4), 116–126.

Edmunds, J., Willse, J., Arshavsky, N., & Dallas, A. (2013). Mandated engagement: The impact of early college high schools. *Teachers College Record, 15*(7), 1–31.

Elmore, R., & City, E. (2007, May/June). The road to school improvement. *Harvard Education Letter, 23*(3), 1–3.

Falk, J. K., & Drayton, B. (2009). *Creating and sustaining professional learning communities*. New York, NY: Teachers College Press.

Ferriter, W. (2010). Preparing to teach digitally. *Educational Leadership, 67*(8), 88.

Feynman, R. (1997). *Surely you're joking, Mr. Feynman.* New York, NY: Norton.

Fox, S. (2013, August 7). 51% of U.S. adults bank online. Retrieved August 25, 2017, from http://www.pewinternet.org/2013/08/07/51-of-u-s-adults-bank-online

Fullan, M. (2012, February). *Q&A with Michael Fullan* [Lead the Change Series, Issue No. 16]. Washington, DC: American Educational Research Association. Retrieved from https://michaelfullan.ca/wp-content/uploads/2016/06/13514675730.pdf

Fullan, M., & Langworthy, M. (2014). *A rich seam: How new pedagogies find deep learning.* London, England: Pearson.

Goodlad, J. (2004). *A place called school: Twentieth anniversary edition.* New York, NY: McGraw-Hill.

Goodman, J. (1995, Spring). Change without difference: Schools restructuring in historical perspective. *Harvard Educational Review, 65,* 4.

Goodwin, B. (2011, February). Research says . . . One-to-one laptop programs are no silver bullet. *Educational Leadership, 68*(5), 78.

Great Schools Partnership. (n.d.). 21st century skills. Retrieved August 16, 2017, from http://edglossary.org/21st-century-skills

Green, J. (2014). *The fault in our stars.* New York, NY: Penguin.

Grolnick, W. S., & Ryan, R. M. (1987). Autonomy in children's learning: An experimental and individual difference investigation. *Journal of Personality and Social Psychology, 52,* 890–898.

Grossman, P., Wineburg, S., & Woolworth, S. (2000). Towards a theory of teacher community. *Teachers College Record, 103*(6), 948.

Gulamhussein, A. (2013, September). *Teaching the teachers: Effective professional development in an era of high stakes accountability.* Retrieved from http://www.centerforpubliceducation.org/Main-Menu/Staffingstudents/Teaching-the-Teachers-Effective-Professional-Development-in-an-Era-of-High-Stakes-Accountability/Teaching-the-Teachers-Full-Report.pdf

Guskey, T. R. (2002). Professional development and teacher change. *Teachers and Teaching: Theory and Practice, 8*(3/4), 381–391.

Hargreaves, D. (2004). *Learning for life: The foundations of lifelong learning.* Bristol, England: Policy Press.

Hattie, J. (2015). *What doesn't work in education: The politics of distraction.* London, England: Pearson.

Hattie, J., & Timperley, H. (2007). The power of feedback. *Review of Educational Research, 77*(1), 83.

Hirsch, E. D. (2009–2010, Winter). Creating a curriculum for the American people: Our democracy depends on shared knowledge. *American Educator, 33*(4), 10.

Johnson, D., & Johnson, R. (1994). *Leading the cooperative school* (2nd ed.). Edina, MN: Interaction.

Karpinski, A., & D'Agostino, J. (2013). The role of formative assessment in student achievement. In J. Hattie & E. Anderman (Eds.), *International Guide to Student Achievement* (pp. 202–204). New York, NY: Routledge.

Klein, J. (2011, June). The failure of American schools. Retrieved from https://www.theatlantic.com/magazine/archive/2011/06/the-failure-of-american-schools/308497

Kohn, A. (1999, March). From degrading to de-grading. Originally published in *High School Magazine*. Retrieved from http://www.alfiekohn.org/article/degrading-de-grading

Kohn, A. (2001, January). Fighting the tests: A practical guide to rescuing our schools. *Phi Delta Kappan*. Retrieved from http://www.alfiekohn.org/article/fighting-the-tests

Kohn, A. (2004). Challenging students—and how to have more of them. *Phi Delta Kappan, 86*(3), 189.

Kohn, A. (2011, November). The case against grades. *Educational Leadership*. Retrieved from http://www.alfiekohn.org/article/case-grades

Kohn, K. (1997). How not to teach values: A critical look at character education. *Phi Delta Kappan*. Retrieved August 17, 2017, from http://www.alfiekohn.org/article/teach-values

Lederer, R. (1987). Student bloopers. *Language Quarterly, 13*(4).

Lipman, M. (1988). Critical thinking: What can it be? *Educational Leadership, 45*, 38–43.

McQueen, S. (Director). (2013). *Twelve years a slave* [Motion picture]. United States: Regency Enterprises.

Menéndez, R. (1988). *Stand and deliver* [Motion picture]. United States: American Playhouse.

Nater, S., & Gallimore, R. (2010). *You haven't taught until they have learned: John Wooden's teaching principles and practices*. Morgantown, WV: Fitness International Technology, Inc.

National Center for Education Statistics. (2013, June). *The nation's report card: Trends in academic progress 2012*. Washington, DC: Author.

National Education Association. (n.d.). *Preparing 21st century students for a global society: An educator's guide to the "Four C's."* Retrieved from http://www.nea.org/assets/docs/A-Guide-to-Four-Cs.pdf

National Governors Association Center for Best Practices and the Council of Chief State School Officers. (2010). *Common Core State Standards for English language arts & literacy in history/social studies, science, and technical subjects*. Retrieved from http://www.corestandards.org/ELA-Literacy

National Research Council and Institute of Medicine. (2004). *Engaging schools: Fostering high school students' motivation to learn*. Washington, DC: National Academies Press.

Newmann, F. (1992). *Student engagement and achievement in American secondary schools*. New York, NY: Teachers College Press.

Newmann, F., Bryk, A., & Nagaoka, J. (2001). *Authentic intellectual work and standardized tests: Conflict or coexistence?* Chicago, IL: Consortium on Chicago School Research.

Organisation for Economic Co-operation and Development. (2015). *Students, computers and learning: Making the connection*. Paris, France: Author. Retrieved from http://dx.doi.org/10.1787/9789264239555-en

Osborne, K. (2004). *Canadian history in the schools: A report prepared for Historica Foundation*. Toronto, ON, Canada: Historica Foundation.

Palmer, P. (2007). *The courage to teach: Exploring the inner landscape of a teacher's life*. Toronto, ON, Canada: Wiley.

Parker, W. (1989). How to help students learn history and geography. *Educational Leadership, 47*(3), 41.

Partnership for 21st Century Learning. (2007). *Framework for 21st century learning.* Washington, DC: Author.

Paul, R. (1993). The logic of creative and critical thinking. In R. Paul (Ed.), *Critical thinking: How to prepare students for a rapidly changing world* (pp. 195–216). Santa Rosa, CA: Foundation for Critical Thinking.

Pellegrino, J. W., & Hilton, H. L. (Eds.). (2012). *Education for life and work: Developing transferable knowledge and skills in the 21st century.* Washington, DC: National Academies Press.

Perkins, D. (1993). The connected curriculum. *Educational Leadership, 51*(2), 90.

Peters, W. (Producer and Director). (1970). *The eye of the storm* [Motion picture]. United States: PBS.

Peters, W. (Director). (1987). *A class divided* [Television series episode]. In *Frontline.* United States: PBS.

Pirsig, R. (1999). *Zen and the art of motorcycle maintenance: An inquiry into values.* New York, NY: HarperCollins.

Planche, B., & Case, R. (2015). Critical, creative and collaborative (C3) thinking: A three-sided coin? *OPC Register, 17*(1), 8–13.

Raths, L., Harmin, M., & Simon, S. (1966). *Values and teaching: Working with values in the classroom.* Columbus, OH: Merrill.

Reaney, J. (2010). *A suit of nettles.* Erin, ON, Canada: The Porcupine's Quill.

Ritchhart, R. (2002). *Intellectual character: What it is, why it matters and how to get it.* San Francisco, CA: Jossey-Boss.

Rotberg, I. C. (2014, October 16). The endless search for silver bullets. *Teachers College Record, 1-2.* Retrieved October 24, 2014, from http://www.tcrecord.org. ID Number: 17723.

Rotherham, A. J., & Willingham, D. (2009). 21st century skills: The challenges ahead. *Educational Leadership, 67*(1), 16–21.

Rotherham, A. J., & Willingham, D. (2010, Spring). "21st Century" skills: Not new, but a worthy challenge. *American Educator, 34*(1), 17–20.

Ruggiero, V. R. (1996). *Becoming a critical thinker.* Boston, MA: Houghton Mifflin.

Ryerson, E. (1847). *Report on a system of public education for Upper Canada.* Montreal, QC, Canada: Lovell & Gibson.

Schleicher, A. (2016, September 26). Educating for innovation and innovation in education [Web log post]. Retrieved from http://oecdeducationtoday .blogspot.ca/2016/09/educating-for-innovation-and-innovation.html

Schools Program Division, Manitoba Education. (2010). *Engaging middle school students in learning: Transforming middle years education in Manitoba.* Winnipeg, MB, Canada: Manitoba Education.

Seely Brown, J. (n.d.). Learning in the digital age. Retrieved April 12, 2015, from http://www.johnseelybrown.com/learning_in_digital_age-aspen.pdf

Sener, J. (2011, February 22). Do we really need a core curriculum? Retrieved from http://etcjournal.com/2011/02/22/7347

Sergiovanni, T. (1994). *Building community in schools.* San Francisco, CA: Jossey-Bass.

Shanker, S. (2013). *Calm, alert, and learning: Classroom strategies for self-regulation.* Toronto, ON, Canada: Pearson Education Canada.

Shulman, L. S. (2002). Making differences: A table of learning. *Change: The Magazine of Higher Learning, 34*(6), 36–44.

Soley, M. (1996). If it is controversial, why teach it? *Social Education, 60*(1), 10.

SparkNotes Editors. (n.d.). Romeo and Juliet [plot overview]. Retrieved August 15, 2017, from http://www.sparknotes.com/shakespeare/romeojuliet/summary.html

The State Education Department and the University of the State of New York. (2014, November). *The New York K–12 social studies framework: Introduction* (revised). Retrieved from http://www.p12.nysed.gov/ciai/socst/documents/ss-framework-k-12-intro.pdf

Statista. (2017). Global number of digital buyers 2014–2021. Retrieved August 24, 2017, from https://www.statista.com/statistics/251666/number-of-digital-buyers-worldwide

Steinberg, L. (2015, February 16). Failings of American high schools. *Teachers College Record.* Retrieved March 6, 2015, from http://www.tcrecord.org. ID Number: 17864.

Sternberg, R. (2008). Assessing what matters. *Informative Assessment, 65*(4), 23.

Student Achievement Division. (2013, September). *Student voice: Transforming relationships* [Capacity Building Series, Secretariat Special Edition #34]. Toronto, ON, Canada: Ontario Ministry of Education. Retrieved from http://www.edugains.ca/resourcesLIT/ProfessionalLearning/CBS/CBS_StudentVoice.pdf

Tapscott, D. (2008). *Grown up digital: How the net generation is changing your world.* New York, NY: McGraw-Hill Professional.

Tishman, S., Perkins, D., & Jay, E. (1995). *The thinking classroom: Learning and teaching in a culture of thinking.* New York, NY: Pearson.

Tomlinson, C. A. (2015, April). Communication that powers leadership. *Educational Leadership, 72*(7), 90–91.

Tyler, R. (1969). *Basic principles of curriculum and instruction.* Chicago, IL: University of Chicago Press.

Understanding. (n.d.). In *Merriam-Webster's online dictionary* (11th ed.). Retrieved from http://www.merriam-webster.com/dictionary/understanding?show=0&t=1357871911

Washoe County School District. (n.d.). *21st century competencies: A guide for planning instruction for 21st century learners.* Reno, NV: Author. Retrieved August 15, 2017, from https://www.washoeschools.net/Page/8186

West Windsor-Plainsboro Regional School District. (n.d.). *21st century competencies.* West Windsor, NJ: Author. Retrieved August 15, 2017, from http://www.west-windsor-plainsboro.k12.nj.us/departments/Curriculum/21st_century_competencies/

Wiggins, G. (2015, March 30). On reading, Part 5: A key flaw in using the gradual release of responsibility model [Web log post]. Retrieved August 15, 2017, from https://grantwiggins.wordpress.com/2015/03/30/on-reading-part-5-a-key-flaw-in-using-the-gradual-release-of-responsibility-model

Wiggins, G., & McTighe, J. (2005). *Understanding by design*. Alexandria, VA: Association for Supervision and Curriculum Development.

Wiliam, D. (2007). Keeping learning on track: Formative assessment and the regulation of learning. In M. Coupland, J. Anderson, & T. Spencer (Eds.), *Making mathematics vital: Proceedings of the twentieth biennial conference of the Australian Association of Mathematics Teachers* (pp. 20–34). Adelaide, Australia: Australian Association of Mathematics Teachers.

Wiliam, D. (2010, March 4). *Teacher quality: Why it matters and how to get more of it.* Unpublished paper, Schools Revolution Conference, London, England.

Wiliam, D. (2011). *Embedded formative assessment.* Bloomington, IN: Solution Tree Press.

Wineburg, S., & Schneider, J. (2010). Was Bloom's taxonomy pointed in the wrong direction? *Phi Delta Kappan, 91*(4), 56–61.

Wiske, M. S. (Ed.). (1998). *Teaching for understanding.* San Francisco, CA: Jossey-Bass.

Wolcott, S. (1997). *Student assumptions about knowledge and critical thinking in the accounting classroom.* Unpublished paper, Southwest Regional Meeting of the American Accounting Association, Lakewood Ranch, FL.

Wolters, C. (2011). Regulation of motivation: Contextual and social aspects. *Teachers College Record, 113*(2), 265–283.

Index

A SAGE Publishing Company

Helping educators make the greatest impact

CORWIN HAS ONE MISSION: to enhance education through intentional professional learning.

We build long-term relationships with our authors, educators, clients, and associations who partner with us to develop and continuously improve the best evidence-based practices that establish and support lifelong learning.

Solutions you want. Experts you trust. Results you need.

Author Consulting

Author Consulting

On-site professional learning with sustainable results! Let us help you design a professional learning plan to meet the unique needs of your school or district. www.corwin.com/pd

Institutes

Institutes

Corwin Institutes provide collaborative learning experiences that equip your team with tools and action plans ready for immediate implementation. www.corwin.com/institutes

eCourses

eCourses

Practical, flexible online professional learning designed to let you go at your own pace. www.corwin.com/ecourses

Read2Earn

Read2Earn

Did you know you can earn graduate credit for reading this book? Find out how: www.corwin.com/read2earn

Contact an account manager at (800) 831-6640 or visit **www.corwin.com** for more information.

Praise for *Creating Thinking Classrooms*
by Garfield Gini-Newman and Roland Case

I loved the book and highly recommend it. This book can help school leaders, teachers, and professional developers understand and appreciate what it means and what it takes to promote a thinking classroom. It is substantive, practical, well grounded in theory and practice. A must-read.

Giselle O. Martin-Kniep, PhD, President,
Learner-Centered Initiatives, Garden City, New York

My work with The Critical Thinking Consortium, Garfield Gini-Newman, and Roland Case spans almost two decades. As a former principal and community superintendent, I observed firsthand how transformational their work is in the classroom, in the school community, and on a system level. *Creating Thinking Classrooms* takes theory and research and places it directly into the hands of practitioners by offering thoughtful and immediately useful strategies. Not only does this work transform student engagement and achievement, but it also transforms thinking for both teachers and their students. The knowledge and act of teaching and learning goes from passive acquisition of information to active, purposeful, and deliberate interaction with the curriculum and instructional experience in the classroom. It is a must-read!

Ursula A. Hermann, PhD, Retired Principal
and Community Superintendent, Montgomery
County Public Schools, Rockville, Maryland

Creating Thinking Classrooms is a must-read for all instructional leaders wanting to use a new lens on sustained school improvement. Establishing a thinking orientation, enriching goals, and invigorating practices form the straightforward and effective framework of this book. Too often there is a focus on abandoning practices rather than strengthening them in educational reform. However, Garfield Gini-Newman and Roland Case challenge such thinking by suggesting a renovation mindset. Through such a mindset, a renewal takes place in classrooms that is transformational, actionable, and meaningful.

Barbara Woodward, PhD, Principal, Hallie Wells
Middle School, Montgomery County Public Schools, Maryland

Creating Thinking Classrooms is an outstanding resource for educational leaders. There are many things I like about it, but what impressed me most is the notion of framing the retooling of schools as renovation or reinvigoration rather than as revolution—twinned with the message of targeting a limited number of strategic areas to focus on in a sustained, systemic way.

Too many are asking too much of schools in terms of "reform," seeming to ignore that there are many good things worth preserving and others that need to be reframed or recast to give them greater currency. In that connection, I liked the analogy with improving medical care/procedures. You build on what has worked, making it better. This message—being purposeful and patiently focused on long-term success—is a powerful one that needs to be heard above the din.

The plethora of charts and examples illustrate in practical detail how some concepts can show up or be implemented. Very practical, very user friendly.

David Chojnacki, Former Executive Director,
Near East South Asia Council of Overseas Schools

There has been a shift in the culture of our school. We used to believe our students were not capable of doing the work; now we worry we are not challenging them enough.

Nora Dietz, Principal, Captain James E. Daly Elementary School,
Montgomery County Public Schools, Germantown, Maryland

Creating Thinking Classrooms offered our faculty practical and powerful ways to nurture creative, critical, and collaborative thinking across our inquiry-based school. Our teachers found the ideas clear, concise, and relevant, offering ways to "make little tweaks to the good things we are already doing to enhance the learning substantially." The student-centered approach of "launching into the learning straight away through interesting provocations" coupled with setting clear criteria were the most impactful takeaways from our reading and application of *Creating Thinking Classrooms*.

Teresa Belisle, Director of Learning Research and
Development, International School of Prague